Charles Dickens

THE PROGRESS OF A RADICAL

T.A. Jackson

D1648568

International Publishers New York

©1987   International Publishers Co., Inc.
1st printing of this edition, 1987
All Rights Reserved

Manufactured in the United States of America

Library of Congress Cataloging-in-Publication Data

Jackson, T. A. (Thomas Alfred), 1879-1955.
Charles Dickens: progress of a radical.

Originally published: London: Lawrence and Wishart, 1937.
1. Dickens, Charles, 1812-1870—Political and social views. 2. Radicalism
in literature. 3. Social problems in literature. I. Title.

PR4592.R27J3   1987   823'.8   87-4159

ISBN 0-7178-0654-5 (pbk.)

CONTENTS

TO
STELLA
and
VIVIEN
Who made me read Dickens to them by the
hour, while they perched on each side and
looked at the pictures.

Foreword

The reappearance of T. A. Jackson's classic study of the novels of Charles Dickens is a welcome event. Dickens, the greatest popular writer in English since Shakespeare, continues to be of lively interest to American scholars as well as those who read for pure pleasure, no less appreciated today than in the 1930s when Jackson's book was first published. American college students are required to read Dickens and discover he is worth reading. His novels, which were converted into plays during his own lifetime, have long been recognized as legal plunder for film-makers. An abundance of books and articles continues to be written about Dickens and his novels, and interest in the man and his work shows no sign of abating. The return of Jackson's book is, then, especially timely, because his Marxist approach brings to current discussion a perspective not generally in favor today in American colleges and universities.

When it was first published fifty years ago, Charles Dickens: the Progress of a Radical *had a mixed reception. American literary critics applauded the work for its knowledgeable treatment of the details of Dickens' novels and their relation to the historical events of Victorian England, that is, his own time. They also praised Jackson's account of Dickens' literary career: the novel-by-novel development of a man who was at the same time a participant in his society and a keen critic of it. "Mr. Jackson presents a fine study in violence as he traces the industrial functioning of Victorian virtue," wrote Maxwell Geismar in the* Nation. *Malcolm Cowley, in the* New Republic, *was especially pleased that Jackson's work "...gives you so much of Dickens himself. It ... proves that the later [novels] are ... closely knit together and calculated to produce a single effect." Edmund Wilson, in his perceptive essay "Dickens: The Two Scrooges", called Jackson's analysis of* Little Dorrit *"the best thing that has been written on this novel."*

But the critics, without exception, were distressed by the energy with which Jackson pursued his reading of Dickens. "Mr. Jackson rides his argument too fast and too far," wrote Malcolm Cowley. Maxwell Geismar said much the same: "In an excess of zeal he is not content with explaining what is obviously a large part of Dickens. Like the daring Oliver Twist himself, he 'wants some more'." Although he found merit in Jackson's approach, Edmund Wilson criticized him for ignoring facts and themes in Dickens' novels which did not fit the framework, for failing to "carry to fundamental findings the line which he undertakes." And in England George Orwell, in a critical essay in Inside the Whale, *convinced that Dickens was merely a bourgeois moralist at odds with the excesses, not the system, of industrial capitalism, accused Jackson of "spirited efforts to turn Dickens into a bloodthirsty revolutionary."*

What most annoyed these 1930s literary critics was not Jackson's use of a Marxist framework but, rather, what they considered its excessively rigid application. Most agreed that the Marxist perspective illuminated themes in Dickens that otherwise might have remained in the shadows. But Jackson wrote with an adamant 1930s faith in the masses and the future ("... the march of history has forced the petit-bourgeoisie to yield the hegemony of the onward march of humanity to the militant proletariat....."), disappointed in Dickens' failure to acquire a similar faith. The critics argued that Jackson's political commitments shackled his study at times, advancing only one interpretation where others were possible.

The criticism as well as the praise was sound. One can agree that Jackson's language is occasionally perturbing and his analysis at times a bit forced. But the worth of his work on Dickens is as obvious today as it was 50 years ago. The limited exposure to the Marxist perspective among American college students in literature and social science only adds to the value of Jackson's approach in our time.

The focus of the book is the relationship between Dickens' work and the period in which it was written. It shows how the social conditions of Victorian England helped shape Dickens' imagination and how political and social changes in that society helped move him away from the facile optimism of his youth, expressed in his early novels, toward an ever more radical and troubling pessimism, evident in the great novels of his later years. Jackson argues that the radicalism of Dickens' later years "stiffened, hardened, and deepened into something that with a little outside aid might easily have emerged as positive Socialism or Communism," and he concludes on the basis of an examination of internal evidence in Dickens' novels that Dickens became progressively "more ready to appreciate the need for a mass uprising" in England. This judgment was not shared by most of the literary critics of the 1930s. One need not agree with Jackson's every conclusion, however, to appreciate his challenging insights.

*Having announced his allegiance to the Marxist critique of nineteenth century society and briefly described the injustices of that society, Jackson considers each of Dickens' novels in detail, providing plot summaries and analyses of all of the major works. He traces the development of Dickens' view of class and class relations, beginning with the bourgeois optimism of his early novels (*Pickwick Papers, Oliver Twist, Nicholas Nickleby, Old Curiosity Shop, *and* Barnaby Rudge*), in which classes are viewed as subjective and accidental divisions "whose ill effects would disappear if only the rich used their power and wealth sympathetically...." Jackson shows that this "naive optimism" received a severe jolt when Dickens visited the "classless" United States and encountered the corrupting influence of its commercial aristocracy. Real, rather than subjective, class divisions begin to appear in the novels of the middle period (*Martin Chuzzlewit, Dombey and Son, *and* David Copperfield*), although it is a class structure without class struggle. About* Dombey and Son, *for example, a novel of Dickens' middle period, Jackson writes:*

The class-implications ... are different ... from those of the earlier novels. There is a greater readiness to see a real ... distinction between the aristocracy of blood and the aristocracy of commerce and finance. If the latter are shown as dehumanized by their wealth, where they are not vulgarized by the process of its acquirement, the former are shown as dehumanized by heartless idleness and conventional frivolity....

There is ... no clear recognition of class conflict.... But there is the beginning ... of a recognition of class as a positive fact.

It is in Dickens' third phase, Jackson argues, the period of his greatest novels *(*Bleak House, Hard Times, Little Dorrit, Tale of Two Cities, Great Expectations, *and* Our Mutual Friend*)*, that an increasingly embittered Dickens confronts the class realities of bourgeois society. Jackson here is at his best, as he charts the development of a maturing class conception in these carefully constructed novels, showing their essential unity of purpose ("Hard Times ... stands to Bleak House and to Little Dorrit as a furious raid does to two systematic campaigns."). He concludes that Dickens' ideas of class and class structure in the later novels reflected a complete loss of faith in the promise of bourgeois society without a corresponding acceptance of "the only possible alternative—faith in the proletariat and its revolutionary mission," which is, for Jackson, "the real tragedy of Dickens."

Jackson's study is certainly provocative. It sheds light on central but often hedged themes in Dickens' novels, notably those of class structure and conflict and their effect on the individual. Jackson is a stimulating guide through the complexities of the novels, making valuable connections among characters and themes, always anchoring the works in the social and political struggles of the times in which they were written. And in a finely crafted comparison of Our Mutual Friend, *Dickens'* last completed novel, with Pickwick Papers, *his first, Jackson observes the change in Dickens' social and political outlook over the course of his writing career:*

Certainly we miss profoundly (in Our Mutual Friend*) the whole multitude of delightful freaks and oddities who play their pranks and tumble over each other in every chapter of* Pickwick.... *But no less certainly the whole riotous company ... who frisk their way through* Pickwick *would have been as out of place in the world of* Our Mutual Friend, *as a Hitler, or a Goering in fairy-land.*

It was not that the sense of fun had died down in Dickens or that his power of creation had been exhausted. It was that the world had changed for Dickens, and with it his sense of responsibility to, and for, that world.

FOREWORD

For students of social science, Jackson shows how great literature is a rich source of social commentary, a mirror on the social structure and politics of society and, as such, a valuable aid in social analysis. For all readers of Dickens, Jackson provides fuel for rich thought and lively discussion. If used judiciously, his is an approach that could well be applied successfully to literature of more recent vintage.

June, 1987

John Murray
Purchase, New York

Preface

By common consent Charles Dickens is one of the most significant of English novelists; definitely one of the three greatest English novelists of the first half of the nineteenth century, along with Scott and Thackeray; certainly of all English novelists, other than those still living, the one who most continues to be read, and the one who is most "popular" in the widest sense of the word.

In 1936, for instance, on top of the centenary celebrations of his Pickwick Papers, *his* David Copperfield *appeared as a serial in* Humanité, *the French Communist daily; a Belgian Communist journal gave, as part of its fourteenth of July celebration, large extracts from his* Tale of Two Cities, *and so on. Dickens is of all non-Russian novelists the one most often translated into, and read in the Russian language; and plays based upon his works are as popular in Russia as films based upon them are popular in Hollywood. Three of his novels are listed as "set books" for the high schools of the U.S.A. and (per contra) the very latest English writer on prison life (Macartney, in* Walls Have Mouths) *testifies that his works head the list of popular novelists among long-term convicts in British prisons.*

The antinomical character of his popularity—among State officials, bourgeois moralists, Communists, convicts, and the unlettered generally—is emphasised by the sharp division which persists, and has from the first persisted, among literary critics as to Dickens' true place in the hierarchy of his art. For some he is far and away the supreme English *novelist. For others he is the supreme example of English incapacity for High Art. He is, say these latter, thin, banal, grotesque, maudlin, exaggerated, extravagant; not to be spoken of in the same breath with Balzac, Dostoievsky, Turgenev or Flaubert, not anywhere near the excellence of Henry Fielding, Jane Austen, Thomas Hardy, Thackeray or even Walter Scott.*

His very popularity is, to these critics, a proof of his inferiority. He reached popularity at a bound, while still a youth. He never surpassed the high-water-mark of his first novel the Pickwick Papers. *That he kept on writing, without developing, and retained his popularity to the end—as he still to a large extent retains it—is, to this school of critics, a proof of his fundamental inferiority. No man, they say, could become so instantly and remain so widely popular and be really great.*

To which, another school, headed by G. K. Chesterton, makes the obvious reply—that his abiding popularity proves that, for good or-ill, he struck a chord which never fails to excite a response in the emotions of common humanity everywhere. High Art or Low, his was the art for which the common man has always an appetite. And J. B. Priestley caps the moral by supplying the public with Dickens-and-water garnished up-to-date—thereby achieving the distinction of a best-seller. Let us leave this critical problem to the critics and ask what exactly was the relation of Dickens' work to the period in which it was produced?

T.A.J.

CHARLES DICKENS

Progress of a Radical

PART I.

DICKENS' DEVELOPMENT IN GENERAL

CHARLES DICKENS was born—the son of a clerk in the Naval Pay office, and of his wife, whose relatives were also of the minor, professional class (the "lower gentry")—in 1812. Owing to parental vicissitudes his schooling was intermittent and varied.

Periods of no schooling at all, alternated with spells of tuition in various "scholastic establishments for the sons of gentlemen," and with one horrible spell of employment at manual labour, as a child in a blacking factory.

We know the sort of thing well; since Dickens has described it all for us in *David Copperfield.* Other aspects of his childhood experiences can be traced in *Little Dorrit*—for Dickens' father, like Mr. Micawber (who is largely modelled upon him, as Mrs. Nickleby is largely modelled upon Dickens' mother) was imprisoned for debt in the Marshalsea prison, as was also Edward Dorrit, the father in *Little Dorrit.*

He was (and most humiliatingly for one of a family aspiring to "gentility") forced quite early to leave schooling altogether for clerical work in a succession of lawyers' offices. Eventually he qualified for a post as reporter in the ecclesiastical law-court of "Doctors' Commons," (a court long since abolished), and from thence he graduated as a member of the Parliamentary reporting staff of the *True Sun.* From thence he passed to the service of the *Mirror of Parliament* and finally to that of the *Morning Chronicle*—being, in fact, one of the "crack" shorthand writers of his day. In his earlier reporting days he had hankerings after the stage—which he retained all his life—and made an unsuccessful attempt to get engaged as an actor at Covent Garden. During his later reporting days he blossomed out as an original writer by contributing under the pseudonym of "Boz"—a family pet name—a series of descriptive sketches (humorous and satirical) of men and manners to various journals. These sketches were thought sufficiently highly of to be collected and reprinted in volume form as *Sketches by Boz* which (in its first series) duly appeared early in 1836. Before it appeared, however, the author had already contracted to write a work in monthly parts, the first of which appeared in April 1836. This work was the now famous *Posthumous Papers of the Pickwick Club.*

At first, so far as Press notices would seem to indicate, *Sketches by Boz* was far more highly esteemed than was the newcomer. And, indeed—as is apparent to the most casual of readers—if ever a work changed under the hands of its author, and as though in spite of him, that work was *Pickwick*.

Intended by all concerned to be a collection of ephemeral sketches, whose chief point was their comicality, it gradually took on form and consistency and ultimately emerged as the supreme comic epic of English literature—with Mr. Pickwick as a nineteenth-century English Quixote and Sam Weller as his Sancho Panza—only more so. Of the first number of *Pickwick* the binder was instructed to bind up 400 copies; of the fifteenth part he was ordered to bind more than 40,000. Its sale continued steadily during the whole of its author's life—every fresh novel creating a fresh demand for *Pickwick*. And it is still (though, naturally enough, on a diminished scale) steadily in demand a century later.

Pickwick decided Dickens' fate. He had married on the strength of the £50 for which he had sold outright the copyright of *Boz*, and on his established position as a parliamentary reporter. *Pickwick* broke his connection with the reporters' gallery—he left it at the close of the session of 1836 never to return.

Thereafter, until the closing years of his life, when he took to giving public readings of his works, Dickens lived wholly by the sale of his writings.

The progression of the novels

To appreciate the historico-social significance of Dickens' work, two things must be kept constantly in mind: (1) the chronological sequence of his works; (2) the form in which they were issued.

The former is indispensable for an appreciation of the then current circumstances which prompted the direction of Dickens' thoughts, as it is for that of the development in his attitude to the problems of his time. The second is necessary as explaining much that would otherwise be inexplicable—much that critics able to consider each novel as a whole find to be artistically objectionable—Dickens' seemingly needless overcomplication of his plots, his over-emphasis upon purely subsidiary matters and characters; a certain staginess and theatricality of artifice; his indulgence in a sentimentality we now deride. If it be remembered that Dickens was nearly always writing for serial publication, either in monthly or even weekly parts, or weekly instalments in a magazine—that he was often less than a week ahead of the day of publication—in fact once or twice, when overtaken by accident, or domestic calamity, he was compelled to suspend publication for a month or two—if all this is remembered much that is apparently eccentric and purposeless in his construction will become explicable. The baseless charge that Dickens' work is "formless" is, when this mode of publication is taken into account, turned into its opposite. Not for Dickens did there exist such luxuries as Flaubert's week-long search for the "exact word," or Anatole France's seven resettings. If anything Dickens' work suffers from the tyranny of form—from an over-conscientious endeavour to confine himself within the limits of a rigid space, a drastic time-limit and a preconceived plan.

Here is a list of Dickens' chief works, the time at which they were written, and their mode of publication:

1836	*Sketches by Boz* (first series); reprint of sketches written during previous three years.
1836-7	*Pickwick Papers;* monthly parts.
1837-8	*Oliver Twist;* magazine serial.
1838-9	*Nicholas Nickleby;* monthly parts.
1840-1	*Old Curiosity Shop;* weekly parts.
1841	*Barnaby Rudge;* weekly parts.
1842	*American Notes;* 2 vols.
1843-5	*Martin Chuzzlewit;* monthly parts.
1843	*A Christmas Carol;* a Christmas book.
1844	*The Chimes;* a Christmas book.
1845	*The Cricket on the Hearth;* a Christmas book.
1846	*The Battle of Life;* a Christmas book.
1846	*Pictures from Italy;* reprint of articles issued in *Daily News.*
1846-4	*Dombey and Son;* monthly parts.
1848	*The Haunted Man;* a Christmas book.
1849-50	*David Copperfield;* monthly parts.
1852-3	*Bleak House;* monthly parts.
1854	*Hard Times;* serial in *Household Words.*
1855-7	*Little Dorrit;* monthly part.
1859	*Tale of Two Cities;* serial *All the year Round.*
1860-1	*Great Expectations;* serial *All the Year Round.*

| 1864-5 | *Our Mutual Friend;* monthly parts. |
| 1870 (Ap.-Sep.) | *Edwin Drood;* monthly parts (left unfinished at death). |

To this list must be added the Christmas stories Dickens wrote annually for various journals every Christmas from 1850-67, as well as a great many articles, stories, sketches, etc.

Ignoring the unfished *Edwin Drood* (since the break of five years between it and *Our Mutual Friend* seems to signify—as does Dickens' preoccupation with public readings during those years—that *Edwin Drood* should properly be regarded in the light of an afterthought or "come back") we have here twenty-two volumes produced in twenty-nine years, along with much other journalistic work. Of these volumes fourteen take rank as major novels; and many would claim that one or possibly more of the Christmas books *(The Chimes, The Cricket on the Hearth,* etc.) should also be counted as major works; while others again would bespeak a place in the major list for each of the three non-fictional volumes included above.

The only one of Dickens' works of fiction which is generally regarded as a failure is—surprisingly enough for those who think Dickens "invented Christmas"— one of his Christmas books, *The Battle of Life.* Be this as it may, it will be agreed, however, that speaking broadly, his non-fictional work, all interesting as it is unquestionably, is so mainly as indicative of the manner in which Dickens prepared the raw material for working up into novels.

His *American Notes,* for instance, is by many thought to be a failure. But the same material imaginatively treated and presented in *Martin Chuzzlewit* was (and is) an unqualified success.

A distinct progression is perceptible in the works in this list, and one of considerable importance for the establishment of Dickens' relationship to his time. A clear break can be made by means of those very Christmas books which (mistakenly) are supposed to be Dickens' most characteristic and heartfelt productions. These begin to appear in 1843 and end with Christmas 1848. In 1843 Dickens began *Martin Chuzzlewit;* hard upon the publication of *American Notes* in 1842. In 1848 he completed *Dombey and Son* and finished the year with *The Haunted Man*—the last of his Christmas "books" (as distinct from Christmas stories).

If now we divide Dickens' output at these points, putting all before 1842 and his first visit to America into one category, and all after 1848 into a third category, we get the following result:

Class I includes *Pickwick, Oliver Twist, Nicholas Nickleby, Old Curiosity Shop* and *Barnaby Rudge*.

Class II includes the Christmas books, the *American Notes, Pictures from Italy, Martin Chuzzlewit* and *Dombey and Son*.

Class III includes *Copperfield, Bleak House, Hard Times, Little Dorrit, Tale of Two Cities, Great Expectations,* and *Our Mutual Friend*.

It can hardly be questioned that the works in this third class are the works of Dickens' greatest maturity and power; nor can it be doubted that, this notwithstanding, there is, towards the last, a perceptible falling off in the spontaneous exuberance which characterizes *Pickwick* particularly and in general all the works of the first class. In the first period fun, high spirits, a tendency even to literary horse-play—alternating, it is true, with spells of sentimentality—strike his dominant note. It is the period of Dickens "genial unveracities."

In the third period although there is plenty of fun, it comes only as a relief to the growing sombreness of the prospect as a whole, and it has increasingly a sub-acid satirical content. *Pickwick* is not more characteristic of the first period than *Hard Times* (by many regarded as the least successful of Dickens' major works) is characteristic of the third period. If we shift our line of demarkation slightly to allow for a time-lag, transferring *Chuzzlewit* to the first period, and *Copperfield* to the middle or transitional period the classification becomes unimpeachable—a period of youthful optimism leads to a period of excitement and irritation from which emerges in turn a period of steadily intensifying pessimism. That is the sequence observable in the list of the works of Charles Dickens.

Is this sequence purely personal to the author?—an expression of purely subjective development?—of growing weariness and satiation? It is true that Dickens suffered a good deal of domestic discomfort, which culminated in his separation from his wife in 1855. The strain of this discomfort, and its culmination may have helped, say, to intensify the general gloom of his *Hard Times*. But if this were all the release should have shown a corresponding rebound in the post-separation years; which, quite conspicuously, does not appear. More still: as this domestic discomfort began quite early it should have shown itself in the works of the first period.

A truer explanation is to be found in Dickens' Radicalism and its relation to the history of his time.

His first period '36-'42 coincides with the period of the rise and culmination of the Chartist movement. His middle period covers the period of the temporary revival of Chartism, and the whole upheaval of 1848-9. It ends with the definitive triumph of European reaction in 1850; a triumph which endured unshaken during the whole of his third period.

To whatever extent personal-subjective influences may have modified Dickens' development it is more than a little noteworthy that these three periods of (1) optimism; (2) qasi-realistic-romantic excitement followed by defeat and depression; and (3) a final relapse into exacerbated pessimism, reflect exactly the moods of English Radicalism in just those years.

With a slight overlap at each end Dickens' literary lifetime *(Edwin Drood* excepted) falls in the interval between the collapse of the English Socialist movement led by Robert Owen and its revival under the hegemony of the International Working-Men's Association by Karl Marx in 1864.

It is here that we may seek, profitably, for the significance of Charles Dickens.

Dickens was born during the Napoleonic wars; to be precise, in the year of Napoleon's disastrous Moscow campaign. He entered the Press gallery of the House of Commons just after the triumphant passage of the Reform Bill in 1832 and seems to have shared to the full in the Radical enthusiasm for that measure—and also in the Radical recognition of its shortcomings. He had completed his first period of productivity before the repeal of the Corn Laws in 1846; and before the first great operative Factory Act the Ten Hours' Bill of 1847. His early experience as a reporter was gained as a contributor to Radical journals and in Radical circles. That he shared to the full in the ardour of this period is known from sources other than his later-written novels. It is known, for instance, that he took a prominent part in organizing a strike of the reporting staff of the *True Sun*—the first paper he worked upon—and that he acted successfully as the spokesman for the strikers. His early years had given him experience of poverty, and of that embittering aspect of poverty, the attempt to maintain a shabby "gentility" in the face of financial adversity. Quite early, however, he met with success beyond his wildest dreams; and for the rest of his days he was able to live in circumstances of more than comfort—of all but affluence. The fact, however, that he had to maintain his position by unremitting labours—that even if he earned much the need to maintain a position such as was demanded by the standards of gentility of his mother, his wife and her relations, made it imperative for him to be always earning more, seems to have helped to keep him from being in any way spoiled or corrupted by his success. On the contrary though the optimistic exuberance of his early years faded to give place to a decided pessimism—his pessimism was none the less a *Radical* pessimism—the pessimism of a Radical who was

all the more stubbornly Radical because he could see no immediate prospect of a Radical political triumph. In fact, the Radicalism which begot the
famous description of the Eatanswill election (in *Pickwick*) with its derision of the rival factions of Buffs (Whigs) and Blues (Tories) deepened in
this third period into what Macaulay called the "sullen Socialism" of *Hard
Times,* and the kindred atmosphere of the remaining works of this period.

As Richard Garnett observed (without properly understanding its significance) the attack upon the Fleet prison in *Pickwick* and upon the Poor Law
and Bumbledom in *Oliver Twist*—and upon the "Yorkshire" schoolmasters
in *Nickleby*—is in each case merely incidental to the novel. In *Bleak House*
the attack upon the Court of Chancery, in *Little Dorrit* the attack upon the
Circumlocution Office, and upon money-worship generally; and in *Hard
Times* the attack upon Manchester School Utilitarianism is part of the
essential ground-work of the story itself.

Dickens' Radicalism instead of mellowing in the sunshine of prosperity
into a mere benevolent Liberalism—or worse, into the self-satisfied
humbug he satirized (in *Our Mutual Friend*) as Podsnappery—did the
reverse. It stiffened, hardened and deepened into something that with a
little outside aid might easily have emerged as positive Socialism or
Communism.

Not for nothing did the highly respectable Whig, John Forster deplore
the fact that Dickens' private inclinations were for "low" company and
towards "low" courses—that his opinions were much more "subversive"
than it was expedient to publish—that his hatred of social inequalities was,
more than anything else, the reason why Dickens avoided, wherever possible, any sort of "going into society."

Those who say that Dickens "could not depict a gentleman" have a good
deal of reason for their saying. But it is not in the least to Dickens' discredit
as a man, and still less to his disparagement as a writer, that such should be
the case.

That Dickens always thought of himself as one of the common people
needs no proof. Nor does the fact that his very inability to distinguish the
proletariat as a distinct social formation proceeded, as did a similar blindness in all his contemporary humanitarian Radicals, from a subconscious
refusal to admit that anything so evil as positive class divisions could,
really, exist—except as a stupid prejudice, and a transitory relic of an evil
past. This very limitation in him, however, has another and a more revolutionary side. He is so full of the sense that the common, working-people
ought not to be discriminated against either by law, by convention, or by
economic circumstance, that he is driven continually and by instinct, to

champion the cause of the common people against each and every one of their enemies. It is this championship of the "lower-orders" which endears him to the common people and forms the basis of his abiding popularity.

A question naturally arises here: was Dickens' Radicalism a matter of doctrinal conviction reached through reasoning? Or was it spontaneous and intuitive?

The answer is easily found. So far as mere schooling and book-learning is concerned Dickens was, at any rate at the time when *Pickwick* was written, one of the least "educated" of writers. Asked after his son had become world-famous how and where Charles had been educated, the elder Dickens made answer: "Well, in a manner of speaking he may be said to have brought himself up."

The bourgeoisie and the rise of the novel

Dickens marks in fact, historically, the definitive triumph in the field of creative literature of what, by eighteenth-century standards, was an "uneducated" school of writers, and a "vulgar" art-form—the novel. Only by degrees did cultured opinion reconcile itself to regarding the novel as other than a trifling means of amusement—fit, possibly, for females, and the literates among the lower orders (who could not be expected to know any better)—but only in very exceptional cases worthy the esteem of a *gentleman* with any pretensions to real taste and learning.

The canons of true taste—in the opinion of eighteenth-century critics—had been established for all time by the foremost writers of Greece and Rome. To be thoroughly steeped in Greek and Latin literature, and to be ready at all times to assert and defend the superior excellence of their foremost writers—the "classics" *par excellence*—was the hall-mark of a man of culture and refinement. It was allowed that other nations and other languages had each their special natural "genius." It was conceded that writers who had had no training in classical studies might produce spontaneously works abounding in "natural" talent. But, these critics contended, only those who conformed as closely as possible to the methods of the classics—and who had achieved this conformity through a prolonged intimacy with them—could hope ever to attain anything near formal artistic excellence.

This contraposed antagonism between "unformed Nature" and "formed" perfection in "Art" became fixed as a convention in the period of the Grand Monarchy—the period of positive and relative reaction after the first great uprising of the bourgeoisie, the Protestant Revolution. It was symptomatric of the gathering forces of a new uprising—one doomed to take form ultimately as the Great French Revolution—when there arose a new Nature-worshipping school, which produced its prophet in Rousseau. And Rousseau avowedly received the stimulus for his *Julie: or New Héloïse* from what is by common consent the foundation work of the modern English novel—Richardson's *Pamela: or Virtue Rewarded.* With Richardson the English novel definitely begins; but, even so, and despite the work of Fielding, Smollett, Sterne, and their successors, the novel though tolerated remained in the esteem even of the novelists themselves a lower form of art; one excusable to men of culture only as a diversion in undress moments; or to women from whom any sort of culture was only to be expected in exceptional cases. It was excusable, too, in so far as it provided a vehicle for the improvement of public morals, either by its employment of satire or by its positively didactic content. But these things notwithstanding the novel remained intrinsically a thing suspect—something only to be tolerated if and when it was found to be the work of men properly respectful to the classic tradition, and to the classic standards of taste.

It was not until after the French Revolution had shaken the world to its foundation, after the fight to prevent the French Revolution from engulfing the whole earth had compelled the reactionaries everywhere to do and tolerate things till then undreamed of, that the cultured classes awoke to a realization of the fact that the old eighteenth-century standards of culture had been completely shattered and a new epoch had dawned. Ironically enough it was from the hands of a Tory—an incurable antiquary; a worshipper of everything past and gone—that the death-blow came. Walter Scott, a highly respectable Edinburgh solicitor, and an aspirant to the ranks of the landed gentry discovered in himself the faculty of writing novels which became "all the rage." It is characteristic of the canons of the time and of the author's conformity thereto that his "Waverley" novels were published anonymously. There was, it was felt, something "low," something essentially ungentlemanly about writing a novel. But, then, it was felt, too, on all hands, that Burke had spoken truly when he had said, in his famous tirade against the French Revolution (which produced a crushing retort in Tom Paine's *Rights of Man)* that "the age of chivalry has gone: the age of sophisticators, of calculators has come." Just as the landed aristocracy found it expedient—all their "chivalry" notwithstanding—to join the ranks of the "calculators" and "sophisticators," the dabblers in the funds,

the manipulators of the currency, and the riggers of tariffs for maintaining
the price of corn (and thereby of their rent rolls)—so the aristocracy of
culture found it expedient to bow the knee in the temple of Rimmon; and,
since a new novel-reading public had undoubtedly come into being, to be
appropriately thankful that the leading caterer for this new demand was
one of themselves, a man of unimpeachable respectability, and an
upholder of the Throne and Constitution.

Scott died, written-out and exhausted, the victim of a combination of
foolish pride, ill judged speculation, and a morbid sense of commercial
rectitude, just before Charles Dickens made his first essays into original
journalism. Five years after Scott's death, *Pickwick* began to appear and the
revolution which opened with Richardson and culminated in Scott entered
upon a new and a more radical phase.

The popular roots of the novel

As we have seen the novel as an art form was, before Scott, regarded as
something inherently "vulgar." It was—there was no disguising it—
indistinguishable from the mere "story-telling" in which the common
people had delighted from time immemorial. In truth, although it was, and
is, hard to extract from "cultured" critics an admission that this is the case,
it was only in a sense, and with qualifications, that Richardson's *Pamela*
was the foundation of a new art form.

Long before *Pamela* the common people had taken into favour, and, by
their patronage, had kept continually in print, such works as Bunyan's
Pilgrim's Progress, Defoe's *Robinson Crusoe,* and Swift's *Gulliver.* True, the
first of these could be technically classified as an allegory; and the second
as a fraudulent pretence at a true story of actual adventure. The third,
could, and did, take "classical" rank in so far as it was a "satire" and its
author a man of undoubted Latinity. But the fact was there none the less.
For the common people the difference between the *Pilgrim's Progress* or
Robinson Crusoe, or, for that matter, between *Moll Flanders, Roxana, Captain Jack, Journal of the Plague Year* or any one of the rest of the works of
that most prolific of writers, Daniel Defoe and *Gulliver's Travels,* was not
one of the classicality or otherwise of their form and diction. For the
common people they were all stories—and very good stories, too—stories
which differed only from the stories of Tom *Thumb, Jack and the
Beanstalk, Robin Hood and Maid Marian, Guy of Warwick* and the *Seven*

Champions of Christendom in that they were more believable as stories and their characters and incidents more such as a plain man might meet with in the course of everyday life. True the Slough of Despond as such was as little a matter of everyday fact as Jack's Beanstalk. But sloughs in which men might get bogged up to the eyebrows were as well-known to every countryman and every traveller as beanstalks were, and the subjective content of the allegory was such that every plain man could easily have experienced it for himself. To an age of growing individualism the self-help moral of *Robinson Crusoe* had a significance for the plain man that men of "culture" and gentility were debarred thereby from seeing—except, "as in a glass, darkly." Contrariwise the murderously mordant satire of Gulliver was apt to be lost on the plain man who could see in it only another, and a more plausible, tale of dwarfs and giants, and of animals, à *la AEsop,* who could talk like men and reason like " Christians." Thus Richardson founded the English novel not in the sense that he made an innovation; but in the sense that he made tolerable to the cultured classes a form of literature which till then had been abandoned to the ale-house, the chimney-corner, the idle apprentice, the nursery, and the servants' hall.

Two things made it possible for the sober-sided and sententious master-printer Samuel Richardson to work this transformation. His leading men characters were all of them fine gentlemen of unimpeachable "quality," his leading women characters were (as in the case of Pamela herself) usually of the "lower orders," rich only in unshakable virtue. The transcending of class-divisions by this " virtue triumphant," like the " true nobility," shown in the generous recognition of this virtue by the gentlemen characters (when repeated failure had shown them the impossibility of succeeding in its seduction!) was pleasing alike to the nobility and gentry and to the not-yet-ennobled commoners in whom advancing wealth and expanding trade were awakening hopes of admission to the ranks of the "quality."

The theme of King Cophetua marrying the beggar maid, and its alternate, the squire of low degree who wed the king's daughter of Hungary, was indeed a theme as old as romance itself. But Richardson gave it a new, and up-to-date, significance by making the marriage a reward of virtue in the humble and a proof of superiority to all mercenary considerations in the upper-classes. Thus in the element of toadyism to class-superiority implicit in his themes, and, simultaneously, in his assertion despite this, of the "natural aristocracy" of virtue, Richardson scored on both sides. Gentlemen and ladies of "quality" had to agree that Samuel Richardson showed a proper deference to rank and social subordination.

On the other hand, commoners could not help but be gratified to find that, after all, the true "aristocracy"—and the palm of victory—was, in the end, found to rest with their order.

For all his would-be gentility Richardson—in spite of himself—counted, as disciple Jean-Jacques Rousseau soon showed, as a force on the side of the new and revolutionary slogan, "Back to Nature."

The death of classicism—the birth of romantic-realism

It is important, too, to remember this also of Richardson—that along with Bunyan and Defoe before him, and Jane Austen and Charles Dickens after him, he is distinguished by an almost total lack of any sort of classical education. Fielding, who found *Pamela* nauseating, and who became a novelist even in spite of himself (since his first novel, begun as a burlesque of *Pamela*, ended, this notwithstanding, as an imitation superior to its original) was not only a gentleman born, but a man of classical education and attainments. He salved his gentlemanly conscience by making his earlier novels elaborate satires, in which his classical learning was turned to account in the form of a ludicrous use of the machinery and diction of the *Iliad* and the *AEneid* to present adventures in low life and brawls between trollops and their paramours.

Fielding found it possible in the end to abandon all subterfuge and disguise, and to produce in his *Amelia*, a "straight" novel, frank and unashamed. Fielding, too, was a man of social sense and understanding; one who knew, and deplored, the actual social conditions then prevailing. As his *Jonathan Wild* shows he had in him much more than Liberal—distinctly Radical potentialities.

Smollett, his rival, was of lower grade of gentility, but of an even higher grade of classicality. He followed, in his earlier novels, and outdid, Fielding in his bias towards the picaresque. But Smollett, too, produced in *Humphrey Clinker* a masterpiece of the naturalistic order in which the burlesque itself becomes transformed into a vehicle of Natureism. His Toryism had worn very thin when he wrote *Humphrey Clinker.*

Where the masters, Richardson, Fielding, and Smollett led, others were not slow to follow. Led by Horace Walpole, one school elevated the *Jack-and-the-Beanstalk* type of fable into a new baroque type of magico-mystical romance; which, while it could not in any sense be called "realist,", was if anything a more radical departure from the canons of classicism than anything in Richardson, Fielding, or Smollett—or in their successor the whimsical sentimentalist Laurence Sterne.

Out of the more everyday realistic side of the work of the great three there developed the school of domestic character-studies which culminated in Jane Austen, whose work, though not published until after Scott had made the novel the supreme literary art-form (*vice* the epic-poem *deceased*), was all written before he began.

Scott sloughing off the baroque, mystico-magical trappings of the Horace Walpole school of pseudo-romance, combined a reversion to the older line of "romantic histories" with the new line of naturalistic-domestic sentiment, and so opened the true, English, romantic school. Dickens, as little of a classicist as Richardson or Defoe, and with none of the toadyism of the one or the didactic sententiousness of the other—as self-taught as Jane Austen, and even more keenly observant; with more humour, more high spirits, more imagination, and more of resilient vivacity than either of them—or than any English novel-writer before him or since, with the only possible exception of Fielding (whom he greatly loved and admired)—Dickens carried the triumph won by Scott a stage further and established the English school of critical-romantic-realism—the school which had as its central merit the shifting of the focus of interest from life as it is for gentlemen of birth, for aristocrats of virtue, for prisoners in parlours or for the entertainingly abnormal, over to life as it is in the gross for plain men and plain women faced with plain everyday ordinary circumstances.

Dickens did not, it is true, always succeed in holding to this, his ideal, without deviating. His keen appreciation of individuality in even the most ordinary of men caused him to make ordinary people so extraordinarily vivid that they became un-ordinary. His ability to sympathize with many moods made him produce melodramatic banalities and maudlin sentimentalities with even greater facility than those writers who could produce nothing else. But with Dickens—as, on a different plane of Art, with Hogarth—the sense of men in the mass in all their intimate multiformity was so ever-present that no man before him in England, and few since, ever gave so convincing a mirror image of what life feels like to plain, ordinary, everyday common people.

Before Dickens the only writers who neglected (or broke) the unwritten law that the leading characters in a novel simply had to be "ladies" and "gentlemen," were those who adventured into the picaresque—those who either had no gentility at all like Bunyan and Defoe, or those who like Fielding and Smollett were of such undoubted gentility that they could be allowed a gentleman's privilege to sow a few literary wild oats and to deal with appreciative realism with scenes of coarseness and vulgarity in low life.

With Dickens, on the contrary, we never lose the sense of his conviction that it is in the lower ranks of life that the really interesting and worthwhile people are to be found;—that it is among the common mass that real life is adventurous and vivid. Since Dickens' time it has been only in the lower grades of fiction—only in the novelette and the serial story for semi-literates that the old tradition of the fine gentleman as the leading character—and the old motif of the village maiden who marries the squire, or the factory girl who marries the millowner—lingers on. Dickens was a petit-bourgeois in social origin; and his standpoint was that of the petit-bourgeoisie. But Dickens never forgot that he had seen his father imprisoned for debt, and had been himself, as little more than a child, condemned to slavery in a blacking factory. He was, ever and always, the petit-bourgeois in revolt.

Now that the march of history has forced the petit-bourgeoisie to yield the hegemony of the onward march of humanity to the militant proletariat it is only natural that the vein of rebellion in Dickens should be sensed by that class which has succeeded to the task in which the petit-bourgeois Radicals of Dickens' day were the pioneers.

The political-historical background to Dickens

That Dickens was, in his social origin, and in his ultimate social position, a petit-bourgeois is too obvious to need proof. That his actual life-experience was, at the outset, so much that of the lower-strata of the petit-bourgeoisie as to coincide, at points, with that of the proletariat, we have seen likewise. We know also, from the dates of his birth, his death, and his period of productive activity, that he was born into the swiftly accelerating period of the industrial revolution, and lived on through its culmination into the period of conservative self-congratulation which immediately preceded the passage of British capitalism into its imperialist phase—the phase of the neo-feudalism of finance capital, of aborted development, disintegration, international wars, revolutions and counter-revolutions.

All these later phenomena, however, lay well ahead and far out of ordinary sight when Dickens ceased his productive activity (except for the afterthought of his unfinished *Edwin Drood)* on the completion of *Our*

Mutual Friend. When Dickens as a youth of nineteen first entered the reporters' gallery of the House of Commons the great political battle of the Reform Bill—the last triumph of the Whigs—had been well and truly won. The Whigs were thenceforward to degenerate steadily, positively and relatively into simple Conservatives, ultimately to fuse with, and become indistinguishable from, plain Tories—except that their Left wing, the Radicals, was to undergo a counterprocess of separation from the main body of Whig Liberalism, which process found expression in the fight against the Corn Laws, the fight for universal Free Trade, and—to the Left of these again—the fight for the Factory Acts and for the Charter.

Dickens as an ardent youth, with his life-prospects rapidly brightening before him, was decidedly with the Radicals—since that was the party most sympathetic to his ardent and generously optimistic nature. But he does not seem to have been, at first at any rate, at all disposed to join with, or to champion, the desperate measures of the more Left-ward Chartists.

That he had acquired, and retained all his life, a supreme contempt for the House of Commons and Parliament generally—a contempt which was later to gain emphasis from his friendship with Thomas Carlyle—seems, at first, to have raised a barrier between him and the arousing masses who were, under the name of the Charter, demanding a new and a more drastic reform of Parliament (manhood suffrage, equal electoral districts, vote by ballot, annual elections, no property qualifications, and payment of members).

In any event Dickens was (until after his visit to America in 1842) preeminently a South of England man, and, by adoption, a Londoner; while the main impetus of Chartism came from the industrial Midlands and North; between which and the South of England generally the difference in social and economic circumstance was so vast as to constitute them virtually "two nations."

It is not surprising therefore that in his earlier novels Dickens' Radicalism was of the moderate order— evincing a tendency to concentrate upon incidental abuses (such as the Fleet Prison, and the blackmailing-pettyfogging aspects of the legal system in *Pickwick,* the "Yorkshire" schoolmasters in *Nickleby,* and Bumbledom in *Oliver Twist)* rather than upon any general reformation of the politico-social system itself. His *Old Curiosity Shop,* in fact, may quite well be read as a moral tract on the theme that it is in the "heart" of man that the source of evil lies. The *Old Curiosity Shop* has, of course, another and a more profound implication to which we will return. Here we are concerned only with the fact that it contains little hint of interest in the Chartist struggle whose first wave of uprising had just previously spent its force in the Newport rising of November 1839. Rather does it seem to imply a deliberate turning away from politics to the more intimate social relations between man and man which may conceivably be altered for the better by a "change of heart" in all concerned. In *Barnaby Rudge*, on the contrary, Dickens takes a political-historical subject as his theme, and handles it in such a way as to imply a total repudiation of the sentiments and methods of the physical-force Chartists.

Since *Barnaby Rudge* and with it the *Tale of Two Cities* are outstandingly exceptional in that they are the only cases in which Dickens attempted a non-contemporary, historical theme, they are worth a special examination.

From John Dennis to Madame Defarge

As its historical background *Barnaby Rudge* has the Gordon Riots in London in 1780. That of the *Tale of Two Cities* is the French Revolution; and particularly the period of the September "massacres" and the opening of the Reign of Terror in Paris in 1792-3. *Barnaby Rudge* was written in the first of the three periods into which Dickens' work falls, the period of exuberant youth and optimism. The *Tale of Two Cities* was written in his third period, that of growing disillusionment and deepening political exasperation.

In *Barnaby Rudge* a violent mob explosion (whose actual social-causation, by the way, no British social historian has, even now, fully elucidated) is handled as an outbreak of pure criminality, set on and inflamed by insanity (religious and congenital) and greed. Dickens is perfectly just, in that he blames the existence of the criminal mob—who for three days held London in their possession, looting and burning at will—upon the savage brutality of the criminal law (which thought nothing of hanging mere children for the pettiest of larcenies) and upon the more-than-criminal neglect of education by the public authorities. Also he is justifiably scathing in his contempt for the cowardice of the municipal authorities who let the outbreak grow beyond all control from sheer ineptitude and panic.

The contrast with the insurrectionary scenes in the *Tale of Two Cities* is extreme —fully as much so as is the actual historical-political contrast in their relative significance. That the Gordon riots were largely, if not wholly, spontaneous—the result of the exploitation of a promising occasion by the desperate criminal population of the slums of London—is an established fact; as much as is the fact that they were occasioned by the fermentation of anti-Popery fanaticism by the maniac Lord George Gordon. But this truth (which gives Dickens his point of departure) is not enough for him. He planned—so his biographer John Forster assures us—to describe the whole *émeute* as organized and led by three men who in the upshot prove to be inmates escaped from "Bedlam" [London's then chief lunatic asylum—officially the "Bethlehem Hospital for the Insane"]. He modified this plan in obedience to Forster's protests, but only to this extent that the occasion was shown to be created, as is historically true, by the paranoiac Lord George Gordon, while the culmination of the riot—the attack upon Newgate prison—is described as led by Barnaby (congenitally mentally deranged) by Hugh (the neglected and halfsavage bastard son of SirJohn Chester by a gipsy mother) and the sadistic monomaniac Dennis the hangman: three men who, though not positively madmen, were at least abnormal. It seems impossible to escape the conclusion that Dickens was, consciously or unconsciously, suggesting that something similar was the case with the then contemporary Chartist movement and its leaders (most of whom were, when Barnaby Rudge was written, in gaol, serving sentences for sedition, or treason). And this conclusion is reinforced almost to a certainty by the part allotted to the disgruntled apprentice Sim Tappertit and his "underground" band. Not only is the whole notion of an apprentices' conspiracy in 1774 one as totally without historical warrant as it is made to appear ludicrous; it is open to serious objection on the ground that it burlesques most unforgivably the genuine "conspiracies"—the earliest form of trade unionism—of the adult journeymen of the period. Dickens in short, cannot be acquitted of the charge of concocting a burlesque of the "underground" Radical clubs of a period of struggle against anti-Jacobin reaction, and of the trade unions of the period before the repeal of the Combination Acts in 1825—a burlesque based upon caricatures circulated by malevolent Tories and reactionaries—and palming this off, by implication, as a picture of the operative machinery of Chartist agitation. This is all the more likely to have been the case because the "moral-force" section of Chartists and with them the anti-Corn-Law school of Radicals (to which Dickens belonged) all habitually spoke and wrote of the "physical force" Chartists, and their leader, Feargus O'Connor, in just such a fashion as Dickens in *Barnaby Rudge* speaks of Sim Tappertit and his "conspiracy."

If now we turn to the *Tale of Two Cities* and study the description of the Faubourg Saint Antoine, of the preparations for the attack upon the Bastille, of its storming and, later, of the September "massacres," and of the revolutionary tribunal, we meet with a totally different tone and atmosphere. Here the revolt of the masses, instead of being treated as a mere *émeute* of desperate greed and criminal insanity, is presented with historical truth, as a just and necessitated uprising of people whose afflictions and privations had grown to be such as could no longer possibly be endured. Whereas in *Barnaby* Dickens' artistic exaggerations of reality were all in the direction of making the riots seem more irrational, more wantonly destructive and more criminal than in fact they were, in the *Tale of Two Cities* the reverse is the case. Tried by the standards of then contemporary English opinion, Dickens went to extreme lengths—beyond those, for instance of Carlyle—in vindication of the French Revolution. True, he could not quite understand the September "massacres"—any more than any of his contemporaries could. And true likewise, he, following contemporary opinion, conceived the "victims" of the purge of the prisons to be mainly aristocrats guilty of nothing but aristocracy, and innocent sempstresses guilty of nothing but innocence and sympathy for the fallen. How much it would have mended matters for him if he had known as we know, that the victims of the purge of the prisons numbered not 15,000, nor even 1,500, but 1,110 all told, that less than half of these were aristocrats and priests (of whom a considerable number were undoubtedly engaged in counter-revolutionary conspiracy) while the remainder were thieves, murderers, and prostitutes, *who were executed as such*—can only be conjectured.

This much alone is certain: that while treating both the Gordon Riots and the French Revolution as alike justly deserved punishments inflicted upon Governments and ruling classes in return for gross misrule, Dickens in the one case showed no sympathy at all for the rioters, and in the other showed a complete and wholehearted sympathy with the revolutionaries; and, up to a point, an entire agreement with, and admiration for, their methods of setting to work.

An admirable test case for comparison is provided by a contrast between Dennis the Hangman and Madame Defarge. Each is shown as possessed by a homicidal monomania. But whereas in the case of Dennis it is the product of the callous, sadistic cruelty of a hangman, ghoulishly infatuated with his craft, in the case of Madame Defarge it is the expression of a cold frenzy, begotten of long brooding over actual sufferings and real injustices too excruciating to be borne. Madame Defarge is a terrible figure—immense with tragic fury to the last. Dennis is horrible in life and despicable in death. In the contrast between their characters Dickens expresses, albeit unconsciously, his change of attitude to the conception of popular armed insurrection and revolutionary civil war.

An interesting clue reinforces this deduction. *Barnaby Rudge,* although not actually completed and published until 1841, was first conceived and provisionally drafted in 1839—that is to say during the Chartist excitements of that year, namely, the first Convention, the Birmingham battle in May, and the Newport rising in November. The *Tale of Two Cities* first entered Dickens' head as a "vague fancy" in the summer of 1857. Dickens was at the time living in France, near Boulogne, and it was in the summer of 1857 that a conspiracy to assassinate the Emperor Napoleon III was discovered. The point to grasp is that Dickens as a good Radical had no great use for "crowned heads" in any case, while, also as a good Radical, he had all the hatred for Napoleon the Little that a modern " Red" has for a Hitler, a Mussolini, a Horthy, or a Franco. Readers of the Marx-Engels *Correspondence* will remember that Marx, for instance, never referred to Louis Napoleon except under an opprobrious nickname. Crapulinsky (the son of a son of excrement), Badinguet (the name of the workman by means of whose papers and garb Louis Bonaparte escaped from prison—and also by a coincidence the name of a famous Parisian clown), Boulstrapa (a name coined from his three *coups d'état* at Boulogne, Strasbourg and Paris)—these were Marx's more printable nicknames for the Emperor of the French whom Swinburne in a published poem describes succinctly as "Bonaparte the Bastard."

This feeling, Dickens seems to have shared to the full: the fact that Dickens while living in Paris, in 1856, had made the acquaintance of Daniel Manin, the heroic leader of the short-lived Venetian Republic—(and had thereupon employed him to teach Italian to his elder daughters)—was not likely to weaken his antipathy towards the Imperial "renegade" and "assassin" of Italian liberation. "Towards the end of January, 1858," Forster tells us, on Dickens' own authority, "the idea 'of the *Tale of Two Cities* as it became in the end' began to take hold of him." And it was on January 14th, 1858 that Orsini made his attempt to assassinate "Badingue"—which very nearly succeeded. Dickens did not however "buckle down seriously to his task" until a year later—that is to say not until after all England had been stirred by the attempt of the British Government to secure the conviction of Dr. Bernard for complicity in Orsini's attempt—and, that failing, to get Parliament to pass an Act to facilitate such prosecutions for the future; in which also they failed.

These dates seem to settle the question why, for the second time, Dickens departed from his usual custom and attempted a full length novel upon an historical theme. They help to reinforce the conclusion supported by the internal evidence of the two novels, *Barnaby Rudge* and the *Tale of Two Cities*—that in between 1839 and 1859 Dickens' Radicalism had modified in the direction of being much more ready to appreciate the need for a mass uprising and much more ready to tolerate the use of armed force. Remembering Dickens' feelings towards Napoleon III the theme of triumphant insurrection handled in the *Tale of Two Cities* might, in modern jargon, be described as a "wish fulfilment."

When we remember too, that this *Tale of Two Cities* followed next after *Little Dorrit*—the novel in which Dickens delivered a thinly-veiled attack upon bourgeois society in general under the image of the Marshalsea (the Debtors' Prison) and upon its governing class under the image of the Circumlocution Office—as this novel, too, followed next upon *Hard Times,* the novel in which "apart from one exquisitely affecting passage" Macaulay found nothing but "sullen Socialism"—the force of the conclusion becomes irresistible.

The significance of "hard times"

An examination of *Hard Times*—generally regarded as the least estimable of his major works—will make the issue clearer.

The scene of *Hard Times* is laid in the North of England, in an imaginary town (Coketown) which may be identified as a composite picture of Manchester, Oldham, Bolton, Blackburn and Preston, as they were in or about 1853. The central action of the book turns on the complete failure of the "perfect" system of education and of ethics carried into effect by Thomas Gradgrind, M.P., Millowner and his friend Josiah Bounderby, Manufacturer and Banker, both of them followers of the "hard-headed" utilitarian Manchester school. "What I want," says Mr. Gradgrind, "is *facts*" And all that children need to be told, or to learn, are "facts"—meaning by "facts" statistical data, modes of formal classification, and a keen appreciation of the need and duty to "buy in the cheapest market and sell in the dearest." Josiah Bounderby boasts himself a man who has got on, and "made himself" entirely without aid. He represents himself (quite falsely) as having been born in a ditch and deserted by a heartless mother and left in the charge of an even more depraved gin-sodden grandmother. As he "got on" entirely without help so others might and could and therefore should do. Any complaint from workers was to him a demand that they should be "fed on turtle and venison with a golden spoon!" Thomas Gradgrind, M.P., indicates his faith by naming his younger sons Malthus and Adam Smith respectively. In the end Thomas Gradgrind's eldest son, falling into dissipation as an inevitable reaction against the dreary monotony of his upbringing, robs Bounderby's bank at which he is employed; while his sister Louisa married to Bounderby and driven distracted—partly by her physical aversion for him, partly by his callous conceit, partly by the general starvation of her emotions, and partly by the persecution of her would-be seducer, a "gentlemanly" protégé of the two friends, with aspirations to represent the manufacturing interest in Parliament—flies for refuge to her father's home in a state of complete nervous collapse.

In the upshot young Tom Gradgrind's theft is detected. But he is enabled to escape from the country and from the legal consequences of his crime by the instrumentality of a group of circus-performers, who, at the opening of the novel, are shown as the objects of the fierce utilitarian scorn and persecution of both Gradgrind and Bounderby. This final liaison with the circus group is effected by one of their number, Sissy, who at the beginning of the novel (after she had been abandoned by her father, who, grown too old for clowning and tumbling, thinks she will have a better chance in life if he disappears) is adopted into the Gradgrind household as a maid-companion first to his daughter, then to Mrs. Gradgrind, the mother. Sissy likewise nurses Louisa back to health; and in thus functioning as the heroine she forms the final concrete revelation of the worse than futility of the Manchester School of Education and Ethics.

The management of the story is notable for the almost complete absence of that vivacious sparkle, which in the novels of his first period seemed inseparable from anything and everything Dickens wrote; and which remained, however restrained he became, second-nature with him to the end. There are certainly flashes of fun even in *Hard Times;* but as a whole it is astonishingly free from humour—as distinct from acidulous satire— in fact, for Dickens, amazingly so. Macaulay's judgment upon it ("sullen Socialism") is not far from the truth—although "coldly furious" would be a better description than "sullen." It is also remarkable in that it contains the one (almost the only) outstanding instance of faulty observation in all Dickens. His description of the trade union—its meetings, its leader, its treatment of the "conscientious non-unionist," Stephen Blackpool, and most of all of Stephen's reason for refusing to join the union—all this is all wrong from beginning to end. So rarely did Dickens take his view of men and things at second-hand that this instance (in which he seems to have been misled by Thomas Carlyle, to whom the book is dedicated, and through Carlyle by the Tory Press and the Whig politicians) is truly remarkable.

In the main, however, this blemish notwithstanding, Dickens presents the relation between employers and employed faithfully and well, and shatters the Manchester School philosophy as effectively as ever it has been done. Moreover, faulty though his description of his trade union is, it is well to remember that to this day, adequate descriptions of the nature and purposes of trade unions, of their mode of operation, of the conduct of strikes and lock-outs, and of the whole phenomena of working-class struggle are, apart from avowedly Socialist and Communist writings, as rare as white blackbirds.

This is true, not only of the novel, but of the cinema, and the ordinary newspaper press. Hence it is remarkable that Dickens shows even in his faults a genuine sympathy for the workers. Stephen Blackpool's refusal to act as informer, and his victimization by Bounderby in consequence, shows an appreciation of the spirit of the workers that few writers even to-day manage to achieve. The few characters in *Hard Times* are well and clearly drawn, with only a minimum of the exaggeration which borders upon caricature. Few would agree with Ruskin in saying that *Hard Times* is "in several respects the greatest he has written." But there is little or nothing to object to in what Ruskin goes on to say:

> He [Dickens] is entirely right in his main drift and purpose in every book he has written; and all of them, but especially *Hard Times,* should be studied with close and earnest care by persons interested in social questions. They will find much that is partial, and because partial, apparently unjust; but if they examine all the evidence on the other side, which Dickens seems to overlook, it will appear after all their trouble, that his view was the finally right one, grossly and sharply told.—RUSKIN: *Unto This Last,* I, 10, note.

In 1860, six years after the publication of the completed *Hard Times,* Ruskin began his attack upon Manchester School economics in the *Cornhill Magazine* under the title of *Unto This Last.* After three instalments had appeared the editor (none other than W. M. Thackeray himself) found it impossible any longer to brave the storm of abuse excited by Ruskin's views. Publication of *Unto This Last* was discontinued, on the frankly admitted ground that it was felt generally to be "too deeply tainted with Socialistic heresy to conciliate subscribers." At the end of 1862 Ruskin tried again, this time in *Frazer's Magazine* edited by Jas. Anthony Froude.

Froude had invited Ruskin's articles expressly because he felt himself to be made of sterner stuff than the softhearted (if satirical) Thackeray. Also, since the readers of *Frazer's* had been tolerating Carlyle for years, it was reasonable to suppose that they would prove more receptive to Ruskin's teaching than the more dilettanti readers of the *Cornhill.* In the end the difference proved to be no more than this: four instalments of the new work, *Munera Pulveris,* appeared (as against the three of *Unto This Last)* before public clamour forced the haughty and unconciliatory Froude to surrender even as Thackeray had done. It would seem from this that Dickens manifested his customarily abnormal acuteness when he felt and showed that exasperated and pugnacious sense of pulling against the stream of a reactionary public opinion which Macaulay notes, but mistakes for "sullenness."

The "main drift and purpose" of Dickens' *Hard Times*—which Ruskin is shrewd enough to see is also to be detected by the discerning as the "main drift and purpose" underlying all of Dickens' work—is the attack upon the Manchester School, *laissez faire,* economics and ethics.

Marx said of bourgeois economics that it holds up as its ideal, "an ascetic but usurious miser, and an ascetic but productive slave":

> Its main dogma, [said Marx], is self-abnegation, the renunciation of life and of all human wants. The less you eat, drink, buy books, the more seldom you attend theatres, dances, the café, the less you write, love, theorize, sing, paint, fish, etc., the more you save, the greater grows your fortune, which neither moth nor rust can corrupt—your capital.

This, as will be perceived, is merely another way of presenting the charge scathingly formulated in the *Communist Manifesto:*

> The bourgeoisie wherever it has got the upper hand has put an end to all feudal, patriarchal, idyllic relations. It has pitilessly torn asunder the motley feudal ties that bound man to his natural superiors, and has left no other *nexus* between man and man than naked self-interest, than callous "cash-payment." It has drowned the most heavenly ecstasies of religious fervour, of chivalrous enthusiasm, of philistine sentimentalism in the icy water of egotistical calculation. It has resolved personal worth into exchange-value, and in place of the numberless indefeasible chartered freedoms, has set up that single, unconscionable freedom—Free Trade.—MARX-ENGELS, *Communist Manifesto.*

There is not the slightest reason to suppose that Dickens had ever seen the *Communist Manifesto*—nor is there any need to suppose it. The passage in the *Manifesto* is little more than a brilliantly forcible summary of the charges which had been hurled at the bourgeoisie and its rule by a number of critics including those of the schools of Robert Owen and the English Socialists—with whose teaching Dickens must have been more or less familiar, though indirectly, through his experience as a Parliamentary reporter—and of that of his friend and admirer, Thomas Carlyle. This gives all the greater force, therefore, to the passages in *Hard Times* in which Dickens takes a ground indistinguishable from that taken by Marx and Engels.

It was a fundamental principle of the Gradgrind philosophy that everything was to be paid for. Nobody was ever on any account to give anybody anything, or render anybody help without purchase. Gratitude was to be abolished and the virtues springing from it were not to be. Every inch of the existence of mankind, from birth to death, was to be a bargain across a counter. And if we didn't get to Heaven that way, it was not a politico-economical place, and we had no business there.—*Hard Times*, III, viii.

This again was one of the fictions of Coketown. Any capitalist there who had made sixty thousand pounds out of sixpence, always professed to wonder why the sixty thousand nearest hands didn't each make sixty thousand pounds out of sixpence; and more or less reproached them every one for not accomplishing the little feat. What I did you can do. Why don't you go and do it?—*Hard Times*, II, i.

[Certain] aspects of Coketown were in the main inseparable from the work by which it was sustained; against them were to be set off comforts of life which found their way all over the world, and elegancies of life which made (we will not ask how much of) the fine lady who could scarcely bear to hear the place mentioned. The rest of its fictions were voluntary and they were these.

You saw nothing in Coketown but what was severely workful. If the members of a religious persuasion built a chapel there—as the members of eighteen religious persuasions had done—they made it a pious warehouse of red brick, with sometimes (but this is only in highly ornamental examples) a bell in a birdcage on the top of it.

The jail might have been the infirmary, the infirmary might have been the jail, the town hall might have been either or both, or anything else for anything that appeared to the contrary in the graces of their construction. Fact, fact, fact, everywhere in the material aspect of the town; fact, fact, fact, everywhere in the immaterial. Everything was fact from the lying-in hospital to the cemetery, and what you couldn't state in figures, or show to be purchaseable in the cheapest market and saleable in the dearest, was not and never should be world without end, Amen.—*Hard Times*, I, v.

The perplexing mystery of the place was, Who belonged to the eighteen denominations? Because whoever did, *the labouring people did not* [our italics]. It was very strange to walk through the streets of a Sunday morning and note how few of them the barbarous jangling of bells that was driving the sick and nervous mad, called away from their own quarter, from their own close rooms, from the corners of their own streets where they lounged listlessly, gazing at all church and chapel going, as at a thing with which they had no manner of concern.

Nor was it merely the stranger who noticed this, because there was a native organization in Coketown itself whose members were to be heard of in the House of Commons every session, indignantly petitioning for Acts of Parliament that should make these people religious by main force.

Then came the Teetotal Society, who complained that these same people *would* get drunk, and proved at tea-parties that no inducement human or Divine (except a medal), would induce them to forego their custom of getting drunk. Then came the chemist and druggist, with other tabular statements, showing that when they didn't get drunk they took opium. Then came the experienced chaplain of the jail with more tabular statements, outdoing all the previous tabular statements, and showing that the same people *would* resort to low haunts, hidden from the public eye, where they heard low singing, and saw low dancing, and mayhap joined in it; and where A.B., aged twenty-four next birthday, and committed for eighteen months' solitary, had himself said (not that he had ever shown himself worthy of belief) that his ruin had begun, as he was perfectly sure and confident that otherwise he would have been a tip-top moral specimen.

Then came Mr. Gradgrind and Mr. Bounderby... who could, on occasion, furnish more tabular statements ...from which it clearly appeared—in short it was the only clear thing in the case—that these same people were a bad lot altogether, gentlemen; that do what you would for them they were never thankful for it, gentlemen; that they were restless, gentlemen; that they never knew what they wanted....—*Hard Times,* I, v.

These extracts have great significance in the light of their parallelism with Marx and Engels, and that of their endorsement by Ruskin as true and as advancing a doctrine implicit in all Dickens', work; also in that of their characterization by Macaulay as "sullen Socialism." They lead naturally to a consideration of two leading aspects of Dickens' critical-realist-romantic attitude towards bourgeois society: (1) his attitude to education and the position of the child, generally; (2) his attitude towards the public authorities, the ruling-class, and bourgeois society generally.

As a prelude to this examination and in further elucidation of Dickens' Radicalism, we will first of all examine his most hotly criticized, nonfictional work, his *American Notes.* This, in turn, requires its prelude—a consideration of its period.

The rise and collapse of victorian radicalism

That Dickens' literary lifetime covered a period of break-neck transformation is evidenced by the novels themselves. In *Pickwick* men travel from place to place by road, in stage coaches, hackney coaches, and hardgalloping post-chaises. How well Dickens knew these roads, and these methods of conveyance is witnessed over and over again in his novels. In *Pickwick*, in *Martin Chuzzlewit*, in *David Copperfield* and in *Bleak House* he gives vivid pictures of England viewed from the road; pictures so vivid, and covering so many moods, times of the day, and varieties of weather—all described as only one with first-hand experience could describe them—that they remain photographed in the imagination for years. The railway begins with *Dombey* and with its coming Dickens seems to feel that something— he is not quite sure what—has gone out of his life. In actual practice he used the railway a lot; but it never grew to fill the same place in his affections as did the older mode of transit. It figures only incidentally in the novels which followed *Dombey*.

With the rise and triumph of the railroad went on that consolidation of the rule of the manufacturing bourgeoisie which was ushered in by their political triumph with the Reform Bill of 1832. The gathering wave of Liberalistic Radicalism which reached its peak in that triumph thereafter broke into a whirl of counter-tendencies. One current set increasingly towards Conservatism; another towards insurrectionary Republican-Radicalism and Chartism. As is well known the crisis came in 1848-9. In that "Year of Revolutions" the Radical-Republican-Chartist-Communist current spent itself; achieving only (in the Repeal of the Corn Laws in Britain; the definite overthrow of the Bourbons in France; and the beginnings of constitutionalism in Germany) the completion of the triumph of the industrial and financial bourgeoisie. The passing of the commercial crisis, the discovery of gold in California in 1849, and in Australia in 1850, opened a period of expanding trade and mass emigration which eased the sociopolitical pressure and began the epoch of Victorian "prosperity." Not until Dickens' literary life had nearly closed did the ferment of revolution begin to show signs of quickening again. Dickens' last (completed) full-size novel, *Our Mutual Friend*, was appearing in monthly parts when in September 1864 the International Working Men's Association was founded.

Up to 1848 it had seemed, to every ardent Radical, as though the triumph of 1832 was to be merely an overture. A section of the Whigs did, it is true, speak of the Reform of Parliament achieved in that year as marking "finality." The British Constitution ("the envy of the whole world") had been, they said, nearly perfect before that Great Reform. That accomplished, and it was quite perfect. To ask for more was preposterous. One of the reasons for the universal popularity of the delicious scene in *Oliver Twist* when the three-parts starved workhouse-orphan asks for "more," was that it lent itself so admirably to use by cartoonists and orators in their derision of the Conservative Whigs and their doctrine of "finality." And one, at any rate, of the reasons why those ardent Radicals, to whose camp Dickens belonged, were so impatient with (and unjust to) physical-force Chartism was because they believed that all those things (extension of suffrage, vote by ballot, etc.) could be won without going to their violent lengths.

What the "American Notes" implied

To appreciate Dickens' reactions to the U.S.A. on visiting the country in 1842, one must remember first of all the Utopianism inherent in the Radicalism of Dickens' day. For them the U.S.A. was the land of their ideal—the land where all were free and equal. They expected more from the U.S.A., by far than modern critical-realist Socialism expects from the U.S.S.R. Dickens' acidulous criticism of men and manners in the U.S.A. (a criticism set out in his *American Notes* and reaffirmed in his *Martin Chuzzlewit)* is, therefore, the criticism of an acutely disappointed Radical-Republican who could not help feeling—or saying out loud that he felt— that the actual state of things then prevailing in the U.S.A. instead of being ideal, bade fair to develop all the vices and all the evils Radicalism and Republicanism were trying to abolish in Europe. It has been suggested— quite without warrant—that Dickens' success and his rapid rise to relative affluence had turned him into a snob and a reactionary. As good a proof as any that this is not so is given by Macaulay's attitude to the *American Notes*— Macaulay being, in the Whig camp of that date, the chief Centrist. Macaulay wrote to the editor of the *Edinburgh Review,* asking that the *American Notes* should be reserved for him to review. After reading it he declines to review it. He cannot praise it, he says, and he will not damn it. If the *American Notes* had been what it is generally supposed to be (by those who have not read it) a disparagement of American Republicanism and democracy by comparison with the "glorious" British Constitution, Macaulay would have leapt to its defence. While Dickens was in the U.S.A.

gathering material for these *Notes* Macaulay fought in Parliament in the vanguard of the opponents of the Charter:

> The dread and aversion, said Macaulay, with which I regard universal suffrage, would be greatly diminished if I could believe that the worst effect which it could produce would be to give us an elective first magistrate and a senate, instead of a Queen and a House of Peers. My firm conviction is that, in our country, universal suffrage is incompatible, not with this or that form of government, but with all forms of government, and with everything for the sake of which forms of government exist; that it is incompatible with property, and that it is consequently incompatible with civilization.—MACAULAY: *Speech*, May 3rd, 1842.

These being Macaulay's sentiments he was not at all likely to be enthusiastic over Dickens' attitude towards "dollar worship" or over his attitude to legislative bodies generally:

> In the first place—it may be from some imperfect development of my organ of veneration—I do not remember having ever fainted away, or having even been moved to tears of joyful pride, at the sight of any legislative body. I have borne the House of Commons like a man, and have yielded to no weakness, but slumber, in the House of Lords. I have seen elections for borough and county, and have never been impelled (no matter which party won) to damage my hat by throwing it up into the air in triumph, or to crack my voice by shouting forth any reference to our Glorious Constitution, to the noble purity of our independent votes, or to the unimpeachable integrity of our independent members. Having withstood such strong attacks upon my fortitude, it is possible that I may be of a cold and insensible temperament, amounting to iciness in such matters; and therefore my impressions of the live pillars of the Capitol at Washington must be received with such grains of allowance as their free confession may seem to demand.—DICKENS: *American Notes*, Chap. VIII.

Dickens goes on to comment with passionate indignation on the treatment meted out by Congress to those who, headed by the aged ex-President John Quincey Adams, continually raised, despite the official ban of the House, the question of Negro-slavery and its evils. Macaulay could not, for very shame's sake, as the son of his father, attack Dickens for his ungoverned and ungovernable hatred of Negro-slavery and all that it entailed. At the same time Dickens' profound contempt for both the House of Commons and the House of Lords, for "independent" voters, and "independent" representatives alike, must have been as shocking to Macaulay (the King of the Whigs) as the very People's Charter itself. Hence he did not review Dickens' *American Notes*—which was, perhaps, all the better for both of them.

The faults of Dickens' *American Notes* are transparently obvious. A completely disproportionate insistence to the point of nausea upon the more repulsive phenomena of the then universal American habit of tobacco-chewing—an all-too-obvious tendency to generalize the "character" of a nation from the people seen in public places and public vehicles—a decidedly querulous reiteration of complaints of dirtiness and discomfort in public conveyances and hotels; these things tend to give the *Notes,* at first glance, the appearance of emanating from a Tory snob.

And, as such, they were naturally resented—notwithstanding those many, more numerous, and far more forcible passages in which Dickens showed himself to be anything but a Tory and genuinely enthusiastic over all the good he saw in the American people, and in the constitution of the U.S.A.

The truth is that Dickens gave himself no chance with his *American Notes.* He was handicapped heavily by his own personal limitations; and still more by the circumstances of his visit. Personally, he was handicapped by a complete lack of historical sense. When he witnessed the barbarous ferocity of party strife in Congress on the slavery issue he did not realize that he was witnessing the opening phases of what, twenty years later, was to materialize as the bloodiest civil war the modern world had till then known. He shows no sign of grasping either the deliberateness or the calculated "provocation" (in the good sense) in the policy pursued by old Quincey Adams.

Quincey Adams, as representative for Massachusetts, returned to public life expressly as an "anti-slavery" man. He was not an "abolitionist"—he was in fact, as Lincoln was later, one of the favourite objects of abuse by the Abolitionists. He did not propose to interfere with slavery in those states in the Union in which it was constitutionally established. But he did propose to prevent—and spent his later years in the forefront of the fight to prevent—any extension of slavery beyond those states. As representative for Massachusetts, however, he felt it his duty to present every petition for the abolition of slavery sent up to Congress by his constituents; and to open a debate upon the issue each petition raised. After the tiny, savagely-bloody, but easily-suppressed Negro insurrection led in Virginia, in 1831, by the half-crazed-by-ill-treatment Negro, Nat Turner, the slave states lived in perpetual fear of similar (but bigger and better-managed) insurrections. Hence in February 1836, the House of Representatives took the step of refusing thenceforward to receive any petitions relating to slavery.

Adams protested fiercely that this was a violation of constitutional right; and although shouted down, thereafter persisted in the teeth of all opposition in waging a fight for the right to petition. From 1836 to 1843—when the House, worn down by Adams' persistence, and the tremendous storm of public approval he aroused, reluctantly gave way and rescinded the "gagging" resolution—Adams continued to present petitions. "During that time," says an American writer, Chas. W. Thompson, in his *Fiery Epoch,*—

> the mere appearance of Adams on the floor of the House, for any purpose, was enough to precipitate what we should now call a riot; resolutions of censure were offered over and over again; but he continued to present all petitions he received, from any quarter, including a letter advocating his own assassination.

When Dickens visited the House the fight was at the stage of extreme exacerbation—the stage immediately prior to the House's surrender. Dickens, from sheer lack of knowledge of the history of the struggle, could only see the shockingly bad manners and vulgarity involved in assailing with hard words and contumely one of the elder statesmen of the Republic. He could only see an old gentleman, whose grey hairs and past record (as an ex-President) should have commanded a respectful hearing even from opponents, met with affronts, interruptions, insults, and savage denunciations. He didn't realize that the old gentleman, for all his grey hairs, was fighting a winning fight; and was deliberately provoking the bad manners of his opponents because of their propaganda value with the electorate at large.

Dickens, too, saw these all-too-obvious " graft" and "corruption" of politics in the U.S.A.; as he saw the only-too-apparent money greediness, and success worship then prevalent there. He did not at first realize that the reason why graft and corruption were not so patent in Britain was because these things had in Britain become *institutionalized;* while money-greediness and successworship were in Britain veiled under the camouflage of "political-economy."

Dickens in short felt, but without understanding—and was horrified at—the logical outcome of the untrammelled rule of the bourgeoisie;— that which Marx and Engels afterwards expressed in a sentence: "the bourgeoisie has substituted for exploitation veiled by religious and political illusions—naked, shameless, direct, brutal exploitation."

Dickens, at the time, did not realize that the things which horrified him most were only the normal consequences of that political emancipation of the bourgeoisie for which as a Radical he was enthusiastic. His American experiences none the less seem to have, in time, brought him to the brink of this understanding. In any event they created a crisis in his political development—the first outcome of which was a period of excited uncertainty in which he was torn both ways.

This vacillation is already evidenced in the *American Notes* (and in *Martin Chuzzlewit,* which followed it) in the things which express, naively, the handicap upon Dickens of the circumstances in which he made his first visit to the U.S.A. He was travelling with Mrs. Dickens and her maid as travelling companions, and Mrs. Dickens was a very genteel person, one not at all easy to please. It is to Mrs. Dickens (it seems fair to surmise) that we owe all that exaggerated over-emphasis upon tobacco chewing and spitting, and all those complaints about dirtiness, untidiness and lack of gentility, which spoil the *American Notes.* Dickens was himself a very spruce and tidy little man; but he had a sense of humour and of proportion. One detects in the *American Notes* the effect of that "nagging" disposition in Mrs. D. which was, in the end, the cause of their separation. In 1842 Dickens submitted to it and even, from mistaken chivalry, adopted Mrs. D.'s petulant fault-finding attitude as expressing his own feelings. Later he revolted against this domestic infliction, and was all the better for doing so.

In any event Dickens could not do himself justice on this American trip. He was "lionized" to the point of extravagance, and he wasn't used to it. He, in fact, did not like it—and actively resented the intrusion upon his privacy that the process of "lionizing" involved. He was determined not to be bought over by flattery. And rather than seem to be so, he over-stressed, and over-drew all the things he found to complain of. Yet when all is said and done the net outcome of Dickens' criticism remained just and valid. Before all he hated Negro-slavery; he hated blatant dollar-worship; he was disgusted at the New York "yellow" press; and he was revolted at the solitary confinement system in the prisons. Also he was, and justifiably, angry at the American refusal to adopt any international copyright law. On all these points history has vindicated him—Americans themselves being the judges.

We have dwelt at length upon Dickens' *American Notes,* because superficial critics have represented it in a light which seems to contradict the thesis that Dickens' standpoint was that of a Radical. If, however, the view be taken that Dickens reacted unfavourably to his first view of the U.S.A. because, as a Utopian Radical, he had hoped for and expected something much better, we get from the *American Notes* a confirmation of his Radicalism, plus a reinforcement. We get, that is to say, reason to believe that Dickens was much more profoundly Radical—much more near to *rev-*

olutionary Republicanism—nearer to the very fringe of Communism—than in his earlier works he allowed himself to appear.

We have noted above that, in his description of the Eatanswill Election, in *Pickwick,* Dickens quite early showed a contempt for English parliamentarianism. In *Nicholas Nickleby* too, there is a murderously scathing description of a Member of Parliament who offers fifteen shillings a week as a fair wage for a secretary and speech scribe. These line up with the contemptuous portrait of the magistrate, Nupkins, in *Pickwick,* the scathing picture of the magistrate Fang in *Oliver Twist,* those of the lawyers Dodson and Fogg in *Pickwick,* and of the lawyer Sampson Brass in the *Old Curiosity Shop*—to say nothing of the descriptions of Sergeant Buzfuz and of the judge in *Pickwick,* of Bumble and of the Poor Law Guardian in *Oliver Twist.* All these satires show Dickens' attitude to the existing order as far from orthodox. But, if Dickens had gone no further, they might well have been regarded as satires directed from the standpoint of such a reactionary Tory-Socialism as was expressed at about this time by Lord John Manners in his celebrated lines:

> Let trade and commerce, laws and learning die,
> But leave us still our old nobility.

This was also, at that time, the standpoint of Benjamin Disraeli; and Tory-Socialism also formed the groundstrata in the philosophy of Thomas Carlyle, as it did also in that of John Ruskin. Dickens was different. From the time of his American visit his Radicalism becomes more subtle, more far-reaching, and more profound.

In regard to Parliament, for instance, he expresses himself freely in a letter written from America to his friend Forster (after a visit to the Pennsylvania State legislature):

> You know my small respect for our House of Commons. These local legislatures are too insufferably apish of mighty legislatures, to be seen without bile....

But a few years later (in March 1844, to be exact) Dickens writes to Forster:

> Heaven help us, too, from explosions nearer home 'he has just predicted an explosion in America on the slavery question'. I declare I never go into what is called "society" that I am not aweary of it, despise it, hate it, and reject it. The more I see of its extraordinary conceit, and its stupendous ignorance of what is passing out of doors, the more certain I am that it is approaching the period when being incapable of reforming itself it will have to submit to being reformed by others off the face of the earth.

The date of this letter suggests a comparison with Engels' *Condition of the Working Class in England in* 1844 —a comparison which enhances our opinion of Dickens' acuteness. But the letter itself, written while Dickens was busy with the concluding chapters of *Chuzzlewit* suggests something else; namely, that in the character of Pecksniff, Dickens was, even more than he knew, summing up his own inner conviction about bourgeois society. •

In *Bleak House* Dickens returns to the theme of Parliament and describes a general election (and the concern therein of Sir Leicester Deadlock):

> England has been some weeks in the dismal strait of having no pilot (as was well observed by Sir Leicester Deadlock) to weather these storm; and the marvellous part of the matter is that England has not appeared to care very much about it, but has gone on eating and drinking and marrying and giving in marriage, as the old world did in the days before the flood. But Coodle knew the danger, and Doodle knew the danger, and all the followers and hangers-on had the clearest possible perception of the danger. At last Sir Thomas Doodle has not only condescended to come in but has done it handsomely, bringing in with him all his nephews, all his male cousins, and all his brothers-in-law. So there is hope for the old ship yet.
>
> Doodle has found that he must throw himself upon the country—chiefly in the form of sovereigns and beer. In this metamorphosed state he is available in a good many places simultaneously, and can throw himself upon a considerable portion of the country at one time. Britannia being much occupied in pocketing Doodle in the form of sovereigns, and swallowing Doodle in the form of beer, and in swearing herself black in the face that she does neither— plainly to the advancement of her glory an morality—the London season comes to an end.

The force of this satire was much more immediate and biting for the original readers of *Bleak House,* since a General Election occurred while the work was in progress (1852)—one which had as its aftermath the hearing of no fewer than ninety-five petitions against the declared results on the ground of bribery and corrupt practices, as well as more than as many again which were talked of but which did not materialize.

Members of Parliament figure in *Hard Times,* in the person of Mr. Gradgrind; in *Little Dorrit* in the person of Mr. Merdle the fraudulent financier who precipitates a crisis by committing suicide (a character modelled partly upon the brothers Sadleir of the Royal Tipperary Bank, who were, with their no less notorious colleague, Keogh, the leaders of the Irish parliamentary party nicknamed the "Pope's Brass Band," and partly upon George Hudson, M.P., these Railway King). In *Our Mutual Friend* Mr.

Veneering is returned to Parliament by his satellites, at the head of whom figures the ineffable Mr. Podsnap. But in all these cases the M.P. is attacked only incidentally, only as part of that general assault upon bourgeois society which develops from *Bleak House* to the end of Dickens' career.

*

Dickens and education

Dickens' contempt for Parliament has its complement in his concern for and interest in that social service which Parliament in his day most scandalously neglected— education in all its phases. As were all the Radicals of his time, Dickens was an ardent advocate of educational facilities for the masses. He expressed himself to this effect in a number of public functions. Even if he had not done so the fact would have been apparent from the way in which he continually returns to the theme of schools and schooling—and the larger aspects of education—in his novels.

In *Hard Times* the novel actually opens in the "model" school (Gradgrind-Bounderby patent) in Coketown. Borrowing a device perennial in English literature— one that Smollett was particularly fond of, but which was common as far back as the Elizabethan dramatists and earlier— Dickens indicates his valuation of this school by the name of the schoolmaster, Mr. M'Choakumchild. Here, however, Dickens' attack is not specially upon the school, as such, but upon the whole Gradgrind-Bounderby philosophy, within which the school and its curticulum were constrained. It was that philosophy, and not congenital predisposition on the part of the schoolmaster, which denied to the children any and every sort of food for their wonder, their affections, or their imaginations—and regarded these things as positive blemishes needing complete eradication. What becomes thus a soul-destroying system in the Coketown school, Dickens also finds in one form or another in most of the schools he describes.

A young ladies' boarding-school forms an ingredient in a comic episode in *Pickwick,* but only in its exterior, non-educational aspect. More pertinent is the workhouse school in *Oliver Twist* (to which, incidentally, Fagin's private-school for pickpockets is a grimly ironical contrast), and also Squeers' School, Dotheboys Hall, in *Nicholas Nickleby.* Another young ladies' seminary, also seen from the outside, is featured in the *Old Curiosity Shop;* as is also a village school with a schoolmaster of an idyllic type.

In the novels of the third period, to which *Hard Times* belongs, school life (that of Esther) is sketched in *Bleak House* (and contrasted mordantly with the absence of any school life for Poor Joe). In addition to this, and the M'Choakumchild school already mentioned, there is a vividly grotesque description of an old-style dame-school in *Great Expectations*, and, in *Our Mutual Friend*, a close study of the schoolmaster, Bradley Headstone, of his pupil teacher, Charlie Hexam, and of the schoolmistress, Miss Peecher.

But it is in the novels of the middle, transitional period — in *Dombey* and *David Copperfield* — that Dickens is most prolific in his studies of school and schoolmasters.

In *Dombey* we have that ogress, Mrs. Pipchin and her establishment. Then we have Dr. Blimber and his academy. Finally, by way of a pendant to these, we have, in the background, the lamentable Rob, and his experiences as a "Charitable Grinder." In *Copperfield* we are richest of all. There is the idyllic home-schooling with Mrs. Copperfield as instructress and Peggotty as both assistant and audience. There is Mr. Murdstone and his cane. There is Mr. Creakle, his school and his savagery. And finally there is the school of Dr. Strong.

It is a commonplace of criticism to say that an author's powers of description are better tested by his similarly situated characters than by those most widely contrasted. Macaulay, quite rightly, argues ardently for the superlative merit shown by Jane Austen in getting such a world of differences out of characters apparently so uniform and so unpromising as the number of Church of England curates who figure in her novels. Yet even Jane Austen, superlatively skilful as she is, cannot with her curates match Dickens' team of schoolmasters.

Squeers in *Nickleby;* Miss Monflathers and also the old schoolmaster in the *Old Curiosity Shop;* Mr. Murdstone and Creakle; Mrs. Pipchin and Miss Blimber; Dr. Blimber and Dr. Strong; Mr. M'Choakumchild and Bradley Headstone, to name only these — although, since Pecksniff is professedly a teacher of architecture, he too should be added, as should Ruth Pinch, since she was a governess — here is a gallery of schoolmasters and schoolmistresses which for variety cannot be matched. And, moreover, all, or most of them (since M'Choakumchild is presented only, as it were, in silhouette) are drawn with such masterly precision of detail as to indicate the author's never-failing interest in, and concern for, the whole question of education and all that it implies.

Dickens' handling of his scholastic characters, too, is such as to give the lie direct to the commonest of all critical objections to his work — that he only drew characters "in the flat." Squeers, Mr. Murdstone and Creakle are all brutes, with a relish for inflicting physical pain upon their child victims. Yet each is totally distinct and different from the others in type. Squeers' savagery to his victims is part of the whole uncouth and illiterate barbarity of his nature; and Dickens' mordant description of him, and of his school at Dotheboys Hall, is not so much an attack upon an individual or upon a type as upon the legislature and the government which allowed such things to be. Murdstone on the other hand is an individual;—cruel and treacherous in grain;—a specimen of that evil type the polished brute —a type which was fostered by, was indeed the necessary outcome of, the industrial revolution. When Joseph Rayner Stephens, in 1839, said that, "every brick and every stone in every factory in Lancashire and Yorkshire was cemented by the blood of the little children done to death within them," he expressed symbolically the truth that the industrial revolution ushered in along with unprecedented luxury and refinement for the possessing classes a period of the most revolting callousness and cruelty ever known for the children of the lower orders. And as a second generation of "gentryfied" millowners grew up—men too "gentlemanly" to take part in the actual work of running the mills, or in the actual flogging of the emaciated and exhausted child-slaves of the mill—but not at all too gentlemanly to demand increases in the "not hundreds per cent, but *thousands* per cent that made the fortunes of Lancashire and Yorkshire"—increases that could only be won by greater and greater intensifications of the cruelty and enslavement of these child slaves and their parents along with them—the habit of cruelty became fixed and exalted into a moral obligation. So grew up the class of gentlemen millowners and investors in industry, who rationalized the conditions precedent for their expanding wealth into a cult of the absolute authority of the parent and the abject submission of the child—a cult for which it was all too easy to find Biblical justification. In Mr. Murdstone, Dickens has pilloried this class for all time. Creakle, on the other hand, though superficially a "gentleman" is in fact a promoted sycophant—such a one as the boy Bitzer in *Hard Times* might have grown into if he had had more virility and less education. Creakle is positively sadistic—and with it is always the sycophant. Nothing even in Dickens is more movingly disgusting than Creakle's sacking of his assistant Mr. Mell on "learning" (say, rather, on being forced publicly to admit the fact) that Mr. Mell had an aged mother who was an inmate in an almshouse. Creakle's public thanking of the fine gentleman Steerforth for making the facts "known" to him is one of Dickens' finest strokes of white-hot irony. That in all the school it is the ludicrously unfortunate but noble-hearted Tommy Traddles alone who cries "shame" on Steerforth completes the picture with a master's touch.

But, as nobody knew better than Dickens, mere physical cruelty is the least permanently injurious cruelty that authority can inflict upon the young. Mr. Murdstone is the revolting ogre that he is because along with his carefully wax-ended cane he knows how to wield the weapon of mental cruelty too. Dickens gives several other masterly studies of mental cruelty inflicted by school-masters and school-mistresses. First in order of execution comes Miss Monflathers, to whose Boarding and Day Establishment Little Nell was sent with a parcel of new bills advertising Mrs. Jarley's waxwork show. This "Establishment" was at:

> a large house, with a high wall, and a large garden-gate with a large brass plate, and a small grating through which Miss Monflathers' parlour-maid inspected all visitors before admitting them; for nothing in the shape of a man—no, not even a milkman—was suffered without special license, to pass that gate. Even the taxgatherer who was stout, and wore spectacles and a broad-brimmed hat, had the taxes handed through the grating. More obdurate than gate of adamant or brass, this gate of Miss Monflathers' frowned upon all mankind. The very butcher respected it as a gate of mystery and left off whistling when he rang the bell.—*Old Curiosity Shop:* Chap. XXI.

A compost of warped gentility, snobbery, bad-temper, and soured virginity Miss Monflathers epitomizes the then prevalent, bourgeois notion of propriety as the keynote in the education of young "ladies." Her interview with Little Nell shows her in full fettle:

> "You're the wax-work child, are you not?" said Miss Monflathers.
>
> "Yes, ma'am," replied Nell, colouring deeply, for the young ladies had collected about her, and she was the centre on which all eyes were fixed.
>
> "And don't you think you must be a very wicked little child," said Miss Monflathers, who was of rather uncertain temper, and lost no opportunity of impressing moral truths upon the tender minds of the young ladies, "to be a wax-work child at all?"
>
> Poor Nell had never viewed her position in this light, and, not knowing what to say, remained silent, blushing more deeply than before.
>
> "Don't you know," said Miss Monflathers, "that it's very naughty and unfeminine, and a perversion of the properties wisely and benignantly transmitted to us, with expansive powers, to be raised from a dormant state through the medium of cultivation?
>
> The two teachers murmured their respectful approval of this home-thrust, and looked at Nell as though they would have said that there indeed Miss Monflathers had hit her very hard. Then they smiled and glanced at Miss Monflathers and then, their eyes meeting, they exchanged looks which plainly

said that each considered herself smiler in ordinary to Miss Monflathers and regarded the other as having no right to smile, and that her so doing was an act of presumption and an impertinence.

"Don't you feel how naughty it is of you," resumed Miss Monflathers, "to be a wax-work child, when you might have the proud consciousness of assisting to the extent of your infant powers, the manufactures of your country; of improving your mind by the constant contemplation of the steam engine; and of earning a comfortable and independent subsistence of from two and ninepence to three shillings per week? Don't you know that the harder you are at work the happier you are?"

"How doth the little——" murmured one of the teachers, in quotation from Dr. Watts.

"Eh?" said Miss Monflathers, turning smartly round. "Who said that?"

Of course the teacher who had not said it indicated the rival who had, whom Miss Monflathers frowningly requested to hold her peace; by that means throwing the informing teacher into raptures of joy.

"The little busy bee," said Miss Monflathers, drawing herself up, "is applicable only to genteel children."

"In work, or books, or healthful play, is quite right as far as they are concerned; and the work means painting on velvet, fancy needlework, or embroidery. In such cases as these," pointing to Nell with her parasol, "and in the case of all poor peoples' children, we should word it thus:

'In work, work, work. In work alway
Let my first years be passed,
That I may give for ev'ry day
Some good account at last.'"

—*Old Curiosity Shop:* Chap. XXXI.

The rest of the interview must be read and enjoyed in the novel itself. We have given sufficient to show Miss Monflathers in all her sententious snobbery and her tyrannical and petulant consequentiality enunciating as a rule for the "lower orders" that which Messrs. Gradgrind and Bounderby—more consistent in their insensitive stupidity—sought to impose as an ethic for all. In the novel she is shown inflicting spiteful cruelties on an unfortunate pupil, Miss Edwards, an unpaid pupil-teacher, who galls her by continually (though unintentionally) throwing into strong relief the congenital stupidity of the star pupil of the Establishment—a *baronet's* daughter.

More advanced along the Murdstone road, and yet different again, is Mrs. Pipchin, "ogress and childqueller" in *Dombey*. Mrs. Pipchin did not keep an "establishment"—it was "not a preparatory school":

"Should I express my meaning," said Miss Tox, with peculiar sweetness, "if I designated it an infantine Boarding House of a very select description?"

"On an exceedingly limited and particular scale," suggested Mrs. Chick, with a glance at her brother

"Oh! Exclusion itself!" said Miss Tox.—*Dombey:* Chap. VIII.

To this exclusive creature and her exceedingly particular and select charge little Paul Dombey was accordingly remitted. She was "a marvellously ill-favoured, ill-conditioned, old lady, with a stooping figure, a mottled face like bad marble, a hook-nose and a hard grey eye, that looked as though it might have been hammered at on an anvil without sustaining any injury."

Forty years at least had elapsed since the Peruvian mines had been the death of Mr. Pipchin; but his relict still wore black bombazine, of such a lustreless, deep, dead, sombre shade, that gas itself couldn't light her up after dark, and her presence was a quencher to any number of candles.

She was generally spoken of as a "great manager" of children; and the secret of her management was, to give them everything that they didn't like, and nothing that they did—which was found to sweeten their dispositions very much. She was such a bitter old lady that one was tempted to believe there had been some mistake in the application of the Peruvian machinery, and that all her waters of gladness and milk of human kindness had been pumped out dry instead of the mines.—*Dombey:* Chap. VIII.

Mrs. Pipchin's special variety of cruelty—on top of her general sourness and selfishness—was the use of a "dungeon" (an empty apartment at the back) in which delinquents were imprisoned in solitude. When Paul Dombey arrived, little Miss Pankey (the only other boarder besides Master Bitherstone) "had that moment been walked off to the castle-dungeon for having sniffed thrice in the presence of visitors":

At one o'clock there was a dinner, chiefly of the farinaceous and vegetable kind, when Miss Pankey (a mild little blue-eyed morsel of a child, who was shampooed every morning, and seemed in danger of being rubbed away altogether) was led in from captivity by the ogress herself, and instructed that nobody who sniffed before visitors ever went to Heaven. When this great truth had been thoroughly impressed upon her, she was regaled with rice; and subsequently repeated the form of grace established in the castle in which there was a special clause, thanking Mrs. Pipchin for a good dinner. Mrs. Pipchin's niece, Berinthia, took cold pork. Mrs. Pipchin, whose constitution required warm nourishment, made a special repast of mutton chops, which were brought in hot and hot, between two plates, and smelt very nice....

After tea, Berry (otherwise Berinthia) brought out a little workbox with the Royal Pavilion on the lid, and fell to working busily; while Mrs. Pipchin, having put on her spectacles and opened a great volume bound in green baize began to read. And whenever Mrs. Pipchin caught herself falling forward into the fire and woke up, she filliped Master Bitherstone on the nose for nodding too.

At last it was the children's bed-time and after prayers they went to bed. As little Miss Pankey was afraid of sleeping alone in the dark, Mrs. Pipchin always made a point of driving her upstairs herself, like a sheep; and it was cheerful to hear Miss Pankey moaning long afterwards, in the least eligible chamber, and Mrs. Pipchin going in now and then to shake her....

The breakfast next morning was like the tea overnight except that Mrs. Pipchin took her roll instead of toast, and seemed a little more irate when it was over. Master Bitherstone read aloud to the rest a pedigree from Genesis (judiciously selected by Mrs. Pipchin) getting over the names with the ease and clearness of a person tumbling up the treadmill. That done, Miss Pankey was borne away to be shampooed; and Master Bitherstone to have something else done to him with salt water from which he always returned very blue and dejected....

At about noon Mrs. Pipchin presided over some Early Readings. It being a part of Mrs. Pipchin's system not to encourage a child's mind to develop and expand itself like a young flower, but to open it by force like an oyster, the moral of these lessons was usually of a violent and stunning character; the hero—a naughty boy— seldom, in the mildest catastrophe, being finished off by anything less than a lion or a bear.—*Dombey:* Chap. VIII

You may, if you please, call this caricature. But it is caricature of an order of genius which reveals the truth more essentially and more justly than any photograph. Mrs. Pipchin is an individual and as such unique. But Mrs. Pipchin's system of management is, in principle, so nearly related to the system of Mr. Murdstone (with a lower grade of positive cruelty set off by a higher grade of personal gluttony) as to be quite of a piece with it. And Mr. Murdstone's system, on examination, reveals itself as touching at the one extreme the system of Squeers and at the other the system of Mr. M'Choakumchild—the Gradgrind system. All are facets of one and the same attitude to the child, and Mrs. Pipchin's formula (plus the necessary variations) covers them all: *find out what the child wants and see that he doesn't get it.* The old *Punch* joke: "go and see what Johnnie is doing and tell him not to" is too apposite, and too much expressive of the period, to be a joke any longer. It was a fixed attitude—born out of Evangelical theology by Manchester school economics, themselves the expression of the vast social transformation imperfectly indicated by the name "Industrial

Revolution." And against this evil thing Charles Dickens fought with every weapon at his command; and fought, with gathering fury, all his life long.

The Blimber system, described in *Dombey,* immediately in sequence to the Pipchin system (of which we have indicated the main points) was a much more refined system of cruelty. But, just because it was a more refined system it was all the more devastatingly cruel. In the Blimber system there is none of the filth, starvation and brutal physical infliction of the Squeers system, none of the petulant, snobbish arrogance and spiteful deprivation of the Monflathers-cum-Pipchin system. Before everything the Blimber system was "genteel." The food was good in quality and unstinted in quantity—though, possibly, by modern standards, ill-chosen—and it was served in the most sumptuously genteel manner possible:

> Grace having been said by the Doctor, dinner began. There was some nice soup; also roast meat, boiled meat, vegetable pie, and cheese. Every young gentleman had a massive silver fork and a napkin; and all the arrangements were stately and handsome. In particular there was a butler in a blue coat and bright buttons who gave quite a winy flavour to the table beer; he poured it out so superbly.—*Dombey,* Chap. XII.

But all this open-handed magnificence is merely the façade. The refined cruelty of the Blimber system becomes apparent as we proceed—apparent as an exquisitely horrible other-side implicit in the farce-comedy with which the dinner culminates:

> Nobody spoke unless spoken to, except Dr. Blimber, Mrs. Blimber and Miss Blimber who conversed occasionally. Whenever a young gentleman was not actually engaged with his knife and fork or spoon, his eye with an irresistible attraction sought the eye of Dr. Blimber, Mrs. Blimber or Miss Blimber and modestly rested there....
>
> Only once during dinner was there any conversation that included the young gentlemen. It happened at the epoch of the cheese, when the Doctor, having taken a glass of port wine, and hemmed twice or thrice, said: "It is remarkable, Mr. Feeder, that the Romans——"
>
> At the mention of this terrible people, their implacable enemies, every young gentleman fastened his gaze upon the Doctor, with an assumption of the deepest interest. One of the number, who happened to be drinking, and who caught the Doctor's eye glaring at him through the side of his tumbler left off so hastily that he was convulsed for some moments, and in the sequel ruined Dr. Blimber's point.—*Dombey:* Chap. XII.

After the farce-comedy of the Doctor's pompous didactitude, inter-rupted by the young gentleman, Johnson's, struggle against strangulation or its alternative explosion—which ends in a victory for explosion—and

the assistant master, Mr. Feeder's, distraction in between polite deference
to the Doctor, and humane fears for the physical integrity of Johnson, had
run its course—and dead silence has been achieved again (after Johnson
had been thumped on the back, helped to a glass of water, and marched
up and down like a sentry by the butler), the Doctor resumed, with a portentous appearance of equanimity:

> "Gentlemen, rise for Grace! Cornelia, lift Dombey down"—nothing of whom
> but his scalp was accordingly seen above the table-cloth—"Johnson will
> repeat to me to-morrow morning before breakfast without book and from the
> Greek Testament, the first chapter of the epistle of Saint Paul to the Ephesians.
> We will resume our studies, Mr. Feeder, in half an hour."—*Dombey,* Chap.
> XII.

When the unwashed, illiterate Squeers leaps upon one of his ragged,
starveling victims and lashes him in brutal fury the cruelty and injustice is
gross, palpable and obvious—the cruelty and injustice of sheer bestiality.
When the sadistic sycophant Creakle (whom Dickens, by a stroke of murderous satire, depicts as finishing his career as a Middlesex magistrate,
childishly vain of his "model" prison—in which transparent hypocrites and
humbugs get favours and an esteem denied to honest men in civil life)—
when this Creakle, sneaks behind an unfortunate boy bent over a desk, and
gives him a wealing cut with his cane just for the sheer pleasure of seeing
his victim writhe in agony, this is, from its purposeless perversity, seen as
an even more unforgivable outrage than is the brutality of Squeers. The
petty egoistic tyrannies and privations inflicted by the Monflathers and the
Pipchins, are no less obviously cruel and unjust—and their ill effects are,
as Dickens shows, likely to be even more permanently, though more
subtly, injurious. Even so, it may be doubted whether, in the long run, the
fundamentally irrational pseudo-"rationality" of the Blimber forcing
system, the system of "bringing them on,"—the system which made the
dead and gone Romans (and Greeks, too, for that matter) the "implacable
enemies" of every child inmate of a school-prison; the system which
sought to load on to a child six years old the learning of "a little English,
and a deal of Latin—names of things, declensions of articles and
substantives, exercises thereupon and preliminary rules—a trifle of
orthography, a glance at ancient history, a bite or two at modern ditto, a
few tables, two or three weights and measures, and a little general information," all to be memorized straight out of a book, with no stimulus to
the imagination or aid other than that of the plain printed page—it may,
we say, well be doubted whether this system is not the most perverse, the

most irrational and the most comprehensively cruel and unjust system of them all.

Dickens indicates as much in one incidental stroke in his description of the night after the dinner above described:

> In the confidence of their own room upstairs Briggs said his head ached ready to split, and that he should wish himself dead if it wasn't for his mother and a blackbird he had at home. Tozer didn't say much but he sighed a good deal, and told Paul to look out, for his turn would come to-morrow. After uttering those prophetic words he undressed himself moodily and got into bed. Briggs was in bed, too, before the weak-eyed young man appeared to take away the candle; when he wished them good night and pleasant dreams. But his benevolent wishes were in vain as far as Briggs and Tozer were concerned; for Paul, who lay awake for a long while, and often woke afterwards, found that Briggs was ridden by his lesson as a nightmare; and that Tozer, whose mind was affected in his sleep by similar causes in a minor degree, talked unknown tongues or scraps of Greek and Latin—it was all one to Paul—which, in the silence of night, had an inexpressibly wicked and guilty effect.—*Dombey,* Chap. XII.

If Squeers' victims are the victims of savagery and selfish greed, abetted by the desire of heartless parents to be rid of their "incumbrances"; if Creakle's victims are the victims of a cruel sycophant and of an evil educational tradition, as those of Miss Monflathers and of Mrs. Pipchin are the victims of snobbery, ill-tempered egoism, and an evil tradition of parental discipline; Dr. Blimber's victims are the victims of a still more evil educational tradition—the tradition of classicism—plus parental vanity, the desire to be parents of a prodigy of mis-called "learning."

> In fact Doctor Blimber's establishment was a great hothouse, in which there was a forcing apparatus incessantly at work. All the boys blew before their time. Mental green peas were produced at Christmas, and intellectual asparagus all the year round. Mathematical gooseberries (very sour ones, too) were common at untimely seasons and from mere sprouts of bushes under Dr. Blimber's cultivation. Every description of Greek and Latin vegetable was got off the driest twigs of boys under the frostiest circumstances. Nature was of no consequence at all. No matter what a young gentleman was intended to know, Doctor Blimber made him bear to pattern somehow or other.
>
> This was all very pleasant and ingenious but the system of forcing was attended with its usual disadvantages. There was not the right taste about the premature productions and they didn't keep well. Moreover, one young gentleman, with a swollen nose and an excessively large head (the oldest of the ten, who had "gone through" everything), suddenly left off blowing one day, and remained in the establishment a mere stalk. And people did say that the

Doctor had rather overdone it with young Toots, and that when he began to have whiskers he left off having brains.—*Dombey:* Chap. XII.

The Blimber system, in short, is a perfect pendant to the Gradgrind system. The grim utilitarianism of the latter is an exact balance of the conventionalized disutilitarianism of the former. Both alike regard nature as of no consequence at all; both alike treat the child as a purely passive subject-matter of whom it would be folly and worse than folly to predicate any such thing as "rights."

Mrs. Pipchin would have approved of either the Blimber or the Gradgrind systems:

> "There is a great deal of nonsense—and worse—talked about young people not being pressed too hard at first and being tempted on and all the rest of it, sir," said Mrs. Pipchin, impatiently rubbing her hooked nose. "It never was thought of in my time, and it has no business to be thought of now. My opinion is: 'keep 'em at it'."—*Dombey:* Chap. XI.

On examination it will be seen that Mr. Murdstone in *David Copperfield* draws together into a single focus all the evil features which are elaborated one-sidedly in each of the evil educational systems we have surveyed. He is, beneath all his veneer—his gentility, his glossy black whiskers, his gleaming teeth, and his fine linen—as greedily savage and as savagely greedy as Squeers; he is as sadistically delighted at a chance to use the cane as Creakle, whom he chooses as a fit agent for carrying out his designs; he is as pettily malignant as Miss Monflathers and as much of a snob; he is as egotistically and as ignorantly tyrannical as Mrs. Pipchin; and as much disposed to the forcing system as Dr. Blimber—without the Doctor's excuse of infatuate-classicality. Mr. Murdstone is, in the whole Rogues' Gallery of Dickens' portraiture, the most unrelieved and most unforgivable scoundrel of all. And it is by a master stroke of clear-sightedness that Dickens makes Mr. Murdstone the one who sends the newly orphaned David Copperfield to child-slavery in a blacking factory. When one reads, in the records of the period, of the millowner who drove a runaway orphan apprentice back to the mill, thirty miles by road, with a horsewhip—the child running sobbing and screaming at the lash's end, as he rode pursuing on horseback— one thinks instantly of Mr. Murdstone.

And by means of Mr. Murdstone Dickens makes artistically a perfect transition from the question of the rights of the child in school to the larger question of the whole right of the child as against its parents, governors, pastors, masters, and those set in authority over it.

Dickens and the rights of the child

Dickens' case for the defence in the great cause of the Child *versus* Tyranny, Cruelty, Injustice and Deprivation, is developed in one form or another in all his writings.

As early as *Pickwick* we have the (only half-ironical) example of the elder Weller who "took a great deal of pains with Sam's eddication"— which means that he "let him run in the streets when he was very young and shift for himself. It's the only way to make a boy sharp."

As Mr. Pickwick remarked, this "seems a dangerous way"; and as Sam assures us, woefully, it is "not at all a certain way," either. For all that, letting a child run wild in the streets is, with all its disadvantages, better than condemning him to imprisonment with stripes, starvation and hard labour under a Squeers, to moral torture under a Pipchin, to physical infliction and mental-starvation under a Creakle, to mental indigestion and exhaustion under a Blimber, to mental and moral malformation under a M'Choakumchild, or to all together under a Mr. Murdstone.

The obverse of which the Weller theory is the reverse is well indicated in one fine stroke early in *Oliver Twist*. When he is taken away by Bumble to the workhouse proper from the hideous baby-farm in which he had spent the first nine years of his existence—the "wretched home where one kind word or look had never lighted the gloom of his infant years"— Oliver bursts into:

> ...an agony of childish grief, as the cottage gate closed after him. Wretched as were the little companions in misery he was leaving behind, they were the only friends he had ever known; and a sense of his loneliness in the great wide world, sank into the child's heart for the first time.—*Oliver Twist:* Chap. I.

The child's right, not merely to the bare necessities of physical existence—to food, fire, clothing and shelter; to free air and sunlight—but to food for the emotions, for the fancy and for the mind—the child's right to affection, to understanding-sympathy and consideration, to companionship;—these things, along with the means of growing, not only in physical stature, but in mental power and emotional range—these things Dickens maintains are the child's absolute *right*. The child's right to *be himself*—the right therefore to be protected against all that threatens his being—against all that impairs, either by positive injury, by deprivation, by paralysing terror, or by coldness, callous indifference, systematic dispar-agement, or active development-arresting hostility, the normal, equable growth and expansion of the self-possession in and by the child of *himself* and *his own powers* of self-support and self-disposal;—these, the fundamental rights of the child, Dickens fights for against every variety of foe, public and private, objective and subjective, whether conventionally known and accepted as foes or whether palming themselves off as public charity, parental right, prescriptive authority or pious duty.

Dickens, for instance, although ardent to the pitch, at times, of mawkishness, in his insistence upon the child's right to affection from his parents, and to a rational liberty in pursuit of happiness, is no friend to the spoilt child. The fat boy in *Pickwick* is hardly an example of this so much as a freak instance. But in his degree Master Bardell is a spoilt child (as is also and most certainly the hideous little griffin, the daughter of the brass-and-copper founder in Camberwell, whom Mrs. Todgers called a "syrup" and who herself calls Ruth Pinch a "beggarly thing," with swift and far-reaching consequences).

Dickens' really "spoilt" children are, however, more subtly spoiled than this. Steerforth is a case; so, too, in their various ways are "pet" (the Meagles' daughter in *Little Dorrit)* and still more Henry Gowan, the man she marries. Bella Wilfer in *Our Mutual Friend* is a partial case; as also temporarily, is Pip the juvenile lead in *Great Expectations.* A more serious case of insanely deliberate child-spoiling is that of Estella, also in *Great Expectations.* And all these must be distinguished from cases of naturally warped dispositions, and frustrated emotions, such as Rosa Dartle in *David Copperfield,* and Miss Wade in *Little Dorrit.*

It is impossible not to see the element of class pride and a snobbish sense of superiority which enters into the process of the spoiling in nearly all these cases, either positively, or as in the cases of Rosa Dartle and Miss Wade negatively—through exciting a morbid personal envy. But most eloquent of all are Dickens' examples of "spoiling" through misapplied discipline and through that evil thing called " charity."

Oliver Twist opens on this theme and shows how Oliver is enabled by circumstances to escape from these evils. But, lest the moral should be lost, Dickens is careful to introduce into *Oliver Twist* the brutish, cowardly, and treacherous dolt Noah Claypole, the "charity boy." There were so many abominations involved in English society in the period of the industrial revolution that one despairs of ever coming to the end of them. But of them all few were more characteristically cruel, few combined in a more perfectly horrible combination, the meanness of the period, with its petty self-seeking, and its unctuous ostentation of righteousness, so much as did this institution of the Charity School (now happily surviving only as a relic, with an entirely altered significance). Well-intentioned benefactors had at various times left money and estates in trust to provide schooling for the children of the poor. These had often, in the period prior to the industrial revolution, made provision for supplying the pupils at the schools they founded with a yearly or twice-yearly suit of clothes, such as were then commonly worn by the common people. The pedantry of lawyers united with the desire for pharisaical ostentation of a later generation of managers of these trust funds to force upon the unfortunate victims of their "charity" a uniform of a colour and a cut so, by then, archaic, as to brand these victims publicly as the recipients of " charity." The ferocious rapacity of the new factory-lords, and that of their allies, the new-gentry—the newly-enriched and ennobled merchants with whom the younger Pitt trebled the membership of the House of Lords and packed the benches of the House of Commons—the classes who combined to impose the "New" Poor Law, and to cover the land with the workhouse "Bastilles for the poor" against which the first fury of Chartism was directed—this rapacity begot the propaganda which spread the outlook expressed in the then-prevalent notion that the acceptance of public charity in any form was, morally, little to be distinguished from plain theft—except in so far as the latter showed a more manly and self-reliant spirit.

And it was at the promptings of this spirit that such free schools as were established during this period by men of this class perpetrated this anach-ronistic abomination of the "Charity" school, with its uniformed and badged "charity" boy or girl pupils.

Noah Claypole is one such. He wears a flat cap and yellow leather "smalls" (meaning "small-clothes," a euphemism for the term "breeches" which the age was too polite to tolerate). Since Noah himself has had to suffer the indignity of being hailed publicly by more fortunate youths as "charity," "leathers" and "yellows," he is delighted to find a victim before whom he can pose as a superior. Hence, to him, Oliver is at once "work'us"—and a butt for persecution. As was artistically inevitable, Noah Claypole reveals himself as a dolt and a cowardly, as well as a servile, brute, who turns thief, and becomes ultimately a professional informer.

But the fullest description of the "charity" boy in Dickens—as also of the evil results the charity school system begot—is in the case of Rob the Grinder in *Dombey*. Rob is, at best, an unlicked cub. But he is far indeed from being vile in grain; and is, in the end, made into something at any rate tolerable. But he comes near to total ruin when his parents in mistaken gratitude accept Mr. Dombey's stiff-necked generosity in the form of an offer of a place for Rob in the charity school, established by the Worshipful Company of Grinders—a school whose unfortunate pupils became at once, in the nomenclature of the uneducated but "unpauperized" mob, "Charitable Grinders."

The announcement of Mr. Dombey's proposed benevolence is made, with proper Dombey-ian pomp and circumstance, to Rob's mother, Polly Toodles, after her six months' faithful service as nurse to the infant Paul Dombey. Mr. Dombey, having learned that Toodles, senior, Rob's father (by trade a locomotive fireman) was unable to read, but hoped to learn from one of his sons as soon as one could be sent to school, thought the occasion an excellent one for recognizing suitably Polly's (officially "Mrs. Richards") meritorious service, and at the same time doing a public service. Having alluded to the "melancholy fact" that Polly's family with Toodles, senior, at the head, "were sunk and steeped in ignorance," Mr. Dombey proceeded:

> "I am far from being friendly to what is called by persons of levelling sentiments, general education. But it is necessary that this inferior classes should be taught to know their position, and to conduct themselves properly. So far I approve of schools...."—*Dombey:* Chap. V.

The reason why interest in the education of the poor, after having been despised as a mere "whimsy" or obstructed as something positively dangerous for centuries, was beginning to dawn upon the ruling class in 1846, is stated here by Dickens with a force as superlative as is its brevity and clarity. No less class-conscious is the manner in which Mr. Dombey proceeds, with the approving chorus of his sister, and his elderly adorer, Miss Tox:

> "Having the power of nominating a child on the foundation of an ancient establishment, called (from a worshipful company) the Charitable Grinders; where not only is a wholesome education bestowed upon the scholars, but where a dress and badge is likewise provided for them; I have (first communicating through Mrs. Chick with your family) nominated your eldest son to an existing vacancy; and he has this day, I am informed, assumed the habit. The number of her son" [this was inscribed on the badge, aforesaid, which in turn was a pewter plaque, or overgrown medal, worn on the chest, or arm, or both] "The number of her son, I believe," said Mr. Dombey, turning to his sister, and speaking of the child as if he were a hackney coach, "is one hundred and forty-seven. Louisa, you can tell her."
>
> "One hundred and forty-seven," said Mrs. Chick. "The dress, Richards, is a nice, warm blue baize tailed coat and cap, turned up with orange-coloured binding; red worsted stockings; and very strong leather smallclothes. One

might wear the articles one's self," said Mrs. Chick with enthusiasm, "and be grateful."—*Dombey:* Chap. V.

How little reason the unfortunate Rob—called also "Biler" in playful allusion to his capacity, when young, for screeching like the "biler" of a locomotive—had for gratitude he learned on his very first day's trial of his "charitable" garb:

> Poor Biler's life had been, since yesterday morning, rendered weary by the costume of the Charitable Grinders. The youth of the streets could not endure it. No young vagabond could be brought to bear its contemplation for a moment, without throwing himself upon the unoffending wearer, and doing him a mischief. His social existence had been more like that of an early Christian than an innocent child of the nineteenth century. He had been stoned in the streets. He had been overthrown into gutters; bespattered with mud; violently flattened against posts. Entire strangers to his person had lifted his blue cap off his head, and cast it to the winds. His legs had not only undergone verbal criticisms and revilings, but had been handled and pinched. That very morning he had received a perfectly unsolicited black eye on his way to the Grinders' establishment, and had been punished for it by the master; a superannuated old Grinder of savage disposition, who had been appointed schoolmaster because he didn't know anything, and wasn't fit for anything and for whose cruel cane all chubby little boys had a perfect fascination.

Naturally, a very little of this sort of thing soon caused Rob to start "wagging" (pretending to go to school and running away to hide and idle instead) and so to get ejected from the school in disgrace, and to fall generally into bad ways. Mr. Dombey on hearing of this ("Mr. Dombey habitually looked over the vulgar herd, and not at them") turned on his heel, saying "the usual return" and marched scornfully away. His friend Major Bagstock comments in his Anglo-Indian military manner:

> "Take advice from plain old Jo, sir, and never educate that sort of people.... Damme, sir, it never does! It always fails."—*Dombey:* Chap. XX.

Partly because Rob the Grinder did not remain a charity-boy for long enough to be ruined in character for life, and partly because of the countervailing influence of his parents, Rob was plucked from the burning in time, and set in the way of making a man of himself. But between Noah Claypole and Rob the Grinder the indictment of the charity school is complete—except that although the badge and the uniform have been dropped (probably on grounds of expense), and although Mr. M'Choakumchild certainly did possess quite an appalling amount of knowledge, and the school in which he functioned did impart quite a deal of education of a sort, it is clear from the fact that Bitzer, the prize product of the Gradgrind-Bounderby school, is recognizably Noah Claypole raised to a higher (and a far more evil) power, that in Dickens' eyes schools run on Manchester School principles were little if at all to be preferred.

By the time the last of Dickens' (completed) novels, *Our Mutual Friend,* was written, the State had interested itself in education to the extent of providing (or subsidizing) training schools for teachers. Dickens does not seem to have viewed the innovation with any cordiality. His Bradley Headstone is one such schoolmaster—and is a movingly tragic study of the growth of exasperation into homicidal insanity in a passionate-natured proletarian who has taken to teaching as a profession because it is the only available way of becoming, even by courtesy, a "gentleman." The implied criticism is two-edged— one edge directed against the basic notion of climbing out of the working class (instead of rising within it), and the other against the State-provided training schools as merely so many State-subsidized factories for producing M'Choakumchilds wholesale.

Dickens died before the first compulsory Education Act—the first provision of elementary schooling by the State—in Britain. But it had been talked of in his time; and he was clearly dubious about its desirability. He appears to have been much of Marx's opinion: "It would be much better to preclude the government and the Church equally from any influence on the schools." (Marx: *Gotha Programme,* 1875.)

To complete the picture of Dickens' attitude to the Rights of the Child it is necessary to take account of the few occasions on which he gives a picture of the kind of schooling more to his liking than those we have noted.

Naturally Dickens was, like the rest of us, more ready to say what he positively disliked and disapproved than what he could suggest as an alternative. Negatively we know very definitely what Dickens wanted; in so far as he wanted the reverse of what he condemned. But to give that which he desired in the form of a positive picture was neither so easy, nor so desirable artistically. He does give, however, such idyllic pictures as those of David Copperfield and his mother (before the advent of Mr. Murdstone); of Little Nell teaching Kit, of Dick Swiveller training the Marchioness, and of the village school in the *Old Curiosity Shop*; and best of all the perfectly delightful system of education invented and carried into effect by Major Jemmy Jackman in *Mrs. Lirriper's Lodgings.* Apart from these and the glimpse we get of the schooldays of Esther Summerson (in *Bleak House*) the only ideal school described by Dickens is that of Dr. Strong (in *David Copperfield*). This is not described in the same detail as are the objectionable types of school, but we are given the clue to its excellence:

> It was very gravely and decorously ordered and on a sound system; with an appeal in everything to the honour and good faith of the boys, and an avowed intention to rely on their possession of those qualities, unless they proved unworthy of it, which worked wonders.—*David Copperfield*: Chap. XVI.

That is Dickens' case in a nutshell. Treat children as well-intentioned, honourable human beings capable (within the limits of their knowledge and powers) of responsibility and trust, and they will, in all but a negligible minority of cases, prove to be all these things. And the converse holds good. "He ordered me like a dog," says David Copperfield of Mr. Murdstone, "and like a dog I obeyed."

The tyranny of parents—and philanthropists

Dickens is quite definite in his conviction that the subjection of the child to arbitrary tyranny and cruel repression in school is prepared for by, and is a continuation and counterpart of, their subjection to arbitrary and tyrannical repression and constraint at home. In many respects Dickens was an outstanding representative of the conventional opinion of his age; but not by any means always so, or in any of his most significant moments. He was well towards the front rank of the then-prevailing opinion (or, as we should say, to the "Left") in his Radicalism. He was definitely in advance of his age in his attitude to education, and he was most of all in advance of it in his attitude towards parental authority. He used every weapon at his command to attack the notion that a school was, and ought to be, a place of torment in which children were punished for the crime of being born or one where they learned nothing beyond the fact that they were reeking with Original Sin. And he attacked no less the notion that parental authority must be based upon the savagely lugubrious creed of spare the rod and spoil the child. In his *Bleak House* he gives a whole series of instances of children victimized by their subjection to the unrestricted egoism of their parents or guardians.

Esther Summerson at the opening of *Bleak House* is shown as a victim, permanently under punishment, mental and moral rather than physical, at the hands of her fanatically pious aunt, for the crime of having been born illegitimate:

"Your mother, Esther, is your disgrace, and you were hers... unfortunate girl, orphaned and degraded from the first of these anniversaries" [of the day of her birth]... "Submission, self-denial, diligent work, are the preparations for a life begun with such a shadow on it. You are different from other children, Esther, because you were not born, like them, in common sinfulness and wrath. You are set apart."—*Bleak House:* Chap. III.

As with his general attitude to education, Dickens is apt nowadays—now that opinion has veered round completely to his standpoint—to seem much less Radical, and much less a champion against a dominant and a domineering creed than he was. Yet a very little study of the rise and fall of the Nonconformist Conscience in English social history shows that here, as elswhere, Dickens is much more courageous than might seem. The attitude built upon the provision in the Mosaic code, that "a bastard may not enter the congregation of the Lord" found, of course, legal expression early. But the full force of its moral and social villainy did not develop until the rise to political and social power of the mercantile and manufacturing middle class—the class of evangelical piety *par excellence*—the class of Wilberforce in his later, pious and reactionary phase.

In his free-thinking youth Wilberforce championed Negro emancipation: in his old age, after he became reconverted to Christianity, he championed the suppression of trade unions, the suppresion of "blasphemous" and "seditious" literature, the suppression of working-men's political clubs, the Six Acts of Sidmouth and Castlereagh, and vigorously compulsory Sunday Observance. So too did the class of Sidmouth, ally and confidant of Bloody Castlereagh; the class on the one side of the Gradgrinds and the Bounderbys, and on the other of the Stiggins, the Melchizedek Howlers, the Pecksniffs, and the Chadbands. Against them Dickens waged, and in the days of their ascendancy, a neverending war.

What Esther Summerson's aunt did from piety, Mrs. Jellyby and Mrs. Pardiggle did from egotistical and vainglorious devotion to moral and philanthropic crazes. Superficially Dickens might seem to belong to the school of bourgeois Socialists scathingly described by Marx and Engels in the *Communist Manifesto*—the school to which belonged

economists, philanthropists, humanitarians, improvers of the condition of the working class, organizers of charity, members of societies for the prevention of cruelty to animals,temperance fanatics, hole and corner reformers of every imaginable kind.—*Communist Manifesto:* III, 2.

Actually, anyone really familiar with Dickens knows that he hated the whole brood just as Marx and Engels did. He pilloried the temperance fanatics (though himself, in practice, a very abstemious man), in Stiggins (*Pickwick*), and in Chadband (*Bleak House*). But his most furious assault upon the whole brood was deployed in his onslaught upon Mrs. Jellyby, who left her children to tumble up and down stairs in dirt and neglect, except the eldest girl, Caddy, who was doomed to a permanent saturation in ink as her mother's amanuensis, while she, Mrs. Jellyby, occupied herself night and morn in the moral regeneration of the Africans by means of, "the settlement of a hundred and fifty to two hundred families to cultivate coffee and educate the natives at Borrioboola-Gha on the left bank of the Niger."

Mrs. Jellyby's absorption in this, and kindred philanthropic schemes, was absolute; so much so as to totally inhibit any concern for, or interest in, the management of her household or the condition and upbringing of her children:

> All through dinner, which was long, in consequence of such accidents as the dish of potatoes being mislaid in the coal-scuttle, and the hand of the corkscrew coming off and striking the young woman in the chin, Mrs. Jellyby preserved the evenness of her disposition. She told us a great deal that was interesting about Borrioboola-Gha and the natives; and received so many letters that Richard, who sat by her, saw four envelopes in the gravy at once. Some of the letters were proceedings of ladies' committees, or resolutions of ladies' meetings, which she read to us; others were applications from people excited in various ways about the cultivation of coffee, and natives; others required answers, and these she sent her eldest daughter from the table three or four times to write. She was full of business, and undoubtedly was, as she had told us, devoted to the cause.—*Bleak House:* Chap. IV.

Mrs. Jellyby's is a bad enough case; and the state of her shamefully neglected offspring (as of the shamelessly overworked Caddy) is disgusting enough. But by the side of Mrs. Pardiggle, Mrs. Jellyby shines as an angel of light. In the whole crowded gallery of Dicken's characters, one woman character alone is fit to stand beside Mr. Murdstone as an equal and she is Mrs. Pardiggle.

Mrs. Pardiggle's version of the prominent point in her own character is that she is, she freely admits, "a woman of business."

> "I love hard work; I enjoy hard work. The excitement does me good. I am so accustomed and inured to hard work that I don't know what fatigue is."—*Bleak House:* Chap. VIII.

Hard work in her case meant, in the times when she was not occupied with committees of one kind and another, visiting the poor in their homes to tell them all the things they had done wrong, all the things they had neglected, and what tracts to read to gain improvement. She was, with the only possible exception of Mrs. Jellyby (whose forte, however, was—through her unfortunate slave-daughter Caddy—correspondence rather than visiting) the most prominent of the ladies "distinguished for rapacious benevolence." Her visit to Bleak House with her five young sons was an event:

> She was a formidable style of lady, with spectacles, a prominent nose, and a loud voice, who had the effect of wanting a great deal of room. And she really did, for she knocked down little chairs with her skirts that were a great way off. ... She seemed to come in like cold weather, and to make the little Pardiggles blue as they followed.
>
> "These, young ladies," said Mrs. Pardiggle with great volubility after the first salutations. "are my five boys. You may have seen their names in a printed subscription list (perhaps more than one) in the possession of our esteemed friend Mr. Jarndyce. Egbert, my eldest (twelve), is the boy who sent out his pocket-money, to the amount of five-and-threepence, to the Tockahoopo Indians. Oswald, my second (ten-and-a-half), is the child who contributed two-and-ninepence to the Great National Smithers Testimonial. Francis, my third (nine), one-and-sixpence-halfpenny; Felis, my fourth (seven), eightpence to the Superannuated Widows; Alfred, my youngest (five) has voluntarily enrolled himself in the Infant Bonds of Joy, and is pledged never, through life, to use tobacco in any form."
>
> We had never seen such dissatisfied children. It was not merely that they were weazened and shrivelled—though they were certainly that, too—but they looked absolutely ferocious with discontent. At the mention of the Tockahoopo Indians, I could really have supposed Egbert to be one of the more baleful members of that tribe, he gave me such a savage frown. The face of each child, as the amount of his contribution was mentioned, darkend in a peculiarly vindictive manner, but his was by far the worst. I must except, however, the little recruit into the Infant Bonds of Joy who was stolidly and evenly miserable.—*Bleak House:* Chap. VIII.

Mrs. Pardiggle goes on to explain that much as she admires Mrs. Jellyby she disapproves of her in one respect—she does not do as Mrs. Pardiggle does and "take her family everywhere" in the prosecution of benevolence. Mrs. Pardiggle explains all this with her "choking eyes" and her "demonstrative hard tone"—which makes her voice "seem to have spectacles on, too." And we learn too, that not only have all the wretched little Pardiggles contributed to the African project, but that going "everywhere" with Mrs.

Pardiggle is no light task. (The eldest child started to yell at its very mention, but managed to turn the yell off into a yawn):

> "They attend matins with me (very prettily done) at half-past six o'clock in the morning all the year round, including of course the depth of winter," said Mrs. Pardiggle rapidly, "and they are with me during the revolving duties of the day. I am a School Lady, I am a Visiting Lady, I am a Reading Lady, I am a Distributing Lady; I am on the local Linen Box Committee, and many general Committees, and my canvassing alone is very extensive—perhaps no one's more so. But they are my companions everywhere; and by these means they acquire that knowledge of the poor, and that capacity of doing charitable business in general—in short the taste for that sort of thing—which will render them in after-life a service to their neighbours and a satisfaction to themselves."—*Bleak House:* Chap. VIII.

How much self-satisfaction these unfortunate brats were likely to get out of such a life, and what sort of service they were likely to render their neighbours, after being soured for life by such an upbringing, soon appears:

> "My young family are not frivolous. They expend the entire amount of their allowance in subscriptions, under my direction; and they have attended as many public meetings, and listened to as many lectures, orations, and discussions, as generally fall to the lot of few grown-up people. Alfred (five), who, as I mentioned, has of his own election joined the Infant Bonds of Joy, was one of the very few children who manifested consciousness on that occasion after a fervid address of two hours from the chairman of the evening."
>
> Alfred glowered at us as if he never could, and never would forgive the infamy of that night.—*Bleak House:* Chap. VIII.

Mrs. Pardiggle insists upon taking the whole company off to visit a colony of brickmakers in the vicinity. On the way Esther (who has taken charge of the children, with Mrs. Pardiggle temporarily out of hearing ahead) learns at first hand that this treatment has had the sort of effect upon the brats that might have been expected:

> As soon as we were out of doors, Egbert, with the manner of little footpad, demanded a shilling of me, on the ground that his pocket money was "boned" from him. On my pointing out the great impropriety of the word, especially in connection with his parent (for he added, sulkily, "by her!") he pinched me and said, "Oh, then! Now! Who are you? *You* wouldn't like it, I think? What does she make a sham for, and pretend to give me money, and take it away again? Why do you call it *my* allowance and never let me spend it?" These exasperating questions so inflamed his mind, and the minds of Oswald and Francis that they all pinched me at once, and in a dreadfully expert way:

screwing up such little pieces of my arms that I could hardly forbear crying out. Felix at the same time stamped on my toes. And the Bonds of Joy, who, on account of always having the whole of his little income anticipated stood pledged, in fact, to abstain from cakes as well as tobacco, so swelled with grief and rage when we passed a pastry-cook's shop, that he terrified me by becoming purple. I never underwent so much both in body and in mind in the course of a walk with young people, as from these unnaturally con-strained children when they paid me the compliment of being natural.—*Bleak House:* Chap. VIII.

It is some sort of recompense when Mrs. Pardiggle finds at her first place of visitation that the more unregenerate proletariat has a way of being natural and free-spoken too. She visits a brickmaker's hovel, and finds the lord and master, reclining, from lack of a sofa, on the floor. After some preliminary exchanges he speaks his mind:

"I wants an end of these liberties took with my place. I wants an end of being drawed like a badger. Now you're going to pool-pry and question, according to custom—I know what you're a-going to be up to. Well. You haven't got no occasion to be up to it. I'll save you the trouble. Is my daughter a-washin'. Look at the water. Smell it! That's what we drinks. How do you like it, and what do you think of gin instead? Ain't my place dirty? Yes, it is dirty—it's nat'rally dirty, and it's nat'rally unwholesome; and we've had five dirty and unwholesome children, as is all dead infants, and so much the better for them, and for us besides. Have I read the little book wot you left? No, I ain't read the little book wot you left. There ain't nobody here as knows how to read it; and if there was it wouldn't be suitable to me. It's a book fit for a babby, and I'm not a babby. If you was to leave me a doll I shouldn't nuss it. How have I been conducting of myself? Why I've been drunk for three days; and I'd a been drunk four days if I'd a had the money. Don't I never mean for to go to church? No, I don't never mean for to go to church. I shouldn't be expected there, if I did; the beadle's too gen-teel for me. And how did my wife get that black eye? Why, I give it her; and if she says I didn't she's a lie!"

He had pulled his pipe out of his mouth to say all this, and he now turned over on the other side and smoked again. Mrs. Pardiggle who had been regarding him through her spectacles with a forcible composure, calculated, I could not help thinking, to increase his antagonism, pulled out a good book, as if it were a constable's staff and took the whole family into custody. I mean religious custody, of course; but she really did it as if she were an inexorable moral Policeman carrying them all off to a station house.—*Bleak House:* Chap. VIII.

Marx in his *Capital* gives a grim description of the condition of the brickmakers at this period. Dickens at the same time when Marx was gathering the materials for this chapter, was independently exposing, in connection with brickmakers (as here set out), just how all the ostentatious charity-mongering of the pious, pseudo-reformers, whether Nonconformist or Anglican (Mrs. Pardiggle one perceives is an Anglican, and a Puseyite at that) functioned as an auxiliary police force and a smoke screen of moralizing behind which the rapacity of Capitalism could develop without stint.

The case of poor Joe

The question of the rights of the child and of the reasonable limits of parental authority which is raised so sharply in *Bleak House*, by the cases of Esther Summerson's aunt, of Mrs. Jellyby, Mrs. Pardiggle and their respective families and also from another angle, by the case of that ineffable humbug the elder Turveydrop—who makes his son and his daughter-in-law slave to maintain him and his "deportment"—forms a natural and inevitable transition to the whole question of governing authority, and the relation between those governing and those they govern. In *Bleak House* the transition is made with great ease and artistic restraint. The Jellyby household has its counterpart in the Skimpole household—the "telescopic benevolence" of Mrs. Jellyby (who always looked at her daughter, her mind, the while, dwelling in Africa, "as if she were a steeple in the distance") is set off by Harold Skimpole's "charming" incapacity for practical affairs, from which incapacity everybody around him suffers except the "artless" and "engaging" Harold himself, so that the Skimpole "artlessness" achieves the same result as the Jellyby "benevolence." The Pardiggle horror has as her pendant and complement, partly, Jarndyce himself, the guardian of Esther, partly the finely drawn and altogether admirable household of Bagnets, and partly the household of little "Charley" who herself a child, mothers her orphaned, and still more infant, brother and sister. Over against all these is the household of the childless Sir Leicester Deadlock with his concern for the government of the country—his recurring fear lest the floodgates should be burst open and the proper safeguards of society be swept away. Thus Sir Leicester links the question with that of the government of society itself.

Bleak House is, probably, the most important of all Dickens' works, for the study of his point of view on this question. It is certainly one of the most carefully constructed of all his novels, and contains first-class examples of all his various levels of writing. The murder of Tulkinghorn, and the whole Nemesis-drama of Lady Deadlock's secret, shows Dickens as more than the equal of the most lurid of his contemporaries in the art of melodrama—and with a capacity for realistic plausibility that few of them could equal, and none surpass. The death-bed of Poor Joe is as reekingly sentimental as anything even in Dickens. Neither the protracted dying of Little Nell, nor the prolonged fading-away of little Paul Dombey, with all the sob-fantasias they provoke, scores anything in point of sob-ology over the death of Poor Joe. In fact, since it is got over much more quickly, and does not arise (as does the doing-to-death of Paul Dombey and also that of Little Nell) from a mechanical inevitability foreseeable in advance, the death of Pool For if anything wins the medal. Little Nell must die—so much is apparent from the very outset of the *Old Curiosity Shop*—to point the moral of her grandfather's insane hope to make poor Nell a "lady" by a gambling coup. This, it is true, is a fine conception artistically (even though its working-out in the early Victorian manner does involve the laying on of sentiment with a treacle-ladle) and it gives a fore-indication of Dicken's permanent conviction that children suffer, at the hands of their parents and guardians, as much, at times, from their good intentions as from their bad ones. Little Paul Dombey is even more obviously than Little Nell doomed from the very start. He must die to give his father's personal, family, and commercial pride the knock-down blow from which it never wholly recovers; and also to prepare the way for the "descent into hell" and the "glorious resurrection" of his sister Florence.

There is, indeed, something almost ghoulish about the zest, reminiscent of his own Mr. Mould (the undertaker in *Martin Chuzzlewit*) or Jerry Cruncher (the body-snatcher in the *Tale of Two Cities*), with which Dickens adds stroke after stroke to his drawing of Paul Dombey, expressly to emphasize to the uttermost the superpathos of his demise. It is not at all surprising to learn from Forster, that acting on a suggestion from that amiable but obtuse admirer, Dickens decided, in order to introduce a fresh incident or two, "not to kill little Dombey until the next part." Poor Joe, on the other hand, dies as an act of supererogation. He has performed the function for which he was introduced, and is no longer needed for the development of the novel. Hence he dies, mostly as the quickest way he could be disposed of without leaving a loose end; but, in dying, he gives Dickens a chance, not only for the sentimentalizing without which his readers would have considered themselves defrauded of their just due, but also—and this marks a real growth in Dickens—for a fierce affront to the whole system of society as then established.

Little Nell was killed by her devotion to her insane grandfather, and by her efforts to save him, on the one hand from the asylum, and on the other from his own insane efforts to make her fortune. Paul Dombey is killed, directly and indirectly, by his father's stiff-necked infatuation for perpetuating the tradition of "Dombey and Son." The point of the implied condemnation is in each case levelled against a parent and a guardian. But in *Bleak House*, and in the case of Poor Joe, who has neither parent nor guardian, the implied censure is levelled against society itself. Joe is harried to death for no other crime than that of having become, inadvertently, drawn into a plexus of contending forces. Lady Deadlock's secret; Sir Leicester Deadlock's aristocratic dignity and importance, family and personal; Mr. Tulkinghorn's dislike and suspicion of Lady Deadlock as one who has, by mere good looks, gate-crashed into a station in life to which she was not born; Mrs. Snagsby's ridiculous, Chadband-exacerbated jealousy of Mr. Snagsby; the maniacal malevolence of Mademoiselle Hortense; the professional efficiency of Detective-Inspector Bucket; and the "artless" love of beauty—and, on occasion, of five-pound notes—of Harold Skimpole; all—along with, of course, the great Chancery suit of Jarndyce *v.* Jarndyce, which links everybody together at some point or another—play their part in harrying Poor Joe into the grave.

It is this significant difference, even in the handling of his mst conventionally orthodox theme—that of sentimentalizing over a dying child—that enables us to distinguish the period of Dickens' literary life which opens with *Bleak House* his third and final period.

PART II

DICKENS' WORK CONSIDERED IN DETAIL

DICKENS' novels, as we have said, can be discriminated into three periods: (1) Early; (2) Middle; and (3) Late. The mode of discrimination is again threefold: (a) literary-technical; (b) the relative preponderance of optimism or its converse in the general world-outlook; (c) the class-sympathy implicit in the working-out of each novel.

In the novels of the first period—*Pickwick, Oliver Twist, Nicholas Nickleby, Old Curiosity Shop, Barnaby Rudge, Martin Chuzzlewit*—the craftsmanship is predominantly that of youthful exuberance. Like a high-spirited youth on a well-mettled hunter he dashes at every obstacle without a moment's hesitation. What he can't get over he crashes through. And though his neck is in peril continually, he manages, as much by luck as by judgment, to emerge, breathless but triumphant, at the finish. This is, of course, most true of *Pickwick*. Undertaken in a spirit of light-hearted self-confidence, it was intended by its promoters to be something of the kind of thing that R. S. Surtees, the creator *of Jorrocks,* had already begun to write. Dickens, while shifting the field of action from that of sporting and hunting (about which as he said he was as big a Cockney as anybody) none the less intended originally to take a parallel line, exploiting the vein originally opened with masterly effect by Molière in his *Bourgeois Gentilhomme*. But, after a few episodes had been written, Dickens' creations took command of him; and *Pickwick* grew into a coherent whole almost despite its author. Having discovered in himself powers beyond anything he had suspected, Dickens set to work to supply the clamour for "more." *Oliver Twist, Nicholas Nickleby, The Old Curiosity Shop,* and *Barnaby Rudge* followed without a break, the new novel being in each case begun before its predecessor had been finished. Finding that he possessed the ability to invent a life-like character at a moment's notice—or none at all, since he does it almost in spite of himself, with people who appear only to disappear and play no further part—Dickens in his first period hardly bothered to invent a plot. His inveterate fondness for the theatre (in his pre-*Pickwick* days, he went, he tells us, to see a play almost *nightly)* is manifest in the plots he adopts and the situations which give him his points of departure. In *Oliver Twist* the plot basis is simply the old theme of the love-child, the destroyed will, and the lost heir who in the end triumphantly enters upon his own, despite the scheming of his wicked (but legitimate) half-brother.* In *Nicholas Nickleby* the plot is that other old favourite theme, the wicked uncle who in trying to make pliant and profitable tools out of the children of the brother whom he had cheated, defeats himself and in the end drives himself to suicide. In the *Old Curiosity Shop* the basic plot is again a well-worn theme: that of the crazy gambler who ruins himself and his dearly loved grand-daughter by his insane notion that by gambling he can win a fortune that will make her a "lady." In *Barnaby Rudge* the main plot is an exercise in the Nemesis theme: Barnaby, born mentally deranged in consequence of the shock to his mother of a double murder committed by his father (a house steward who murders his master and a fellow-servant) meets his father again in the course of the Gordon riots in which Old Rudge and Barnaby both figure as minor ring-leaders. Barnaby first of all rescues his father (knowing nothing of his early guilt) along with the other prisoners released by the burning down of Newgate. But both are betrayed by their fellow ringleader, the hangman Dennis. Barnaby is reprieved and released by the good offices of friends (an inverted Nemesis), while Old Rudge, who has for years been supposed to have been murdered in defending his master from the fellow-servant whom in fact he murdered, and whose "widow" has been paid a pension on that score by the brother and guardian of the heiress daughter of the master he had murdered, is left to be hanged.

A sub-plot repeats the Nemesis motive: the heiress daughter, Emma Haredale, is courted by Edward Chester, the son of Sir John Chester, an old enemy alike of the deceased Haredale and still more of his brother, Emma's guardian. The elder Chester bans the marriage and disowns his son. He also, taking advantage of the fact that the Haredales are a Catholic family, bribes the leaders of the Gordon riots to attack and burn down the Haredale mansion—thereby, he hopes, inflicting final ruin upon his enemy. In the upshot the burning down of the Haredale mansion not only occasions the capture of Old Rudge—drawn back to the scene of his crime by the fascination supposed to obsess murderers—but also occasions a meeting and a duel between Haredale and Chester in which the latter is killed. An agent in this culmination is Hugh, the son of a gipsy woman who years before was hanged for robbery. Hugh, whom early neglect has brutalized to the point of savagery, is the ring-leader of the rioters whom Chester bribes to lead the attack upon the Haredale mansion, as he had bribed him earlier to intercept the correspondence between Emma and

---

*In the melodrama of the period wicked half-brother was usually the "bastard"—a significant difference.

his son Edward. Hugh, who is hanged for his share in the riots, turns out to be Chester's son by the gipsy woman. His son Edward is the chief agent in the rescue of Gabriel Varden, who in turn leads the suppression of the riot and effects the reprieve of Barnaby.

In *Martin Chuzzlewit* the main plot is an exercise in the theme of obstinate selfishness. Old Martin Chuzzlewit quarrels with his grandson, young Martin, because he will not submit entirely to his imperious will. Being as self-willed and as imperious as his grandfather, young Martin first of all tries to make a living by qualifying as an architect, under the tuition of his relative, the humbug Pecksniff—but is turned out of his house by that humbug who thinks that doing so will please old Martin and so procure for him (Pecksniff) a substantial legacy. Young Martin, in desperation, emigrates to America, where his sufferings, and the example of his servant, Mark Tapley (who is as obstinately cheerful and unselfish as the Martins are, at first, imperious and selfish), effect a complete change for the better in his character and disposition. A similar change is produced in old Martin by the patient forbearance and unselfishness of his adopted ward, Mary Graham, whom young Martin wishes to (and in the end, does) marry.

The sub-plot is motived by the parallel selfishness of the miserly brother of old Martin—Anthony Chuzzlewit —who has an unselfish affection for only one object, his son Jonas, whom he has taught to be even more selfish and money-greedy than himself. In the end Anthony dies broken–hearted because he finds his idolized son, impatient for his decease, tries to poison him. Jonas, in turn, blackmailed by an adventurer who believes (as Jonas believes) that he had in fact poisoned his father, murders the blackmailer; and then, being detected, poisons himself to escape the gallows.

The sub-plot is linked with the main plot through Pecksniff. When Jonas is left his father's fortune he marries (in spite) that one of Pecksniff's daughters who has been most contemptuous to him; she being morally coerced into the marriage by her greedy hypocrite of a father. Jonas is drawn into contact with the adventurer by his murder plot. He makes the acquaintance of the adventurer's firm in consequence of a quarrel with the company in which he had insured his father's life; and is induced, firstly, to invest his own money in the concern, and, then, to induce Pecksniff to invest his money therein also. (Pecksniff, by a characteristic double-cross, leads Jonas to believe that it will be bequeathed to him and his wife, anyway.) The murder of the adventurer by Jonas brings the whole flimsy financial structure down with a crash. Jonas, if he had lived would have been all-but pauperized and Pecksniff is similarly ruined.

Meanwhile, old Martin who is, secretly, only awaiting the return of young Martin from America to effect a reconciliation, fills in the interval by planning the self-exposure of Pecksniff. He goes to live in his house; affects to be feeble-minded and entirely under his influence; and in this way induces him to reveal himself as (under the cover of his hypocrisy) the greediest, the most unprincipled, and the most heartless of all the harpy-swarm of expectant relatives who had, before the novel opens, driven old Martin into his frantic misanthropy. The novel ends with the exposure (as well as ruin) of Pecksniff; and with wedding bells all round for the juveniles—except poor, pathetic, Tom Pinch, who is left to exemplify the somewhat ambiguous truth that, "Virtue is its own reward."

The teaching of Dickens' first period

Taking these novels as a group it will be seen that their general presupposition is bourgeois society—a society based upon the private ownership of the means of existence, upon competition, and individual freedom qualified only by the law on the one side and the exigencies of competition on the other. The wealth of potentiality in human nature is exemplified by the enormous variety of characters revealed in the working out of these simple themes. From the standpoint of rigid plot economy whole groups of these characters are the merest of irrelevancies. In *Oliver Twist* the fact of being born in the workhouse leads to vividly realistic descriptions of a parochial baby-farm, of a workhouse orphanage, of a Board of Guardians, and above all, of the quintessential parish beadle, Bumble. Oliver being apprenticed to an undertaker gives an occasion for similarly vivid descriptions on the one hand of funerals, and of the circumstances attending parish relief and parish burials, and on the other hand, of the undertaker's household—the hysterical shrew wife, the foolishly amorous maid-of-all-work, and the treacherous, brutal, and gluttonous charityboy. Driven to run away, Oliver makes his way to London, which occasions descriptions of the weary starving tramp to London; the meeting with the Artful Dodger, the introduction to the thieves' kitchen, and the first glimpse of London. Later developments lead to flashlight photographs of thieves' haunts, of the Hatton Garden magistrate, Mr. Fang (an unmistakable likeness of a real Hatton Garden magistrate named Lang— deliberately inserted in support of the public campaign for his removal), of a servants' hall; of detectives; of Sykes' murder of Nancy; of his remorse-ridden tramp round the outskirts of London; of the hue and cry against Sykes; and of his death. All these are on a strict construction, irrelevancies—just as are the Dotheboys Hall scenes, the scenes in which Crummles and his company of strolling players appear, and the Kenwigs-Lilliwick-Petowker scenes, all in *Nicholas Nickleby*. But it is these scenes which in each case make the novel—*are* the novel in fact. Dickens' technique is faithfully and enthusiastically copied from that of his idols Henry Fielding, and (even more) Tobias Smollett. It is a picaresque technique devoted, however—especially in *Oliver Twist*, but more or less in each and every member of the group—to antipicaresque purposes. Dickens can find plenty of pity for the weak and the unfortunate, and a kindly feeling for the shifts of the impecunious—as witness the immortal Dick Swiveller in the *Old Curiosity Shop* (who is in some respects a farcical caricature of Dickens himself). But he hates a rogue; and has no mercy for roguery of any kind. In this first period all his rogues are either so chastened that they repent (e.g., Jingle in *Pickwick)* or they are, like the wicked uncle, Ralph, in *Nickleby*, like the wicked, step-brother Monks in *Oliver* (and with him the whole Fagin-Sykes gang), like Quilp and Sampson Brass in the *Old Curiosity Shop*, and like Jonas and Pecksniff in *Chuzzlewit*, brought to complete ruin, and destitution, or death. The moral illustrated by all the novels of this group is, " Cheats never thrive," "Be sure your sin will find you out," " Virtue will triumph in the long run."

An apparent exception is the death of the virtuous Little Nell in the *Old Curiosity Shop*. But even here the exception is only apparent, since Nell does succeed, even at the cost of her own life, in saving her grandfather from both crime and the asylum. For her, as for him, death is a release. And also, in terms of evangelical ideology, the attainment of heaven's bliss.

This naive optimism is reinforced by the implied class standpoint of the novels of this group. For the petit bourgeoisie in its ascendant phase—the phase in which, though the fight against feudalism has been won, it is still necessary to fight to secure the fruits of the victory—from this class standpoint, social classes have only a relative subjective reality. "A man's a man for a' that!" There is, it is true:

...yon birkie, called a "Lord,"
Wha struts an' stares, and a' that.

but as Robbie Burns made haste to add:

Though hundreds tremble at his word
He's but a coof for a' that.

There were still "Lords" (and, in Wolfe Tone's phrase, "the gentry as they affect to call themselves") but they were in the Hegelian sense, *unreal.* They existed, only so far as men still foolishly gave them existence by recognizing them as a superior class. In reality there are no classes, only humanity. And the true line of policy for humanity is (to revert again to Burns' words) that, "man to man, the world o'er, should brothers be for a' that." In a word—all the preventable ills of the world would be remedied if only men behaved to each other with kindliness, justice, and sympathetic understanding. There were, of course, rich people and poor; but these were casual, accidental, and transitory divisions whose ill effects would disappear if only the rich used their power and wealth sympathetically to assist the poor to escape from poverty, and the poor took example from the manly and intelligent self-reliance of the deserving rich.

Mr. Pickwick, for instance, who ends as a radiating centre of general benevolence, is a well-to-do city merchant—retired. Mr. Brownlow and his friend Grimwig, who function as the "good fairies" in *Oliver Twist,* are of the same class; as are also the brothers Cheeryble in *Nicholas Nickleby,* whom modern readers find incredible to the point of nausea, but whom Dickens swore (and truthfully) that he had drawn from life.

Certainly these first-period novels show virtue as existing also among the poor. Sam Weller, for instance, carries off the honours of Pickwick, equally with his master. If Squeers, Quilp and Dennis the hangman, are all villains drawn from the lower stratum of society, as also are Sykes, Fagin, and Sairey Gamp, contraposed to them are a score of characters in each novel, exemplifying as much native virtue in the poor as can be supposed to exist among the well-to-do and rich. In fact, the relations of employer and employed are presented ideally in those between Samuel Pickwick, Esq., and his man Sam Weller, quite as much as in those between those monstrosities of benevolence, the brothers Cheeryble, and their many employees.

The same moral is preached by direct comparison. The savage ill-treatment and starvation of the poor orphan drudge, the Marchioness, by her employer Sally Brass, contrasts, glaringly, at all points, with the treatment of Kit, by his employers, the Garlands. The part played by the Marchioness in thwarting the villainy of Sampson Brass and Quilp drives the moral home.

It is not possible to escape the conclusion that at this stage Dickens believed, as did most of his humanitarian-Radical contemporaries, that the whole social question would be solved if only every employer of every degree modelled himself upon the Cheeryble–Pickwick–Garland example.

Optimism gets a shock — the second period

This optimism meets with a severe shock in *Martin Chuzzlewit.* The ingrained hypocrisy of Pecksniff, whose heartless self-seeking and crafty greed is habitually hidden under a cloak of universal benevolence, seems to mark the collapse of Dickens' faith in the Cheeryble ideal. The American scenes — in which, by the way, the basic theme of the heartless swindling of emigrants by fraudulent real-estate dealers is, in essence, only exaggerated in the inverse sense that this sort of thing happened in fact on an even bigger scale than indicated; while the portrait of Colonel Driver, the editor of the *Rowdy Journal,* and of his assistant, Jefferson Brick, is recognizably based upon a real original, the founder of the Gordon Bennet dynasty — these scenes show that Dickens' optimism had received a severe shock from his visit to a land which boasted as its chief virtue the refusal to recognize class divisions.

The effects of the shock upon Dickens were profound. It may, of course, be argued, that he never fully worked out the logical consequences of what he had seen — but it is certain that he never again emerged with a completely reconstructed optimism.

His first reaction was in the direction of partly recognizing the enormously corrupting influence of wealth and power; which partial recognition is made manifest in the two full-length novels of his second period, *Dombey and Son,* and *David Copperfield.*

As self-worship and its evil consequences was the basic theme of *Martin Chuzzlewit* — a theme, by the way, clearly suggested by Dickens' American experiences — so the basic theme of *Dombey and Son* is pride — the pride of the head of the firm of that name in its wealth, its good repute, and its unshakeable perpetuity. Just as the ostentation of vulgar self-seeking which Dickens found to his disgust to be the cant fashionably paraded in the cities of the U.S.A. — a cant which occluded and hid the innumerable finer qualities which he also found there — just as this stung him into writing in *Martin Chuzzlewit* a novel-tract on the vice of Selfishness in all its forms, so his return to England seems to have brought him a further shock in his recognition that the Pride prevalent in Britain—being, basically, *purse*-pride—was an even more obnoxious vice.

Pride of birth was a folly he felt no need to attack: it was so little fashionable in England in 1848 that Macaulay, for instance, doubted whether the House of Lords would survive another couple of Parliamentary sessions. The pride of the new commercial-financial aristocracy, the victorious upper-strata of the bourgeoisie, was another thing altogether. Dickens saw, to his horror, that instead of expanding trade and commerce leading, *via* a growth of Cheerybleism, to a new benevolent-equalitarian harmony, it was leading to the creation of "Great" commercial houses whose heads wielded a power as great as that of Roman Emperors; and who, in their pride of wealth and power, exacted from their connections and dependents a deference and an obedience greater than those for which the Emperor Caligula had had his throat so deservedly cut. That this pride was in itself a self-less pride—since it was pride in the house to which, and to whose glory, the head himself was as subservient as were the humblest of his underlings—made it all the more shocking. As Bernard Shaw was to say, sixty years later, " Self-sacrifice enables us to sacrifice other people without blushing." It was their own complete self-effacement before the claims and needs of the House, whose standing and honour was in their keeping, that made these financial-commercial magnates so ruthlessly imperious in exacting an equivalent self-effacement from all beneath their sway.

Vulgar, conscienceless, dollar-chasing was revolting enough; but this conscientious exaction of deference to, and of service on behalf of, great wealth already amassed —an enslavement to its impersonal process of gaining— this was even more shocking, in that it opened up no obvious prospect of remedy.

The ground plot of *Dombey and Son* is conceived in this spirit. It is, in fact, an exercise in the Biblical theme: "Pride goeth before a fall, and a haughty spirit before destruction." Mr. Dombey is shown as completely obsessed with his function as the head of the Great House of Dombey and Son. Only at long last, under the battering of mischance, does the man himself emerge, distinct from, and independent of, the Head of the House—and then only when the pride has been brought to a fearful fall and the House itself brought totally to destruction.

To secure the perpetuity of the House, Mr. Dombey needs a son, that the House's name may correspond to actuality and its continuance be ensured. His wife is of importance to him only as the means of producing the son. He was "Mr. Dombey" to her when she married him, and "Mr. Dombey" he was to her when she died — in giving birth to the son. That she did in the end produce the son, went a long way towards effacing her earlier indiscretion in producing, not a son, but a daughter—at best, an irrelevance; at the worst, an impertinence. If she had, however, been really worthy the honour, the joy and pride in having done her duty and produced, however tardily, the son, would have sustained her for years of further honorific service. As it was, she died—and so proved herself not fully worthy.

In the end, as might have been expected, the son (whom the father idolizes as the Future Head of the House) proves frail in constitution, and his hopes of survival are extinguished when his father tries to "bring him on" at Dr. Blimber's " forcing house."

Heavily shaken by his loss, Mr. Dombey marries again; taking, as his wife, Edith, the handsome daughter of a vain, frivolous, self-seeking woman of aristocratic connections who has already from mercenary motives, forced her daughter into one previous, loveless marriage. Mr. Dombey is not deterred by Edith's frankly avowed lack of affection for him. All he wants is a woman who, in birth and appearance, is suited for public recognition as the wife of the Head of the Great House of Dombey and Son; and who has the physical capacity of producing the needed son. In the end his imperious pride meets with a pride and a will as imperious as his own, and all his hopes are brought to nought.

In his obtuseness Mr. Dombey offends Edith from the start; and the rift between them is artfully widened by the villain Carker, his manager, whom he employs as his messenger to convey offensively imperious demands. The breach widens, and culminates in a crisis. Edith leaves him, ostensibly with Carker—but really intending, as she does, to spurn Carker with hatred and loathing once she has allowed him to ruin his credit with his employer by seemingly eloping with her. Carker meanwhile has allowed, deliberately, Mr. Dombey—who is all but distracted by the insubordination of the intractable Edith—to enter upon reckless commercial speculations which he knows will bring the House to ruin. Dombey, furiously in pursuit of Edith and of revenge, meets Carker, equally furious, as he returns from the meeting at which Edith had spurned him and escaped him. In the sudden surprise Carker, shocked and startled, stumbles from a station platform before an oncoming express train and is killed. Dombey, baffled and thwarted of personal vengeance, returns to face the failure of the House upon which his whole life and pride had been built.

The sub-plot is provided by the adventures of his unwanted daughter. From being ignored until the infant son, Paul, grows to love her as his favourite companion — and thereafter regarded with jealous irritation because of little Paul's avowed preference of her before everybody else—the daughter Florence grows increasingly to be a thorn in Mr. Dombey's flesh. When his second wife, Edith, who is as cold as marble to him, shows a keen affection for Florence, his jealous anger grows beyond all restraint. His angry demand that Edith shall cease to show a preference for Florence over himself, precipitates the breach between them which ends in the final break. His rage at Edith's fight impels him to strike a blow at Florence and drive her from his house. She takes refuge with friends in humble circumstances—the old seacaptain, Cuttle, his friend the spectacle-maker, Sol Gills, and their nephew Walter, who is an employee of the firm of Dombey and Son. In the end Florence becomes married to Walter, who has prospered as a supercargo. Eventually, she is reconciled to her father who for his part, has been brought to humility and repentance by the crash of all his hopes. Edith ends her days in voluntary seclusion.

What marks *Dombey* out as opening a new transitional period in Dickens' development is its recognition of the infinite complexity of the issues raised in social life. The basic plot of *Dombey* departs widely from the stock themes which had contented Dickens up till then. There is much less working to formula—pride and its fall is the basic theme, but in a different sense entirely from that in which selfishness is the theme of *Martin Chuzzlewit*. Whereas in *Chuzzlewit* every character, almost without exception is made deliberately to give an example of some form of selfishness or of its reverse, in *Dombey* the pride *motif* covers at most the two main characters, Dombey himself and Edith. But in each of their cases the pride was far other than one of self-satisfaction. Mr. Dombey's pride was imposed upon him by his devotion to his position as Head of a Great House. It was, in fact, a form of abject humiliation before the great god, Wealth; just as Edith's pride was the mask worn by an outraged nature, cruelly hurt and tormented into suppressed fury by a self-seeking mother—the pride of a furious heretic who, from suffering, had learned to hate the devotees of the great gods Wealth and Social Standing, with a hatred scornful beyond all bounds. If Florence stands, as she does, for a continuance of the Little Nell motive of simple, affectionate, kind-hearted devotion to duty—and in her eventual triumph is evidence of Dickens' clinging to the belief that unselfish goodness is bound to win in the end—Mr. Dombey and Edith stand each of them as types of good qualities perverted into instruments of evil under the impulsion of an evil state of society; while Carker, whose smooth plausibility covers an active Iago-like malevolence, stands as a type of positive evil to which that society lends a cover of virtue, and which, barring accidents, it usually rewards with success.

The net outcome of *Dombey* is neither predominantly optimist nor predominantly pessimist. As the case is presented, Mr. Dombey deserves his fall for his stupid lack of sensitivity; and it might be counted for optimism that after his fall, he, though broken, discovers his truer self. But the discovery is not made until he is past making any use of it. And Edith from first to last is a tragedy—a fine spirit that has been allowed no chance from the start, and who, in the end, wins only the peace of a voluntarily-adopted solitary confinement. Carker is, it is true, thwarted and killed; but only after he has done the maximum of mischief—to his discarded mistress, to his brother and sister, to Rob the Grinder, to Walter, to Florence, to Edith, to the House, and to Dombey himself—and the evil he has done in great measure lives after him. In fact, the moral of *Dombey*, instead of being the, "God's in his Heaven, all's right with the world" moral of the first period novels, is, at most, the pathetic moral, "little children, love one another." Or, in other words—there is so much incurable evil in the world, that it is a positive sin not to make the most out of whatever has in it any measure of good.

The class implications of *Dombey* are different, too, from those of the earlier novels. There is a greater readiness to see a *real,* as distinct from a merely conventional, distinction between the aristocracy of blood and the aristocracy of commerce and finance. If the latter are shown as dehumanized by their wealth, where they are not vulgarized by the process of its acquirement, the former are shown as dehumanized by heartless idleness and conventional frivolity.

As against both of these aristocracies—with the Wilkinsons and Pipchins, their flunkey imitators and hangers-on—the whole group of common people, the lower strata of the petit-bourgeoisie and the proletariat stand out in striking contrast. Old Sol Gills, Captain Cuttle, Susan Nipper, Polly Toodles and her husband, all figure in an admirable light. Susan Nipper in fact, in her bearding of Mr. Dombey and her out-facing of the Pipchin ogress, comes near to being a banner-bearer of class war. True, the old hag, Mother Brown, is an unforgivable wretch—but she, unquestionably, belongs to the slums, and Dickens, to do him justice, never mistakes the *lumpen-proletariat* for the working class. Broadly speaking, all the characters of wealth and social position turn out to be " bad eggs"; and, with similar reservations, all the characters from the lower orders prove to be "good eggs."

There is, it is true, no clear recognition of class conflict, as such, and no indication of a function for political struggle. But there is the beginning at any rate of a recognition of class as a positive fact.

"David Copperfield"

A similar conclusion can be drawn from *David Copperfield.* Here the plot is tenuous to non-existence, showing, in fact, an even more complete reversion to the picaresque method—the method of events succeeding events as in a journey of exploration—than do his earlier novels, since it is told in the first person and is in form a quasi-autobiography. If *Oliver Twist* shows most clearly the influence of Smollett, *David Copperfield* shows no less clearly the influence of Defoe. Such plot as there is must, on this method, seem to be fortuitous and extraneous, since the main theme is the arrival of the hero at his selfappointed end—in this case prosperity and happiness with his second wife, Agnes. It would be, however, equally true to say, on this method, that the hero himself was fortuitous and extraneous to the incidents in which he happens to be involved. On the whole, it would be truest to say that the incidental plot and the hero's progress-plot are complementary aspects of the implied plot which is to present under the image of one man's journey through life a many-faceted picture of life-asit-is. Almost any reader must, in some mood or another find it possible to identify himself with David Copperfield, who might as well, from this standpoint, have been named " Everyman." It is this more or less complete achievement of universality which distinguishes *Copperfield* from all the other novels of Dickens, and marks it out as pivotal in his development. Even less than is the case with *Dombey* can it be said of *Copperfield* that its moral is optimist or pessimist. It is, so far as it is anything, positively meliorist. The total balance of good and evil in the Universe is, on the meliorist view, fixed in sum, since each implies its opposite and any increase in the one implies an increase, actual or potential, in the other. The utmost that human endeavour can achieve is to modify the incidence of the evil in such wise as to insure that avoidable evil is reduced to a minimum; even though, in doing this, mankind's enhanced sensitivity will make the unavoidable evil more intense and more apparent, and on the whole greater in bulk. So that it be borne in common—each according to his power comforting his neighbour, giving by kindness encouragement to those affected by inescapable ills—that, seemingly, is the utmost that it is within the power of man to achieve. This, which is, in part, the moral of *Dombey*, is even more, and wholly, the moral of *Copperfield*.

The balance of good and evil, and their mutual interconditioning runs all through the novel. To David's idyllic childhood succeeds his widowed mother's marriage to the vile-natured Mr. Murdstone; who proceeds, under the guise of teaching and "forming David's character" to use the affection of each for the other as a means of torturing both David and his mother. Incidentally also, the occasion of the wedding causes David to begin an acquaintance with the Peggotty household, and with Little Em'ly, which has in the end far-reaching consequences.

David, driven to revolt by Mr. Murdstone's torments, is sent away to the school of the sadistic brute Creakle. Here he is badly treated physically; but, after a time finds the atmosphere much more congenial in that he makes friends with the tearful but buoyant hearted Tommy Traddles, and with the handsome and wilful Steerforth, the spoiled son of a foolish and aristocratic mother. When David's mother dies, crushed under the moral tortures of the Murdstones—brother and sister—David is taken from school, and, child as he is, set to work as a child labourer in a blacking factory. This infliction has its set-off in that it causes him to make the acquaintance of the inimitable Mr. Micawber, who, however, soon falls into the clutches of his creditors. When Micawber, after compounding with his creditors, is forced to remove to Plymouth with his family, David decides to stand it no longer; and sets off to appeal for help to his great-aunt in Dover, Betsy Trotwood—of whom he knows only by repute. Robbed on setting out, he makes his way to Dover on foot. His aunt decides to adopt him; and thereafter he begins a new life. His aunt sends him to a good school, and, his education concluded, gets him articled to a proctor in Doctors' Commons (an ecclesiastical Court nearly all of whose functions have been absorbed by the High Court of Justice).

From this point the main, autobiographical, thread proliferates into a succession of dramatic and melodramatic sub-plots, each of which would have been, in the hands of almost any other writer, sufficient for an independent novel.

On the main line, so to speak, are David's own love adventures. He falls in love with his employer's daughter, and, after her father's sudden death, marries her. After a brief comedy-idyll of married life the child-wife, Dora, dies. Later on David does what he might have done in the first place, and marries Agnes, the daughter of his aunt's lawyer-agent, Wickfield; and so achieves the "happy ever after" terminus of his adventures.

This final *dénouement* is complicated by the sub-plot of Uriah Heep, a less polished, more hypocritical, and even more villainous Carker. Under a pretence of cringing humility, Heep conceals an active malevolence that places him above either Squeers, Quilp, Dennis, Jonas Chuzzlewit, or even Carker in Dickens' list of villains in grain. Heep aspires, on the one hand, to get complete control of his employer's business; and on the other to use that power to force Agnes to marry him. He uses as his means to that end, his employer's weakness for drink; and all but succeeds. He is, however, thwarted, exposed, and forced to disgorge by the detective enterprise of Mr. Micawber, whom he has employed as a clerk—as a means of spying upon David.

Moving simultaneously with the Uriah Heep sub-plot (which, in its turn, progresses during, and in incidental contact with, the main autobiographical love-plot), goes on the chief sub-plot, that of Little Em'ly. Meeting Steerforth again, prior to taking up his duties in Doctors' Commons, when on his way to visit his old nurse Peggotty at Yarmouth, David invites Steerforth to accompany him. They visit the home of the fisherfolk and find Little Em'ly engaged to be married to her cousin, Ham Peggotty—who like herself, is an orphan whom Daniel Peggotty has brought up. The handsome villain Steerforth, induces Little Em'ly to elope with him, under a promise of marriage—which, of course, he does not intend to fulfil. Ultimately, Steerforth, who has abandoned Em'ly (he offers to give her financial compensation if she will marry his servant, Litimer) is shipwrecked and drowned off Yarmouth on his return to England. Ham Peggotty is drowned at the same time in an attempt to rescue him—not knowing who he is trying to save. Em'ly is found by her uncle, Daniel, and they, with friends, and with the Micawber family, emigrate to Australia—where they also live (more or less) "happily ever after."

Each of these sub-plots is, of course, like the main plot, complicated further by subsidiary ramifications, so that in the upshot the effect is achieved of a vastly ramified plexus of incident and character symbolical of the current of human life itself.

The moral of *David Copperfield* is elusive. In the main it is expressed in the words of Betsy Trotwood (the best-drawn character in the novel, and the most pleasing) "Never be mean in anything; never be false; never be cruel." But it is apparent from the course of the novel that Dickens has lost his old naive faith that these injunctions alone will ensure peace, prosperity and happiness to all who live their life in their practice. On the contrary: every character in the novel who, tried by this standard, passes muster as "good," is forced to face hardship, disappointment, trial and affliction; and only in the end—and with chastening qualifications—attains to peace, happiness, and a moderate prosperity. It is, on the showing of *David Copperfield,* the good who are forced to suffer most cruelly; and it is their very goodness which provides the means whereby their pain is inflicted. The bad characters, on the other hand, while they, too, are checked and thwarted—and, in the case of Uriah Heep, forced to disgorge their ill-gotten gains —do not, in fact, suffer anything like so much. Steerforth, for instance—who, though a villain, is so, more as a result of a foolish upbringing than by reason of natural wickedness—works mischief far beyond any power of recompense. He suffers, in that he is never happy, is haunted by remorse, and is, in the end, drowned. But he does not suffer anything like so much as does Little Em'ly, or as do her relatives, and David on her account. Steerforth's mother, too, stricken into paralysis and loss of reason, by her son's death, suffers a far more drastic penalty than he.

More telling still on the pessimist side of the account is the fact that, though Uriah Heep does, in the end, land in gaol, he is shown there as swindling still, and still gaining benefits by the exercise of hypocritical pretences. Most telling of all is the fact that Murdstone is shown not only as surviving but as practising profitably on a fresh victim the very deceits and cruelties he had inflicted fatally upon David's mother.

The politico-social moral of *David Copperfield* seems, therefore, to be identical with that of *Dombey and Son.* Life in general is an inexplicable muddle, of which it is possible to make the best or the worst. It is finer and nobler to make the best of it; but such rewards as this course will bring are moral and subjective, only; and even they must be bought with a price.

There is, however, in *Copperfield,* a change in Dickens' class-orientation. The only quasi-aristocratic characters in the book—the Steerforths, and also certain connections of Mrs. Strong, the wife of the benevolent schoolmaster—fall definitely into the " bad" category. The well-to-do bourgeois characters, are, with the exception of Betsy Trotwood—and her amiable, but deranged, companion, Mr. Dick—either scoundrels, as Murdstone is, liars like Mr. Spenlow, or moral weaklings like Mr. Wickfield. It is the lower middle-class and proletarian characters, such as Micawber and Tommy Traddles in the first category, and the whole Peggotty family in the second, who occupy the centre of the stage and reap all the laurels. In fact, the juxtaposition of the Steerforth and Peggotty families issues in something very near to natural class antagonism—a fact which Dickens himself suggests through the mouth of Steerforth.

When the proposed visit to Yarmouth and the Peggotty family is mooted to Mrs. Steerforth and her companion Rosa Dartle—who, we learn in the end, is secretly Steerforth's discarded mistress (torn continually between infatuation for him, hatred for herself for having been his mistress, and hatred for him for having discarded her, as well as for those who have taken her place) Rosa Dartle asks whether "that sort of people," meaning the Peggotty family, are really "animals and clods, and beings of another order." Steerforth answers in a way that, at the time, David takes to be ironical:

> "Why, there's a pretty wide separation between them and us," said Steerforth with indifference. "They are not to be expected to be as sensitive as we are. Their delicacy is not to be shocked, or hurt very easily. They are wonderfully virtuous, I dare say—some people contend for that, at least, and I am sure I don't want to contradict them—but they have not very fine natures, and they may be thankful that, like their coarse rough skins, they are not easily wounded." —*David Copperfield:* Chap. XX.

In the subsequent working out of the whole Little Em'ly sub-plot, Steerforth is shown as acting fully in the spirit of this proposition; while every member of the Peggotty household down to and including even Mrs. Gummidge (the "lone, lorn, creature," always lamenting "the old'un," her lost husband), shows each in a different way how revoltingly false it is. The Peggotty household, in fact, contains by far the finest, most delicate, and most sensitive natures to appear in the novel; and the contrast is heightened to the pitch of absolute antagonism when both Mrs. Steerforth and Rosa Dartle, the one with self-centred aristocratic scorn, the other with jealous fury, refuse to believe that any sort of injury, physical, mental or moral, could be inflicted on "that sort of people" which money would not more than compensate.

This class moral is reinforced by a number of side strokes. One of the most obvious is that given by the casually introduced character, Mrs. Henry Spiker, the wife of a Treasury solicitor, who "looks like Hamlet's aunt." At a dinner table she follows the lead of her hostess, Mrs. Waterbrook, and discourses on the Aristocracy and Blood:

> "I confess I am of Mrs. Waterbrook's opinion," said Mr. Waterbrook, with his wine-glass at his eye. "Other things are all very well in their way, but give me Blood!"
>
> "Oh! There is nothing," observed Hamlet's aunt, "so satisfactory to one! There is nothing that is so much one's *beau idéal* of—of all that sort of thing, speaking generally. There are some low minds (not many I am happy to believe, but there are *some)* that would prefer to do what I should call bow down before idols. Positively Idols! Before services, intellect and so on. But these are intangible points. Blood is not so. We see Blood in a nose, and we

know it. We meet with it in a chin and we say, 'There it is! That's Blood!' It is an actual matter of fact. We point it out. It admits of no doubt."

The simpering fellow, with the weak legs, who had taken Agnes down, stated the question more decisively yet, I thought.

"Oh, you know, deuce take it," said this gentleman, looking round the board with an imbecile smile, "we can't forego Blood, you know. We must have Blood, you know. Some young fellows, you know, may be a little behind their station perhaps in point of education and behaviour, and may go a little wrong, you know, and get themselves and other people into a variety of fixes —and all that—but deuce take it, it's delightful to reflect that they've got Blood in 'em! Myself, I'd rather at any time be knocked down by a man who had got Blood in him, than I'd be picked up by a man who hadn't!"

This sentiment, as comprising the general question into a nutshell, gave the utmost satisfaction, and brought the gentleman into great notice until the ladies retired.—*David Copperfield:* Chap. XXV.

There is here expressed more than the ordinary bourgeois-Liberal contempt for the aristocracy of Blood and an exaltation, as against it, of the (so-called) aristocracy of talent. The company are none of them aristocrats; hence their deference to "Blood" is manifestly the most contemptible of toadyism. More than that; since these words were written towards the end of 1849, at a time when the completeness of the defeat of the revolution of 1848 was apparent (and the corresponding exaltation of the reactionaries was at its height), it is impossible not to see in the vapid imbecile who would rather be knocked down by a man with Blood than picked up by a man without it, the spokesman of that very petit-bourgeoisie which had deserted to the reaction rather than allow themselves to be saved by the revolutionary proletariat. The whole episode expresses in an imaginative-burlesque form the very spirit of Engels' chapter on the "Smalltraders" in his *Revolution and Counter-revolution in Germany, 1848.*

Dickens' third period—"Bleak House"

David Copperfield is outstanding among Dickens' novels on several grounds. It was his own favourite. It was his first attempt at a novel in the first person; and is, probably in consequence of this, much more genuinely autobiographical than any of his previous—or, for the matter of that, any of his later—novels. His powers had clearly, in *Copperfield,* reached their maximum expansion. His ability to invent a character at a moment's notice is not, perhaps, so obvious as in his earlier work. But it is more definitely under control. His plan undergoes much less modification in progress than did that of *Pickwick,* for instance, or even that of *Dombey* (where Walter was on the original scheme intended to come to as lamentable an end from a deficiency of proper pride as Mr. Dombey does from an excess of it). Dickens' mastery of his chosen medium is shown at its completest in *Copperfield.* This is not to say that any falling off is to be detected in his later work. On the contrary; his later work is less liked by one school of critics precisely because, in the full consciousness of his powers, he tackles bigger and bigger problems—those arising from the fundamental composition of bourgeois society—which these critics think are outside the scope of the novel as a work of art. What makes *Copperfield* pre-eminent, by comparison, does, however, arise from the fact to which these critics point. Though his powers are at their height there is in these later novels a pervading consciousness of effort—not in the invention of character and episode, but in the sense that Dickens, consciously and subconsciously, shows himself more and more at odds with bourgeois society and more and more aware of (and exasperated by) the absence of any readily available alternative.

In *Bleak House,* which opens Dickens' third period, the whole novel is dominated by the Court of Chancery and the Great Case of Jarndyce *v.* Jarndyce, which has been going on for years, setting relatives quarrelling with relatives, and driving some to ruin and others to suicide. The ground-basis, as it were, of the novel, is the fate of this cause; which, in the end, collapses because the lawcosts have gobbled up the entire estate.

The action of the novel has as its main thread the lifestory of Esther Summerson, who is the illegitimate child of a mother she believes to be dead, and who was brought up in infancy by an aunt whose death precedes the action of the novel. Esther is brought from the boarding-school in which she has completed her education and attained to young womanhood to be the companion of Ada Clare, a ward of Chancery (interested as a minor in the suit of Jarndyce *v.* Jarndyce). Esther has been adopted and chosen to be Ada's companion by her relative, John Jarndyce of Bleak House, in Hertfordshire, who is also "interested" legally (but the reverse of *interested* personally) in the Great Suit; and who has been appointed Ada's guardian, and that of her distant cousin Richard Carstone, by the Lord Chancellor. The action proper of the novel, opens with them all installed together in Bleak House under the common guardianship of John Jarndyce.

The action thereafter divides into a series of closely interwoven threads. Along one line Esther at first agrees —after a suitable interval—to marry the benevolent John Jarndyce; but both she and her guardian (who is much her senior) realize independently that such a marriage would be a mistake; so the novel ends with Esther married to the ideal of her choice, an altogether praiseworthy medical gentleman, Dr. Woodcourt.

A more pronounced thread is provided by the love entanglement of Ada and Richard. The latter, a youth of many good qualities, is shown as completely unsettled, morally, by the uncertainty of his financial prospects; which, in turn, are wholly conditioned by his expectations in the Great Suit. He will not take the advice of his guardian and settle to some occupation, and abandon all hope of any good coming from this accursed suit. On the contrary, Richard, after various false starts, abandons everything else to become absorbed in "aiding" (as he thinks) the settlement of the case. In pursuit of this infatuation he uses up his small fortune; and that, too, of Ada, who marries him. He dies, crushed, in the end, by the ignominious collapse of the suit—when the estate has been swallowed up by the law costs. Ada and her (posthumous) child return to Bleak House and to the custody of John Jarndyce, who has built a replica of Bleak House in Yorkshire as a wedding present for Esther.

Most dominant and melodramatic of all is the strand which involves Sir Leicester and Lady Deadlock of Chesney Wold, in Lincolnshire. Lady Deadlock is, in her own right, interested in the Great Cause; being herself a connection of the Jarndyce family. She shows an unguarded interest in the handwriting in which a lawpaper in the suit (produced by the family solicitor, Tulkinghorn) has been written. Tulkinghorn who dislikes her ladyship, follows up the clue. After a prolonged chain of inquiries he discovers that the writer (who, after living wretchedly, under an assumed name, as a law-writer, has died of an overdose of laudanum before Tulkinghorn can set eyes on him) had been one Captain Hawdon. In dying he left behind him a bundle of letters which reveal the fact that he had been, years before her marriage, the lover of Lady Deadlock, and that she had had a child by him—which child proves to be none other than Esther Summerson.

The evidence which establishes this sequence is scattered in a number of hands. The links of the chain are brought together by a succession of chances devised with extraordinary skill. Mr. Tulkinghorn is, at first, merely curious to get hold of some information that will give him a hold over Lady Deadlock. The calf-like infatuation for Esther of a law clerk, Guppy—and his recognition of an astonishing likeness between her and Lady Deadlock—causes some of the links to be gathered. The insane jealousy of Mrs. Snagsby, the wife of a law stationer (who is a disciple of the preacher Chadband, who has married Rachel, once the servant of the aunt who brought Esther up) brings other links together. The death of the illiterate waste-paper dealer, Krook, and the inheritance of his effects by the Smallweèd family, brings other facts to light. Finally, the threads being all in Tulkinghorn's hands, he threatens Lady Deadlock with the exposure of her secret past. She, meanwhile, to her amazement and terror, has learned that the child she thought still-born was actually living, and was indeed then her neighbour. At this critical moment Tulkinghorn is murdered.

Suspicion falls first of all upon an ex-soldier, George (the son of Sir Leicester's housekeeper) who has been in the clutches of Tulkinghorn on account of a small debt, which Tulkinghorn buys from Smallweed as a means of squeezing from George proof of the handwriting of his old captain, Hawdon. Then suspicion falls upon Lady Deadlock. She knows that she is not guilty, but fearing the exposure of her past, and the indignation of Sir Leicester, she flees away, to die of exposure at the gate of the graveyard where her lover is buried. The actual criminal was her discharged maid, Mademoiselle Hortense, who had in fact, been arrested for the crime, unknown to Lady Deadlock, before her flight. Also, as it turns out, Sir Leicester though terribly stricken and paralysed by the shock, promises full forgiveness if she can be found and induced to return. Esther, who has been called in by the Detective-Inspector, Bucket, to assist in tracing her mother, catches up with her, only to find her dead.

There are other ramifications in this, the melodramatic strand in *Bleak House;* and all are linked together with a constructional skill Dickens never surpassed. And it is not only in construction that *Bleak House* challenges comparison with any of Dickens' work. If there is no single comic character that stands out on the scale of Pickwick, the Wellers, Dick Swiveller, or Micawber—and no villain buffoon of the dimensions of a Squeers, a Quilp, or a Pecksniff—there is, as more than a compensation, the whole amazingly-multiform aggregate of the representatives of the law. Conversation Kenge, Mr. Vholes, the Lord Chancellor, the young man Guppy, his friend Jobling, young Smallweed and his family, Krook, the rag-and-paper dealer (called also the "Lord Chancellor" by the facetious—as he says, "There's no great odds between me and my learned brother across the way; *we both grub on in a muddle!")* the sinister, vulture-like Tulkinghorn, Snagsby the law-stationer, Nemo the law-writer (really Captain Hawdon), and the full-time clients, Gridley and little Miss Flite—taken in their aggregate they constitute collectively and in detail, a feat of characterization that Dickens, even, could not better. All are so saturated with the law and legality—so completely subordinated to the legal machine—that either of them might have been taken as, and would have served the purposes of most novelists as typifying, either the law or litigation. Even the horrible Krook, yammering in his filth, with his savage cat, is inextricably part of, and essentially expressive of, Law, Lawyers and Legality. So, too, is the repulsive old miser-usurer, Grandfather Smallweed, and those grotesque, living parodies himself, his grandchildren, young Smallweed and his sister. Yet each in the group is for all their common legalistic essence, as markedly individual as any character Dickens, even, ever drew.

They must be considered in their aggregated collectivity, too, for another reason. The villain of *Bleak House* is no single individual. Neither a Ralph Nickleby nor a Quilp—nor a group of individuals like the Fagin gang performs this function. The villain whose villainy conditions the whole action, and in the end precipitates the culminating catastrophe, is The Law, and the actively malevolent Vested Interest which it both protects and typifies. In the immediate foreground so far as the action of *Bleak House* is concerned, it is, of course, the Court of Chancery, with its special technique of obstructive mystification, which appears as the primary villain. But the villainy of the Court of Chancery, as it was then constituted, grew out of, and was part of, the greater villainy of the British legal system in gross. It was, for example, the arbitrary division between courts of "Law" and courts of "Equity"—between actions in the Court of Common Pleas, and pleadings at the Chancery Bar—with their incompatible modes of procedure and rules of evidence—which gave the Court of Chancery its peculiar powers of working mischief. And behind the whole legal system, maintaining it, and protecting it from all innovation, was the whole governing system of the country—the system which was defended and upheld by the Boodle Party no more than, or less than, by the Buffer Party—the system which, in the opinion of Sir Leicester Deadlock and his swarm of parasitical cousins, could not be altered in any iota except for the worse, or without risk of opening the floodgates of revolution and anarchy. And, as Dickens shows (with or without conscious intent), this system is reinforced on the one side by a grim, gaoler-like, theology which also in the eyes of its devotees, could not be altered except for the worse, or on peril of fearful evils; and on the other by a system of spurious philanthropy which both diverted attention from real evils and real remedies to false ones, and also provided the established order with an additional defence as against the poor and the oppressed. The Miss Barbarys and the Chadbands, on the one side, and on the other the Mrs. Jellybys and the Mrs. Pardiggles must be counted in with that total apparatus of evil of which the Lord Chancellor and his Court are only the most obvious and most immediate symbols.

Dickens makes this evident in various ways. In his description of Mr. Vholes, the attorney who, much to his own profit, abets professionally Richard Carstone's infatuate endeavours to expedite a settlement of the case of Jarndyce *v.* Jarndyce, he makes it evident in direct terms. Mr. Vholes is, he explains, a "very respectable man," who has a father dependent on him in the Vale of Taunton, and who "is making hay of the flesh which is grass for his three daughters." Dickens continues thus:

> The one great principle of the English law is to make business for itself. There is no other principle distinctly, certainly, and consistently maintained through all its narrow turnings. Viewed by this light it becomes a coherent scheme, and not the monstrous maze the laity are apt to think it. Let them but once perceive that its grand principle is to make business for itself at their expense and they will cease to grumble.
>
> But not perceiving this quite plainly—only seeing it by halves in a confused way—the laity sometimes suffer in peace and pocket, with a bad grace, and *do* grumble very much. Then the respectability of Mr. Vholes is brought into powerful play against them. "Repeal this statute, my good sir?" says Mr. Kenge to a snarling client, "repeal it, my dear sir? Never, with my consent. Alter this law, sir, and what will be the effect of your rash proceeding on a class of practitioners worthily represented by the opposite attorney in the case, Mr. Vholes? Sir, that class of practitioners would be swept from the face of the earth. Now you cannot afford—I would say the social system cannot afford—to lose an order of men like Mr. Vholes. Diligent, persevering, steady, acute in business. My dear sir, I understand your present feelings against the existing state of things, which I grant to be a little hard in your case; but I can never raise my voice for the demolition of a class of men like Mr. Vholes...."—*Bleak House:* Chap. XXXIX.

Dickens goes on to show how Mr. Vholes' respectability has been "cited with crushing effect before Parliamentary committees," and how it does duty in private life:

> So in familiar conversation, private authorities, no less disinterested will remark that they don't know what this age is coming to; that we are plunging down precipices; that now here is something else gone; that these changes are death to people like Vholes: a man of undoubted respectability with a father in the Vale of Taunton, and three daughters at home. Take a few steps more in this direction, say they, and what is to become of Vholes's father? Is he to perish? And of Vholes's daughters? Are they to be shirtmakers or governesses? As though, Mr. Vholes and his relations being minor cannibal chiefs, and it being proposed to abolish cannibalism, indignant champions

were to put the case thus: Make man-eating unlawful, and you starve the
Vholeses!

In a word, Mr. Vholes, with his three daughters, and his father in the Vale of
Taunton, is continually doing duty, like a piece of timber, to shore up some
decayed foundation that has become a pitfall and a nuisance. And with a great
many people, in a great many instances, the question is never one of a change
from Wrong to Right (which is quite an extraneous consideration) but is
always one of injury or advantage to that eminently respectable legion,
Vholes. —*Bleak House,* Chap. XXIX.

Here, in so many words, Dickens makes it plain beyond dispute that the
Chancery Court against which his immediate attack is levelled is not only
attacked in itself. It is attacked still more as a type and a symbol of the
whole Wrong embodied in the archaic and rotten constitution of
Society—a wrong that Dickens categorically likens to cannibalism
practised on a vaster and more horrible scale.

And what Dickens says here in words he indicates even more plainly
and comprehensively by his management of the novel as a whole. *Bleak
House* (whose very title is ominous) opens with a masterly description of
London in the grip of a fog. In a few moments we escape from the physically choking and blinding fog into the mentally and morally choking and
blinding fog of the Lord Chancellor's Court and the Great Case of Jarndyce
v. Jarndyce. We escape from here again only to land in the equally
imprisoning, stifling and sight-destroying atmosphere of fashionable
Society typified by Sir Leicester and Lady Deadlock tortured by aristocratic
inanity and *ennui*—and the case of Jarndyce *v.* Jarndyce—to which the
teeming skies, and the flood waters out in Lincolnshire, supply an
harmoniously appropriate physical background. And from this in turn we
escape only to plunge into the choking, blinding, and paralysing piety
amid which little Esther Summerson has her earliest upbringing.

It is highly significant that just as the tragedy of Richard Carstone's
wasted life is directly traceable—like so many other tragedies—to the
Court of Chancery, so the tragedy of Lady Deadlock has its whole origin, as
tragedy, in the merciless piety of her sister—Esther's godmother-aunt. If
Lady Deadlock had known from the first that her love-child was not still-
born, but living, she would never have kept her past a secret, never have
married Sir Leicester, and never have become an object of vulture-like
observation for the implacable Tulkinghorn. Similarly, if the elder sister
had been less fanatically pious, she would not have treated the younger
sister's lapse as an unforgivable sin; to be resented as a personal injury,
and punished by the severance of all relations not only with her sister, but

with her own child. And just as piety is a condition precedent for the origin of Lady Deadlock's tragedy, so too, it plays its part in precipitating its final culmination. When Lady Deadlock has escaped, apparently, every danger of exposure, the hysterical piety of the weak-minded and fantastically jealous Mrs. Snagsby combines with the cupidity of the hypocritical Chadband, the ill-nature of his pious wife, the frantic miserliness of Grandfather Smallweed, and the folly of the ineffable Guppy, to awaken her alarm and so produce the final catastrophe. In noting the infinite care and minuteness with which Dickens causes every tiny incident, however remote, to play its part in producing the ultimate outcome, it would be a grievous error to fail to note that in constituting the vast, omnipresent, impersonal Evil which is the "villain" in *Bleak House,* grim-visaged evangelical piety plays an even bigger part than does personal Greed, Spite, Folly, and everything else—except only that vast plexus of Vested Interest which is manifest in the legal system of Britain.

In respect of class feeling *Bleak House* shows, to some slight extent—or appears to show—a retreat behind the point attained in *David Copperfield.* There is no distinctly proletarian group of characters to play the heroic-sympathetic role played by the Peggotty group in *Copperfield.* Yet, that this reversion is more one of appearance than of reality is shown by all the things listed above which present the established order, and its aristocratic and quasi-aristocratic defenders, in the role of a composite-collective villain. Indeed, in strict fact, the Peggotty group are as much classifiable as petitbourgeois as proletarians. They represent in fact that pre-Capitalist, small-producing class which, in its historical differentiation, begot *both* the bourgeoisie "and" the proletariat; and in making his standpoint identical with that of this class Dickens does what all pre-Marxian Radicalism did—and what in countries where there is still a numerous peasantry, and still a considerable smallproducing class, all Radicalism (French "Radical Socialism" so-called, for instance) continues to do. In *Bleak House:* for example, in the general election which occurs in the background of the main action, Sir Leicester Deadlock is convinced:

> "...upon my honour, upon my life, upon my reputation and principles, the floodgates of society are burst open, and the waters have—a—obliterated the landmarks of the framework of the cohesion by which things are held together."

And all this because the Governmental candidates have not merely been opposed, but been heavily defeated, and by an opposition led, in the industrial North of England, by an iron-master—the son of the housekeeper of Sir Leicester's own ancestral mansion, Chesney Wold, in Lincolnshire—the iron-master being assisted, in turn, by his own son, who aspires to marry Lady Deadlock's personal maid.

This implicit identification of the industrial bourgeoisie with the more successful—because more competent, more enterprising, more persevering or simply more fortunate —members of the proletariat is true to type. That is exactly how petit-bourgeois Radicalism did (and does) envisage the relations of these classes. That this standpoint can be developed into ferociously reactionary, and antirational forms is true—as Dickens, himself, was soon to see and to show. But, at the same time, it was at that time (and in certain circumstances still is) capable of development and application in exactly the opposite direction. And it is this aspect which is apparent from start to finish in *Bleak House*. Not only are the existing social order, its ruling class, its parasites, and its ideological defenders all together presented in the role of implacable " villain"—no hope is held out anywhere that (beyond the purely provisional-personal remedy of each individual making the best possible of a radically bad situation) any remedy is possible, short of the complete annihilation of this evil social system. Some proletarians who do appear in person—the brickmakers for instance—are shown certainly as brutalized types. But their brutalization is specifically charged to the account of bourgeois society, and, despite their brutalization, they are shown as possessing, in the case of their womenfolk, admirable human qualities; potentialities of the highest good. Also, significantly enough, they are shown as begetting, in their most intense misery—in the fever-breeding dens into which destitution drives them— a fearful Nemesis in the diseases which spread to their class oppressors and exact a fearful vengeance.

Bleak House does not seem to be among the best-liked of Dickens' novels—despite the excellence of its workmanship. It is felt to be, in its net outcome, too much like its title—too suggestive of discomfort, hardship, gloom and lack of hope. Certainly its impossibly adorable heroine gets her lover, her wedding-bells, and her darling children—her "happy-ever-after"—as per traditional formula (one, by the way, more insistently demanded by the proletarian novel-consumer to this day than by non-proletarian novel-consumers). But so, too, lives and flourishes the composite evil which functions as Villain. Mr. Tulkinghorn is, it is true, murdered; and his murderess, Mademoiselle Hortense, is placed in train for a hanging. But, even if these incidentals are to be scored to the account of optimism they are more than out-weighed by the fact that the whole crew of Smallweeds and Chadbands positively profit, financially and subjectively, from the torment and tragedy of Lady Deadlock; as Mr. Vholes (and in his way Harold Skimpole) both profit from the self-torment and tragedy of Richard Carstone. Thus, and even in spite of its author— since the compound tragedy of the Chancery suit, of Poor Joe, and of Lady Deadlock (the latter especially) count far more ultimately in dramatic force and effectiveness than do the general benevolence of John Jarndyce, the heroic dutifulness of the shadowy Allan Woodcourt, and the impossible-perfections of Esther—the net outcome of *Bleak House* is defeat, bafflement, and at best, pathetically-sorrowful, indignant, or stoical resignation.

"Hard Times"

In his next novel, *Hard Times,* as we have seen earlier, Dickens' mood has shifted to that of almost truculent exasperation. The employer who has risen from the ranks is, in *Bleak House*—in the person of Rouncewell the iron-master—a minor hero. In *Hard Times,* the manufacturer-banker-employer, who boasts himself as having risen unaided from the lowest ranks is, in Bounderby, the villain. The apparent reversion in *Bleak House* to the traditional standard of the Radical petit-bourgeoisie is in *Hard Times* replaced by a ferocious frontal attack upon the whole ethic of Capitalism as represented by the Manchester school economists. It is, as we have seen, not at all a reversion to an aristocratic or mediaevalist point of view. But it does not yet show any confidence in the proletariat as pioneers of a newer and brighter future. It shows Dickens at his fiercest—in his least placable mood. As Gilbert Chesterton says:

> He describes Bounderby and Gradgrind with a degree of grimness and sombre hatred very different from the half-affectionate derision which he directed against the old tyrants and humbugs of the earlier nineteenth century —the pompous Deadlock* or the fatuous Nupkins, the grotesque Bumble or the inane Tigg. In those old books his very abuse was benignant; in *Hard Times* his very sympathy is hard. And the reason is again to be found in the political facts of the century. Dickens could be half-genial with the older generation of oppressors because it was a dying generation. It was evident, or at least it seemed evident then, that Nupkins could not go on much

---

*From the inclusion of Sir Leicester Deadlock in this connection, it is plain that G.K. C. had overlooked the fact that *Hard Times* followed immediately after *Bleak House*; only a few months separating them.

longer making up the law of England to suit himself; that Sir Leicester Deadlock could not go on much longer being kind to his tenants as if they were cats and dogs. And some of these evils the nineteenth century did really eliminate or improve. For the first half of the century Dickens and all his friends were justified in feeling that the chains were falling from mankind. At any rate the chains did fall from Mr. Rouncewell the iron-master. And when they fell from him he picked them up and put them upon the poor.—G. K. CHESTERTON (preface to Everyman Edition, *Hard Times.*)

In the first half of this passage Chesterton states a truth; in the second half he gives a twisted explanation. His final flourish is quite false; Mr. Rouncewell and his like did *not* "pick up" chains and "put them on the poor." It is as characteristic of the reactionary twist which Chesterton gives to his Liberalism that he should refuse to see any class division other than that into "rich" and "poor" as that he should twist the outcome of a complete social transformation into a deliberate "picking up" and "putting on" of chains upon those who, till then, had been, presumably, "free" men. The matter was both less and more simple than Chesterton suggests. Less simple, in that while the emancipation of the Rouncewells did in time involve an intensification of the enslavement of their wage-workers, it did not of itself create that enslavement. Nor did this consequence follow from any deliberate or conscious treachery on the part of the Rouncewells. It followed, inevitably, from the fact that the bursting of feudal constraints permitted the expansive development which revealed an antagonism till then latent and hidden—that between the bourgeoisie and the proletariat. The matter is more simple than Chesterton suggests, in that, instead of evidencing a mysteriously inexplicable lapse of the Mr. Rouncewells into sin, it evidenced the fact that history in clearing the stage of feudalism, had thereby only created the preconditions for another and a more radical, revolutionary struggle—this time for the overthrow of the bourgeois order which had been reared upon the ruins of the feudal order.

It was not, as Chesterton implies, a *restoration* that was and is wanted; but a *completion of the revolutionary process of emancipation.* And this is the fact that Dickens sees intuitively, and far more acutely than does his quasi-admirer and critic. If in *Bleak House* he represents Mr. Rouncewell as fighting strenuously and competently against the rule of Sir Leicester Deadlock and his class, while in *Hard Times* he shows that Rouncewellism militant emerged in Bounderbyism triumphant, he gives no hint or whisper of anything so supremely foolish as a wish for the return of the past. On the contrary, the aristocratic Mrs. Sparsit, who lives as a decorative-parasite upon the vulgarly brutal exploiter, Bounderby, makes us, in moments, almost pity Bounderby—except for the fact that he deserves all and more than all he gets. The aristocratic James Harthouse, equally a parasite upon the Bounderby-Gradgrind class, completes, in his dandaical boredom, and unprincipled heartlessness, the scornful repudiation of everything aristocratic which Mrs. Sparsit begins. True, no actual revolutionary struggle against the Bounderby-Gradgrind regime is adumbrated. Dickens could not be wiser than his generation; and like most of his contemporaries Dickens saw no more in trade unionism than an aggravation of the evil—the imposition upon the suffering and exploited proletariat of yet another set of parasites, the demagogic agitators. Yet it is as clear as anything can be that the very hardness and bitterness which *Hard Times* expresses arose in Dickens from his acute intuition that something more was at issue than any mere betrayal of the forwardmovement. Another revolution is needed—as drastic and far-reaching as the great French Revolution—and Dickens' harshness arises basically from his intense disappointment and baffled rage at finding no such revolution anywhere in sight.

Hard Times, really, points forward to the theme of revolution—a theme which Dickens took up in the *Tale of Two Cities*. But, before doing so, he controlled his bitterness and exasperation enough to elaborate in *Little Dorrit* an indictment of bourgeois society as comprehensive as, and, in its way, one even more Radical than that elaborated in *Bleak House*. *Hard Times* in fact stands to *Bleak House* and to *Little Dorrit* as a furious raid does to two systematic campaigns. Their community of purpose is plain to the most cursory of inspection.

"Little Dorrit"

The key-note of the Gradgrind system (which we have discussed earlier) is its suppression of every exercise of the imagination, every sort of poetic enthusiasm, and of all enjoyment, as non-utilitarian. The same note is struck at the outset of *Little Dorrit* in the atmosphere created by Mrs. Clennam from motives of acidulous piety—an atmosphere in which all enjoyment is deemed to be sinful *a priori* and all joylessness, down to the most intense suffering, is regarded, *a priori,* as pious, righteous, and pleasing to a joyless God.

A similar inhibition of all spontaneous joy in life is depicted as the atmosphere necessarily pervading and emanating from the debtors' prison, the Marshalsea, in which the main action opens.

The main plot of *Little Dorrit* is provided by the adventures of the Dorrit family in general, and in particular of its most important member (for us), Little Dorrit herself. One, Edward Dorrit, a "gentleman," is, when the novel opens, imprisoned in the Marshalsea. He is imprisoned at the suit of a government department—the Circumlocution Office—his debt being a fine due for failure to execute a given contract; which failure in turn was due to somebody else's failure, which in turn was due to some other failure, and so on. Mr. Dorrit, a mild, meek man, did not at all understand how he got there, and in his weak way imagined at first that somehow or other he would soon be released again. He had soon, however, to bring his wife and two children into the prison—from lack of means to maintain them otherwise. And in the prison his third child, Amy (the Little Dorrit of the story), is born. He is, in the end, released from the Marshalsea—just as inexplicably and without effort on his part as he came in—in consequence of the discovery (by others) that he is the heir to a large and valuable estate. When he is released Little Dorrit is twenty-five years old.

Before this happens, and as the children grow up, they are forced to find employment to maintain themselves and their father, who—his wife soon droops and dies—would have starved but for the assistance given them by his younger brother—who, though ruined financially by his brother's failure, is able to get employment as an instrumentalist in a theatre orchestra—and given them also by sympathizing fellow-prisoners.

Amy's elder sister gets employment as a singer and dancer in the chorus at the theatre in whose orchestra her uncle plays. Amy herself, even as a child, and before her sister followed her example, gets work as a sempstress. Her brother drifts and loafs from casual job to casual job, until he too qualifies for incarceration in the Marshalsea as a "regular" inmate.

All this time, however, the fact that his children go out to work to keep him is (officially) concealed from Mr. Dorrit—he being too much of a gentleman to bear up under the shock of such a happening were it (officially) known to him. He is, for his part, equally discreet and tactful in that he never asks where the food comes from which is placed before him at stated hours, by the patiently affectionate Little Dorrit. It comes, in fact, as often as not, from the meals given to her at the places where she is employed; supplemented, also, from her meagre earnings, and those of her sister and uncle. From lapse of time Mr. Dorrit has come to be the Father of Marshalsea, and it has grown to be a custom for the more fortunately situated inmates to pay ceremonial visits to the Father weekly and "compliment" him with such trifles of cash as they can spare—as each also does as a matter of ritual when each in turn obtains his release. The pitifully-horrible contrast between the pose of gentlemanliness and the dignity with which the faded young-old man maintains his position as Father (with his thin pretence at ignorance that his girls work to keep him), and the eagerness with which he looks forward to his weekly "compliments," and with which he approaches likely newcomers with a gentlemanly request for a " temporary loan," is the abiding shadow upon Little Dorrit's existence.

Her principal employer is the grimly pious Mrs. Clennam. She is an invalid confined to her room, who carries on from her chamber a mercantile business which her husband inherited from his father. This business she intends to devolve in part upon her son, as soon as he returns from conducting the business of the House in the East, where his father (who had quarrelled with Mrs. Clennam) had taken him years before; and where the father had died just before the novel opens. Pious gloom in the Clennam household; sordid, heartbreaking gloom in the Marshalsea; fretful, impatient, tawdry gloom in the lodgings occupied jointly by Little Dorrit's sister and her uncle; and over all the heartbreaking shadow of her father's meanly-eager acceptance of the role of "complimented" Father of the Marshalsea—this is the atmosphere in which Little Dorrit develops her long-suffering diligence and her pathetic patience.

By the discovery of the fact that Mr. Dorrit senior is the heir to a large estate—a discovery made and established legally by acquaintances of Mrs. Clennam's son Arthur—who, for his part, on returning from the East, meets Little Dorrit and is at once attracted by her pathetic little figure—by this lucky chance the Dorrits are converted into people of wealth and members of "good" society. Mr. Dorrit, to avoid all risk of reminding himself (or others) of his once-prized repute as Father of the Marshalsea, takes his family abroad on an expensive tour in France, Switzerland and Italy. In these new surroundings the elder sister, Fanny, and her dissolute brother, instantly blossom out as "fashionable" folk. Their father, too, is able to go admirably through the motions of a severely correct gentility. The uncle does not find it so easy to "keep up appearances" as a member of good society. But his failure is much less than that of Little Dorrit, who is constantly incurring reproof for her "lowness" of taste and inclination—her shrinking avoidance of fashionable society, her inability to rise to the height of "claiming the place" due to her as the daughter of a gentleman of wealth, family and standing.

Fanny meets with, and marries, a young fashionable; one whom she had fascinated in her chorus-girl days, whose mother had become by a second marriage the wife of the great financier Mr. Merdle. (Both Fanny and Mrs. Merdle maintain solemnly—but with an undercurrent of vindictiveness—the pretence that they had never previously met.) Mr. Dorrit senior travels with the young couple to London to see them installed in their new home. There, at Mr. Merdle's suggestion, he invests all his fortune—and that of his children and brother, in Mr. Merdle's enterprises. The excitement of the marriage, of the journey, of the meeting with the great Mr. Merdle and his financial friends—and, also, of his private decision to himself marry again (choosing as his wife the aristocratic lady whom he had engaged as mentor-companion to his daughters) all these things prove too much for Mr. Dorrit. At an immensely fashionable dinner-party on his return to Rome he suffers a mental breakdown. He imagines himself back again in the Marshalsea. Little Dorrit takes charge of him, gets him to his room and to bed, where, in a few days, he dies without recovering from his delirium. His brother, his frail constitution shattered by the sudden shock, is found dead by his brother's bedside.

Within a few weeks of Fanny's triumphant marriage the brief period of prosperity restored for the Dorrit family is brought to a sudden and complete end. Mr. Merdle, the great financier, the exemplar of all that is most to be admired in the British constitution and social system, is found dead in his bath with his throat cut. By this it is discovered that the mysterious complaint from which this Great and Wonderful Man had suffered—a complaint which the most eminent physicians could not diagnose—"had been simply, Forgery and Robbery":

> He the uncouth object of such widespread adulation, the sitter at great men's feasts, the roc's egg of great ladies' assemblies, the subduer of exclusiveness, the leveller of pride, the patron of patrons, the bargaindriver with a Minister for Lordships of the Circumlocution Office, the recipient of more acknowledgment within some ten or fifteen years, at most, than had been bestowed in England upon all public benefactors, and upon all the leaders of all the Arts and Sciences, with all their works to testify for them, during two centuries at least—he, the shining wonder, the new constellation to be followed by the wise men bringing gifts until it stopped over certain carrion at the bottom of a bath and disappeared —was simply the greatest Forger and the greatest Thief that ever cheated the gallows.—*Little Dorrit:* Book II, Chap. XXV.

In the crash of the Merdle enterprises thousands of private fortunes, great and small, were engulfed. That of the Dorrits, the two sisters and their brother was swallowed up whole. Fortunately or unfortunately for

Fanny, one of the last deals of the undetected embezzler was to secure for her husband, Edmund Sparkler (who was also Merdle's step-son), an appointment as one of the permanent "Lords" of the Circumlocution Office. On the salary attached to this sinecure—ample by proletarian standards, but microscopic by those of Grosvenor Square—the two fiercely antipathetic women rivals, Fanny and her mother-in-law, with their husband-son connecting link (who, though a demi-semi-half-wit, is as amiable as the females are not), have henceforward to exist in relative "destitution" and mutual exacerbation.

Also, among the many others brought to ruin is Arthur Clennam, who has invested not only his own small fortune, but that of his business partner, Doyce, in the Merdle enterprises. Within a few days of the crash, Arthur is a prisoner in the room in the Marshalsea in which Little Dorrit had been born.

The resolution of this general collapse into a positive outcome is brought about by one of those elaborately complicated mechanisms of interlocking subsidiary plots in which Dickens delighted, one whose vastly-ramified movement supplies an undercurrent to—and a background for—the development of the main plot.

The first strand in this complex is supplied by Mrs. Clennam, and the unexplained estrangement between her and her husband, Arthur's father. This we meet first as a depressingly ominous mystery at the opening of the novel.

On his father's death, Arthur, instructed by Mrs. Clennam, wound up the branch establishment in the East, and returned home. In an interview with Mrs. Clennam, Arthur declines to take his place as partner, or to help her carry on the business, preferring to take the portion allotted him under his father's will, and set up on his own, in an atmosphere more congenial than that charged with Mrs. Clennam's ferociously vengeful theology. Arthur is finally impelled to do this when Mrs. Clennam refuses to explain the estrangement between herself and his father—the secret of which the latter on his death-bed had said Mrs. Clennam had bound him not to disclose.

In the closing chapters of the novel we learn the secret. Mrs. Clennam who had had her character formed in a school of grim, joyless, punitive theology, had been imposed as a wife upon Arthur's father by his uncle, who also was an ardent adherent of that same theological school, and who, in pursuance of its tenets, had reduced his nephew to a terrified, broken-spirited victim with no will of his own.

The uncle had forced the marriage even though he knew that the nephew had, in secret visits to a house whose well-to-do owner was a patron of the Arts, become devoted to a charming young singer who was equally fond of him. After the marriage Mrs. Clennam made the discovery that the attachment between the young couple had gone further than his uncle had supposed. There had been a secret, free-love, "marriage," and a child. Mrs. Clennam, using the blackmailing threat of exposure—with loss of reputation to the singer, and disinheritance of her husband by his uncle as the consequence—forced the young mother to give up the child which she thereafter brought up as her own. The young singer, terrified and broken-hearted, had been driven insane; and had died, in an asylum, under the charge of Mrs. Clennam's agent. The child had been kept always before his father as a constant reminder of his "sin," and of his wife's unsleeping determination to extort the last possible drop of vengeance for the "wrong" done to her, as lawful wife, and to the moral laws of God—of which she regarded herself as the divinely chosen custodian.

The uncle, not knowing this secret, had in the end proved less implacable. By a codicil to his will he had left one thousand guineas to the young singer as some sort of compensation for the hurt to her feelings; and another thousand guineas to the youngest daughter, or youngest brother's daughter, of the patron of the young singer (at whose house the young couple had met) "as the remembrance his disinterestedness may like best of his protection of a friendless young orphan girl." This patron was Frederick Dorrit—Amy's uncle. Thus Mrs. Clennam's secret was a double-barrelled one. She had, with piously vengeful intent, suppressed the truth about Arthur's parentage; and she had from the same motive suppressed the codicil to his great-uncle's will, and so robbed both Arthur's real mother, and also Little Dorrit, of the legacies due to them.

The secret is disclosed, primarily as a consequence of the treachery of Mrs. Clennam's agent and confederate, Flintwich. Mrs. Clennam for some time would not destroy the codicil she had suppressed. It was part of her system of pious torture to hold out to her husband a half-promise that she might, some day, carry this codicil into effect. (It is part of Dickens' indictment of Mrs. Clennam's theology to show that Arthur's father, though freed of fear of disinheritance by his uncle's death, should have been so will-paralysed by his sense of "sin," that he was still putty in the hands of this imperious woman, and wholly unable to face the disclosure to his own son of the real truth of his parentage.) When, in the end, on Arthur's return from the East, Mrs. Clennam would have destroyed the incriminating document, she was too physically paralysed—as a consequence of her own fearful temper—to be able to get it from its hiding-place. Her confederate, Flintwich (whom she takes into partnership on Arthur's withdrawal) pretends to burn the document; but preserves it—with intent to blackmail. He gives it secretly—with letters from Arthur's real mother which reveal the facts of his parentage—in a locked box, into the custody of his own brother, who had been (unknown to Mrs. Clennam) the keeper in whose custody Arthur's mother had died. From being possessed by this Flintwich-the-Second—who had fled abroad to escape the penalties for ill-treating lunatics under his charge, and who combined dipsomania with his other unamiable qualities—the box passed on his death (by Pistolian-"conveyance"), to a cosmopolitan scoundrel, Blandois, *alias* Rigaud *alias* Lagnier, *alias* etc. He (scenting blackmail from its contents) proceeded to ferret out the facts, and finally approaches Mrs. Clennam with a demand for a thousand guineas in exchange for the documents. As she boggles at the price he applies moral pressure by contriving to disappear in such a way that suspicion is created that he has been lured to her house and there made away with. This suspicion arouses Arthur (who still thinks that Mrs. Clennam is his mother) into action. And the steps he takes to discover the whereabouts of Blandois-Rigaud-etc., have the effect of precipitating the disclosure of the secret.

These steps bring into play two other distinct groups of characters: firstly the group centred in and around Bleeding Heart Yard; secondly, the group centred upon Mr. Meagles, a retired banker, his wife, and their only daughter, "Pet."

Bleeding Heart Yard is a court in the Gray's Inn Road neighbourhood—Ormond Yard off Great Ormond Street resembles it somewhat—of which the outer buildings are shops and workrooms, one set of which is occupied by the works owned by Arthur's partner, Doyce, and himself, while the inner buildings are let out as tenements. The owner of the property is a patriarchal-looking gentleman, Casby, who looks the super-essence of benevolence—but who is, in fact, as greedy and as grasping a rackrenter as he is fat, lazy, self-indulgent, stupid and hypocritical. Casby is known to Clennam as the father of a young woman who was the object of his boyish infatuation, until the parents on both sides interfered, and made an end of the "nonsense." Much comic by-play results from the resumption of the acquaintance between Arthur and Flora. By now she is a widow, and decidedly on the plump side. Arthur suffers no little secret humiliation in comparing her as she is with what he once imagined her to be. (This, by the way, is serio-comic self-criticism on Dickens' part, since Dora in *David Copperfield* and Flora in *Little Dorrit* are, Forster tells us, drawn from the same woman—as seen in the rosy glow of youthful infatuation, and as seen in the cold light of disillusioned maturity.)

Old Casby employs as agent and rent-collector an energetic but fine-natured drudge, Mr. Panks. Mr. Panks (who among other engaging eccentricities has a passion for following the "heirs and relatives wanted" advertisements in the newspapers) was the prime agent in securing for the Dorrits the inheritance which otherwise would have gone unclaimed and unknown—an inheritance of which they were totally ignorant and to which nothing short of Mr. Panks' irrepressible energy and that of his willing assistants (aided by Clennam's money advances) would have enabled them to prove their title.

Among the tenants of Bleeding House Yard is an Italian refugee, to whom Panks is friendly, and whom Arthur employs as a wood-worker. Arthur, agitated by the mysterious disappearance which had thrown suspicion on Mrs. Clennam, consults Panks in the hearing of the Italian (Cavaletto). This leads to the discovery that Cavaletto knows the villain; having been imprisoned (as a smuggler) in the same cell in which Lagnier-Rigaud-Blandois-etc., was imprisoned on a charge (well-based but unprovable) of murder. Cavaletto and Panks find the villain in hiding and bring him to the Marshalsea prison to which Arthur has, in the meantime, been taken. The villain agrees to a date for a meeting with Mrs. Clennam for a final settlement. Arthur does not know what business the villain has to do with Mrs. Clennam. He is concerned only to know that her name has been cleared of suspicion of murder. Blandois, for his part, knowing he has to deal with a woman of amazing determination, from whom it will be hard to extort money, even with such good blackmailing tools as he has, takes every precaution. He has left the box with the documents in safe keeping. And he takes a further precaution. He leaves with Little Dorrit (who has meanwhile returned to nurse Arthur Clennam), an envelope, to be opened by her if it is not reclaimed by the time the prison gate is closed for the night. In the envelope is a statement of the facts he has to disclose, and an offer to sell the original documents for cash. Also enclosed is an envelope addressed to Arthur Clennam with a duplicate statement and offer. He calculates that if Mrs. Clennam will not (or cannot) pay his price, Little Dorrit will be eager to buy his silence for Arthur's sake, while Arthur will be equally eager to do so for his own, and for Little Dorrit's sake. That Arthur is a prisoner for debt does not worry Blandois. Judging him by his own standards he imagines that he will be willing to take all the money he needs from friends who have it to spare.

All Blandois' cunning defeats itself. Mrs. Clennam, in fact, has not the money he demands. And moreover, the excitement of the interview, and the final shock of learning that if something is not done to prevent it the secret will be revealed to Arthur and Little Dorrit that very night, cures temporarily her paralysis. She flies from her house to the Marshalsea, claims the envelope, lets Little Dorrit read the letter addressed to herself; begs her forgiveness; promises the restitution of the withheld legacy; but begs also that Little Dorrit will keep the facts secret from Arthur until she, Mrs. Clennam, is dead.

Little Dorrit gives her forgiveness, readily; and promises not to disclose the facts to Arthur unless she is sure on reflection the disclosure will be for his good. Little Dorrit agrees also to return to Mrs. Clennam's house where Blandois is waiting, and join in persuading him to take less for his silence—since now she knows the truth, the secret is worth so much less.

All through the novel, a curious, semi-demented character, the wife of Flintwich, has been "hearing" curious sounds about the Clennam mansion—rustlings, moanings, creakings, and sounds as of rushing streams of sand. All this has been attributed to her unbalanced fancies. But just as Little Dorrit and Mrs. Clennam come in sight of the mansion (along with Mrs. Flintwich, who has followed Mrs. Clennam to see that she came to no harm), the disregarded "fancies" prove to be thoroughly well-based. Before their eyes the Clennam mansion—(on a window seat of which Blandois is lolling, complacently satisfied that his price will be forth-coming) —splits asunder and crashes into total collapse.

When the excavators have dug far enough into the debris Blandois is found with his skull smashed to pulp by a beam. Flintwich meanwhile has absconded with all the negotiable securities he can lay his hands on. Mrs. Clennam collapses a few moments after the house falls —and this time is completely paralysed and incapable even of speech. She lingered in this statue-like condition until her death, three years later.

The recovery of the original documents upon which Blandois had based his blackmailing attempt brings into play the Meagles' group and the complex sub-plot in which they are themselves involved.

On his way home from the East, Arthur Clennam makes the acquaintance of Mr. and Mrs. Meagles and their beautiful daughter "Pet." They are travelling abroad in the hope of curing "Pet" of an infatuation for an aristocratic painter—good-looking; bored; charming when he pleases; talented enough to set up as a professional artist; but not earnest enough to make any sort of success with his art; at bottom thoroughly selfish and nonmoral—by name Henry Gowan. Arthur meets Mr. Meagles again at the

Circumlocution Office where Arthur has gone to try to discover a way of securing Mr. Dorrit's release, and where Meagles has gone with a friend, Doyce, who has an invention he wishes to offer to the nation. All have been infuriated by their treatment at a public office whose motto is that all it wants is to be "left alone," and which resents nothing so much as people who "want to know you know."

This second meeting with Mr. Meagles leads to a double result. The meeting with Doyce leads to the partnership of Doyce and Clennam—and, later, to Arthur's ill-fated investment of the firm's funds in the Merdle enterprises. The meeting with Meagles leads to a visit to his home, and to Arthur's contracting an infatuation for his beautiful daughter, Minnie (otherwise "Pet"). This infatuation ends in disappointment since Mr. and Mrs. Meagles find it impossible to wean their daughter from her infatuation for Henry Gowan—who is a cadet of the aristocratic family of Stiltstalkings and so, also, connected with the aristo-bureaucratic family of Tite-Barnacles. The Meagles, therefore, though reluctantly, have to agree to, and to arrange for, their daughter's marriage to Henry Gowan.

The newly-married couple travel abroad—partly because travel will, it is believed, facilitate Henry Gowan's art progress; partly (in fact, chiefly) because Henry Gowan wishes to put as big a distance as possible between his wife and her parents. In travelling abroad they meet Blandois (who deliberately makes mischief between husband and wife) and also the Dorrits (which creates an opportunity for Little Dorrit to deliver to "Pet" a letter of introduction from Arthur—which letter Blandois insinuates to Gowan is a covert love letter).

Blandois does not turn up accidentally. He has been bribed to make mischief by Miss Wade—a former mistress of Henry Gowan—a self-tormenting egoist, who, although she is as tired of Henry Gowan as he is of her, hates every other woman upon whom he sets eyes; and, who, from infuriated spite against Minnie Meagles for attracting the notice of Gowan, has induced Minnie's maid Harriet (a foundling the Meagles have brought up from childhood—who also has a fiercely jealous temper) to run away from the Meagles to take service with her. When Blandois goes to London to blackmail Mrs. Clennam—he finds that Gowan has little money, and is not easily to be swindled; also that Miss Wade once she has secured her end will pay only a small dole—he leaves his box of documents in her custody. Arthur, when searching for the missing Blandois—whom he knew had been in communication with Miss Wade—finds out through the industrious Panks (Casby, his employer, being the agent for her property) where Miss Wade lives. When Little Dorrit learns Mrs. Clennam's secret, she, being pledged to reveal nothing to Arthur—who, anyway, at this point sickens under his imprisonment and contracts a brain fever—can consult nobody but Mr. Meagles. He is decidedly of opinion that the original documents must be recovered, and accordingly sets to work to search every place where Blandois has been domiciled to find the missing box. The trail leads him at last to Miss Wade's, where she flouts him and denies all knowledge of the box. He returns to Little Dorrit crestfallen; but is surprised and delighted, before he has had time to confess his failure, by the entry of the runaway maid Harriet (called, affectionately, "Tattycoram") who begs to be taken back into service, and brings with her the box with which she has fled from Miss Wade.

Yet more sub-strands are needed to complete the *dénouement*. Depressed by the Merdle crash, in which he himself had lost heavily and in which Arthur had become involved as a result of his persuasion, Mr. Panks, upon whom Arthur's illness weighs unbearably, can no longer tolerate the insufferable impudence of his brutally greedy humbug of an employer. The thread of his patience snaps when Casby complains, one Saturday evening, that his rent harvest from Bleeding Heart Yard is deplorably low, and orders him to go again on the Monday. Panks knows that Bleeding Heart Yard is at the time heavily hit by unemployment, and knows therefore that it is simply brutal cruelty to try to squeeze more from its inhabitants. Casby, however, issues his decree, and then, as is his custom, takes his benevolent-looking self and his broad-brimmed hat (from beneath which long silvery locks flow down to his shoulders), for a patriarchal, evening parade through the doomed Yard. It is his way of keeping up the pretence that it is Panks who is the merciless grinder, while he, the patriarch, would spare them did he but know the truth. Panks gets to the Yard before him, and when the benevolent-seeming fraud is surrounded by petitioners complaining of Panks' exactions, Panks himself comes forward, tells the crowd the truth, tells Casby just what a fraud he is, and finishes by leaping upon the patriach and shearing off the silvery locks on which his reputation for benevolence has been based. The result is electric. Casby is revealed as a goggle-eyed, lumbering, bare-polled, lump of greedy stupidity and he leaves the Yard amid yells of derision. ("Slapstick," of course; but very welcome, all the same.)

Finally Doyce returns from abroad, where he had found, instead of a Circumlocution Office, a welcome and every encouragement, prosperous enough to laugh at the losses the firm had suffered in the Merdle crash, and to pay off the debts for which Arthur is imprisoned. He completes this good work by getting the licence for the marriage of Arthur to Little

Dorrit—which takes place in the church in which Little Dorrit had been christened, and to which they go direct from the Marshalsea.

Thus Little Dorrit and her Arthur enter upon a "modest life of usefulness and happiness."

The plot-mechanism of *Little Dorrit* has to be set out at fairly full length, because it is of prime significance in a critical evaluation of Dickens' last-period novels to note that the whole of this complexity of tragic and melodramatic themes and incidents forms in fact merely the incidental background to—(so to speak, the purely phenomenal obverse side of)—the *real* substance of the novel.

The real villain of *Little Dorrit* is neither the scoundrel Blandois, nor the treacherous Flintwich, nor the ineffable Casby, nor the forger Merdle, nor the heartless Henry Gowan, nor the self-tormenting Miss Wade, nor is it those rival egoists and social-climbers, Mrs. Merdle and Fanny Dorrit; nor the drifting waster, Amy's brother. Nor is it the tragically wilful Mrs. Clennam. Nor all of these put together. Behind all of these human phenomena, using them as its instruments, is a vaster and more impalpable Evil, of whose true being we get indications in the shadow of the Marshalsea walls, in the heart-breaking immobility of the Circumlocution Office, and in the terrifying gloom of Mrs. Clennam's theology.

Little Dorrit is, in fact, an allegory—of whose true purport its author was only partly conscious. In its first Part, to which the author gives the title "Poverty," we live constrained within the Marshalsea walls. Yet for all their abiding shadow, and the ever-present consciousness of imprisonment, there are within those walls, compassion, courage, and kindliness, unconquerable even amid the heart-break and the despair. In the second Part, which the author entitles "Riches," the prisoners of the Marshalsea escape into Good Society. There, despite wealth, means of enjoyment, travel, Italian skies, luxury, and deference, they meet with heartlessness, callous self-seeking, treachery, malice, envy, greed, cowardice, petulance—everything in short which is mean, contemptible, hateful, and soul-destroying. The degeneration of poverty into mendicancy within the Marshalsea walls—its squalor thrown into sharper relief by the pitifully hollow gaiety of the club room—is pathetic to the limit of pathos. But in contrast with the world of wealth and fashion the Marshalsea and its society or imprisoned debtors stands out as light to darkness, or as heaven to hell. The released prisoners— the Father and the Child of the Marshalsea—find, each in a different way, that they have only changed one prison for a worse. And there is Mrs. Clennam and her victim, Arthur, to prove to them that worse, even, than the Hell of Riches, is the hellishness

of orthodox theology, which turns the universe itself into one huge, inescapable Marshalsea, whose jailer is a fiendishly vengeful God; who holds
all men prisoners for eternity with as little reason, and as little compunc-
tion, as the Circumlocution Office held the Father of the Marshalsea a prisoner for a full quarter of a century.

Only when the riches have been annihilated and the theology has
crashed into ruin, are the long-tormented prisoners set free to make what
they can of what is left of their lives, and of such slender resources as have
been left to them.

Tried by Betsy Trotwood's test—"never be mean, never be false, never
be cruel"—the two categories of the author's own contrasting, Poverty and
Riches, show all these vices flourishing luxuriantly in the latter category,
and the corresponding virtues coming to their fullest flower in the former.

This is most clearly apparent if we try to sort out the actors in *Little
Dorrit* in terms of the conventional classification of Hero and Villain.

Little Dorrit herself is, of course, clearly on the side of Virtue—and is
also, as the central figure, the heroine. But her virtue is that of Andromeda
chained to the rock (of Poverty and Humiliation), the virtue of undeserved
slights and sufferings patiently endured; of humble duty done, for meagre
rewards, or none at all. And Perseus comes to her rescue, not in the
blazing glory of a demi-god, borne on the sweeping wings of a glittering
Pegasus, but in the lowly guise of Arthur Clennam (himself only half-
escaped from the clutches of that Giant Despair, which is his mother's
god), and his supporters, the grubby but indefatigable Panks, the artificer-
inventor Doyce, and the kind-hearted, sorrowing, but businesslike ple-
beian Meagles.

Observe: all of them are victims to the Dragon in one form or another.
Arthur, to the religion-infuriated Mrs. Clennam; Panks to the greedy
impostor Casby; Doyce to the Circumlocution Office; Meagles—through
his affection for his daughter—to the Tite-Barnacles and Stiltstalkings as
embodied in their kinsman Henry Gowan; and all, except Meagles, to the
thief and forger, Merdle. Moreover, this aggregative Perseus has but a
blunt sword with no Gorgon's head, and no Pegasus. Hence the Dragon is
not slain—he is only for the time being beaten off. Andromeda is released
from the rock, and that, so far, is victory. But for her there are no royal
palaces. And even though her rescuer is not a glittering demi-god who will
desert her as soon as the flush of victory has cooled, her prospect holds no
promise brighter than the purely negative blessing of release into a grey,
toil-weary world; a world in which the kindest hearts are found suffering

privations and unemployment in Bleeding Heart Yard, or eating their hearts out in a debtors' prison.

Every character in *Little Dorrit* who counts on the side of Virtue and Heroism is, it will be seen, made to suffer, and that acutely. Arthur Clennam, his dead parents, his partner Doyce, his friends the Meagles, his assistant Panks, the amiable (though adipose) and romantic Flora, the kindly proletarians the Plornishes, the whole population of Bleeding Heart Yard, the cheerful Cavaletto, the lugubriously infatuated, but noble-hearted son of Chivers the jailer—even Henry Gowan's dog—the only admirable thing connected with him—all suffer each in their degree as do the Dorrit family. In fact, beyond the crashing frustration and disaster which overtakes them, the vicious and villainous characters—Blandois, Flintwich, Henry Gowan, Miss Wade, the Merdles, Mrs. General, Mrs. Clennam, etc.—all suffer considerably less, so far as we can see, than do the admirable characters. And the wickedest villains of all, the Circumlocution Office (with its swarms of Tite-Barnacles and Stiltstalkings) and with it Mrs. Clennam's torturing theology, not only do not suffer at all, but show no sign of being capable of suffering or of overthrow.

That the general outlook implicit in *Little Dorrit* is therefore heavily pessimist—and that more so than either *Bleak House* or *Hard Times*—must be admitted. For all its gloom *Bleak House* is redeemed from despair, not so much by the somewhat whimsical goodness of John Jarndyce (to say nothing of Esther and her husband) as by the tragic (even if melodramatic) splendour of Lady Deadlock, by the unsuspected vein of real nobility in Sir Leicester, and by the sturdy, self-reliant competence of Mrs. Bagnet and her "children" (which includes both her husband and his friend George). *Hard Times* shows a break in the gloom both by means of the repentance of Gradgrind, by the unspoiled sympathy and kindliness of Sissy, and by the courageous humanity and buoyancy of her circus friends.

In *Little Dorrit,* while there is a wider and deeper sense of the masses—and a far closer approximation to the proletarian standpoint—there is, in the foreground of the action, little foothold for optimism. Yet, at the same time, too, there is a dawning suggestion of an imminent Doom. In the physical crash of the Clennam mansion—so long the spiritual prison of the young and ardent—so long the stronghold of Wrong inflicted under the guise of Righteousness—one cannot help but sense a prophecy of a like fate awaiting the Circumlocution Office and all that it implies. It would be definitely wrong to say that *Little Dorrit* is revolutionary in the conscious or overt sense. But it would be no less wrong to deny that in the negative or potential sense—in that it shows, by the totality of its implications, what things would be if Fate were just—it is near to being the most revolutionary novel that Dickens ever wrote.

And just as *Hard Times* announces in the Bounderby-Gradgrind warfare against imagination, sympathy, and joyfulness for their own sakes, a theme which, in its theological form, gives the point of departure for *Little Dorrit,* so the implicit (but, as it were, *inhibited)* theme of revolution, which is the net outcome of *Little Dorrit,* finds objective expression in Dickens' next novel, the *Tale of Two Cities.*

The "Tale of Two Cities"

We have noted above that this novel—the most successfully dramatized of all Dickens' novels—has as its background the great French Revolution. We have noted, too, that it demonstrates unmistakably—and one might add, aggressively—Dickens' sympathy with the people in revolt, with their revolt itself, and with, too, within limits, even their infuriated infliction of vengeance upon their oppressors. This was a far bolder, and a far more significant thing to do, in 1859, than might seem possible today.

It is true that the same year saw the production both of Marx's *Critique of Political Economy,* and of Darwin's *Origin of Species.* But the coming of these far-reachingly revolutionary works only the more emphasized the Conservatism, and the anti-revolutionary bias of the mental world into which they were born. That Marx should have retired into relative seclusion to perfect his economic studies was in itself evidence that, at that time, "only a literary battle was possible." That Darwin's work should have been needed, seventy years after the work of Lamarck, proves the same thing; as does the fact that the *Origin* gained its first widespread popularity because it was thought to provide theoretical weapons against any sort of popular revolutionary uprising.

We have noted above what a reception Ruskin met with, and that too, in the year following the appearance of all these three works—the *Critique,* the *Origin,* and the *Tale of Two Cities.* It might, indeed, be argued, that only Dickens' well-established popularity saved him from a denunciation similar to that which befell Ruskin. The supercilious shrugged their shoulders, and put it down to Dickens' ingrained "lowness"—to the fact that he "couldn't understand a *gentleman"*—and noted it as further evidence of the decline of Dickens' genius since *Bleak House,* since *Martin*

Chuzzlewit, or (by the most supercilious) since *Pickwick.* Anyway, since its revolutionary implications were bound up with—and somewhat obscured by—an intensely dramatic story culminating in a finely melodramatic scene of heroic self-sacrifice, the *Tale of Two Cities* could be and was allowed to pass as a moral story in which the horrors of the French Revolution were provided with a suitable corrective in the noble resignation and self-denial of Sydney Carton.

And that view, for bourgeois criticism in general, has remained the dominant view; all the more so as it has been crystallized by the dramatization of the novel under the title of *The Only Way*—in which a first-class actor made a reputation in the role of Sydney Carton.

None the less it is a false view. It is with the *Tale of Two Cities* as it is with *Little Dorrit,* and indeed with all the novels of Dickens' third period—the *real* drama is an implicit drama, which the foreground action-drama serves only to symbolize.

The ground-theme is indicated in the title of its first part (which Dickens originally intended to make the tide of the novel itself): "Recalled to Life." A prisoner imprisoned for more than twenty years, is "recalled to life," only to find that, by the cruel irony of Fate, the very wrong done to him is now used as a means of inflicting further suffering upon him. This, which is the fate of Dr. Manette in the *Tale of Two Cities,* is, it will be perceived, also the fate of the elder Dorrit and his daughter Amy. In the *Tale of Two Cities* the irony is made more obvious and more poignant since Dr Manette is imprisoned, not in association in a Marshalsea, but in strict solitude in the Bastille. In each case, release comes "out of the blue." Edward Dorrit is released by a legacy unearthed and made operative primarily by the energetic (if grubby) Mr. Panks. Dr. Manette is released partly by the fall from court favour of the nobleman who had secured his imprisonment and partly by the tidy (but industrious) Jervis Lorry, manager of Tellson's Bank. Edward Dorrit is for ever tormented by the fear that the wrong done to him—his twenty-five years' imprisonment in the Marshalsea—will become known to his disparagement in the Good Society to which his new-found wealth gives him access. This very anxiety is the proximate cause of the loss of his fortune in the Merdle swindle, which, however, proves a blessing in disguise; since it releases Little Dorrit from the wealth which separates her from her Arthur. Dr. Manette's agony is in one sense more subtle—arising as it does from the fact that his adored daughter loves and marries the son and nephew of the aristocratic brothers who had secured his imprisonment. Edward Dorrit is released from his torment by his collapse and death; his daughter Amy is released by the collapse of the

Merdle enterprises which follows the suicide of the swindler Merdle. Dr. Manette and his daughter are both released together from their torment by the heroic intervention of Sidney Carton into the revolutionary turmoil which had placed Lucie's husband in peril of his life. In each case the novel closes on a note similar to that of Edmund Spenser's lines:

> Sleep after toil: port after stormy seas,
> Ease after war, death after life, does greatly please.
> —SPENSER: *Faery Queen:* Book I, Canto IX, st. XI.

It is impossible to escape the conclusion that this parallelism has an intentional significance. This may possibly have been only partly present to the author's consciousness; but if we are right in seeing in *Bleak House, Hard Times,* and *Little Dorrit* so many phases of expression of one common purpose—a general attack upon the established order of society—we have in the *Tale of Two Cities* a further phase in which Dickens gets nearer than ever to a positive assertion of revolution as the only road to hope, to justice, to peace and to general happiness. In any case the conventional view, which sees Sidney Carton's sacrifice as the primary thematic objective of the novel, is clearly false criticism since it relegates the French Revolution, and the whole dramatic sub-plot of Madame Defarge's vengeance to the status of mere irrelevancies. More than that—it obscures the whole point that Sidney Carton, by sacrificing his life, achieved a triumphantly redeeming escape, from a life which had been, till then, a dreary torment of failure and frustration. And that this latter is the true view is proved by the fact that it harmonizes exactly with Dickens' view of the French Revolution itself, which was, on his showing, and despite its bloody extravagances, the terrible paroxysm of death and destruction whereby the people achieved a triumphantly redeeming escape from a permanent condition of hunger, subjection, failure and frustration.

Dickens leaves no doubt that this is his meaning:

> Along the Paris Streets the death carts rumble, hollow and harsh. Six tumbrils carry the day's wine to La Guillotine. All the devouring and insatiate monsters imagined since imagination could record itself are fused in the one realization, La Guillotine. And yet there is not in France, with its rich variety of soil and climate, a blade, a leaf, a root, a sprig, a peppercorn, which will grow to maturity under conditions more certain than those that have produced this horror. Crush humanity out of shape once more under similar hammers and it will twist itself into the same tortured forms. Sow the same seed of rapacious license and oppression over again and it will surely yield the same fruit according to its kind.

Six tumbrils roll along the streets. Change these back again to what they were, thou powerful enchanter Time, and they shall be seen to be the carriages of absolute monarchs, the equipages of feudal nobles, the toilets of flaring Jezebels, the churches that are not my Father's house but dens of thieves, the huts of millions of starving peasants. — *Tale of Two Cities,* Book III, xv.

The basic plot-theme of the *Tale of Two Cities* is Dr. Manette's imprisonment and its consequences. Dr. Manette, a young physician, a native of Beauvais, but then resident in Paris, is stopped in the streets one night, in December 1767, by two aristocratic gentlemen who request him to come with them to visit a patient. He finds a young woman in a delirium from shock, and also another patient, a young man, dying of a sword thrust. Both are of the peasant class. He learns that they are brother and sister; that they were the serf tenants of the elder of the two (twin) aristocrats. The younger brother had taken a fancy to the girl, and since her husband could not, or would not, coerce her to comply with My Lord's demands, he was claimed by the elder brother, the Marquis, for feudal service — harnessed and driven in a dog-cart by day and kept in the grounds by night to quiet the frogs. After a few weeks of this torment he died, one noon, when he had been liberated from his harness for an hour to find food, if there was any food to find — died in his wife's arms just as the clock struck twelve. Despite the fact that she was demented by her loss, the two noblemen carried her off. Under the blow her father died, heartbroken too. Her brother, after seeing a younger sister safely away to a home among friends, at a distance, tracked the aristocratic villains to their town house. Forcing an entry through an attic window he attacked the younger nobleman with a sword, driving him to draw in self-defence, and give the young peasant his death wound.

When both his patients had died Dr. Manette, who had with indignant politeness refused a fee, returned to his young wife and child, at home, but said nothing of his adventure. Instead he wrote an account of the facts and delivered it to the Minister of State.

Before the letter was finished he received a visit from the wife of the younger aristocrat, who was in deep distress over the whole cruel business (of which she had come to know) and who, being of a compassionate nature, had hoped that Dr. Manette could tell her the whereabouts of the younger sister of his two cruelly ill-treated patients, so that she might befriend her and make such reparation as lay within her power. She was tormented by the fear that her young son, Charles, would never prosper in his inheritance if no reparation was made.

Dr. Manette could not give her the information, and she departed, with her son, lamenting. The next night—the letter having been delivered in the meantime—Dr. Manette was called by a messenger to visit a patient and on his way was seized by the two aristocrats, shown his letter (which was burnt before his face), and then carried off gagged and blindfolded to the Bastille.

During his eighteen years' imprisonment there, in solitary confinement, his reason gave way. He lost his memory and became dead to all else than the craft of shoe-making, which he had begged to be allowed to learn and practise as a means of mental relief. In his madness he became obsessed with the notion that the shoes he was working to complete were urgently needed.

After eighteen years—his wife (an Englishwoman) being many years dead, and his daughter living in England, as the ward of Mr. Jervis Lorry, manager of Tellson's Bank of London and Paris—Dr. Manette was released from the Bastille—since the Marquis at whose request the *lettre de cachet* had been issued had fallen out of favour, and since also Jervis Lorry and Tellson's Bank (who had persisted, discreetly, in pulling such wires as they could) were people from whom authority in its bankruptcy needed assistance.

Dr. Manette was taken, in a condition of mental prostraton, relieved only by his shoe-making obsession, to a lodging under the care of his old servant, Defarge. From this refuge he was taken by Jervis Lorry and Dr. Manette's daughter, Lucie, to London; where, under their care, he recovered his reason, and became able to practise again as a physician. His daughter was courted by a young Frenchman, living in voluntary exile in London, by name Charles Darnay. They were brought together by a charge of espionage brought against Darnay in which the Manettes and Jervis Lorry are cited as witnesses—Darnay having travelled on the same boat with them on the night Dr. Manette was brought from France to England.

On the eve of his marriage to Lucie, Darnay tells Dr. Manette his real name is the Marquis d'Evremond. He is, in fact, the young Charles, son of the younger of the villainous aristocratic twins, whom Dr. Manette saw, with his mother, on the night before he was thrown into the Bastille. The shock of the name brings on a relapse. For ten days Dr. Manette (who could never bring himself to part with his old shoe-making bench and tools) relapses into mental nonentity and his old shoe-making obsession. He recovers, however; without outside aid, and consents to the destruction of his shoemaking kit, as soon as he learns the nature of his relapse.

A few years later Charles Darnay is appealed to by the steward in charge of the family estates he has renounced. The Bastille has been stormed; the Reign of Terror is beginning; the steward is charged with having acted against the People for an emigrant, and is, therefore likely to lose his head. Darnay, responding to his appeal goes to Paris to testify that the steward story is true— that he has instructed him to remit all taxes, and all vexatious imposts and beyond a trifling minimum all rents.

He arrives at an unpropitious moment, on the eve of the "purging of the prisons" in September 1792, and only narrowly escapes being himself involved in the purge. After more than a year's imprisonment he is brought to trial, and, in consequence of the evidence of Dr. Manette (who with Lucie has followed Charles, and Jervis Lorry, who travelled with him, to Paris) he is acquitted and released.

He is, however, immediately re-arrested, on a fresh denunciation. And when the case comes before the tribunal his accusers are found to be Ernest Defarge, Theresa Defarge, his wife, and *Dr. Manette!*

When the Bastille was stormed, Ernest Defarge who was in the forefront of the assault, made his way at once to Dr. Manette's old cell. There hidden in the chimney he found the account written by Dr. Manette, before his reason broke down, of the circumstances which led to his incarceration. The document concluded with a passionate denunciation of the whole race of Evremond down to its remotest progeny. This document Defarge now produces. It is read. It constitutes an unanswerable denunciation of the prisoner, who is sentenced, immediately, to death within twenty-four hours.

It is here that Sidney Carton comes into play. By a freak of fate he resembles Darnay not only facially, but also in build, very closely. He makes his way into the prison, drugs him with a narcotic, changes clothes with him, and sends him out of prison (in the charge of a confederate) to the coach in which Lucie, her daughter, her father (who has relapsed again into complete mental incapacity), and Jervis Lorry wait only for "Carton's" arrival to start for London.

The real Sidney Carton, in the place of Charles Darnay, *ci-devant* Marquis d'Evremond, goes calmly to the guillotine and death.

It will be seen that in this basic theme the stories of Dr. Manette and of the French Revolution are so closely interwoven that each is a condition for the other. Had there been no Bastille, and no ruthlessly arrogant, cruel and vengeful aristocrats, there would have been no French Revolution. But likewise there would have been in that case no story of Dr. Manette. Also, it is as philosophically just, as it is artistically effective, to make Dr. Manette's imprisonment-begotten denunciation of his oppressors serve as an instrument for wounding him, himself, through his own son-in-law, daughter, and granddaughter. Curses do have a way of coming home to roost, and the worst excesses of the French Revolution were no more than a carrying out, in uncritical literalness, of the judgments pronounced in anger by highly refined and philosophical gentlemen who recoiled aghast before the form in which their own theories became concretized.

Moreover, Dickens, who prepares for this culmination with meticulous care and great skill—showing the Defarges as implacable revolutionaries working with never-ceasing diligence to prepare the Day of Wrath whose coming they foresaw—supplies an adequate motive for the merciless pursuit of Darnay-Evremond. Defarge as Dr. Manette's own servant, and himself one of the suffering poor, has taken Dr. Manette's wrongs more to heart than has the Doctor himself. Dr. Manette may, if he chooses, forgive. That is noble in him. But that would be baseness in Ernest Defarge. And even if he should relent, as he does somewhat, it is not for Theresa his wife, the sister of the wronged and murdered sister and brother, victims of the evil house of Evremond, who were the occasion of Dr. Manette's imprisonment— it is not for her to relent. On the contrary, if Dr. Manette weakens so far as, first to let his daughter marry an Evremond, and then to sorrow over his execution, he too is tainted and fit for the guillotine, as is Evremond's wife, and still more, his child. And this culmination is in fact only narrowly averted—partly by the self sacrifice of Sidney Carton, and partly also by an accident in which Miss Pross, Lucie's old servant, plays the chief part.

Left behind to travel with the baggage and a manservant, by a slower vehicle, while Jervis Lorry with Lucie, her child, her father, and her husband (disguised and travelling as Sidney Carton) make their escape by express carriage, Miss Pross is confronted by Madame Defarge, who has come seeking evidence that Lucie and Dr. Manette are showing criminal sorrow over a guillotined aristocrat. To prevent Madame Defarge searching the rooms, and so discovering that her prey has escaped, Miss Pross grapples with her. In the struggle Madame Defarge is killed by the accidental discharge of her own pistol. It is this, as much as Sidney Carton's self-immolation, which finally disposes of the curse pronounced upon the House of Evremond.

Even more ingenuity and skill is shown in the preparation Dickens makes for the final heroic sacrifice of Sidney Carton. His resemblance to Darnay is brought into notice, with telling effect, early in the novel, when Darnay is falsely charged with espionage. The whole case hangs on an alibi which the prosecution try to break down by means of a witness who swore to seeing the prisoner in a certain place at a time when Darnay's witnesses alleged that he was in France. The witness said he "couldn't be mistaken." At Carton's suggestion he was asked to look at him and say whether or not there was no resemblance. The witness had to admit it: everybody in court could see it as an astonishingly close resemblance. The witness's identification of the prisoner being thus destroyed Darnay's alibi was established, and he was acquitted.

That Carton is shown, thenceforward, to be as much an unhappy failure in life as his "double" was the reverse—a contrast made pathetic by Carton's hopeless love for Lucie—is all part of the process of preparation for the grand climax of substitution. But this substitution itself needs its mechanism, and this is supplied by the spy Barsad (who turns out to be a dissolute and unprincipled brother of Miss Pross). Barsad figures as the chief spy-witness in Darnay's trial at the Old Bailey. Discredited there, he loses his worth to the British Government and so makes his way to Paris as a spy of the pre-Revolutionary Government. Later he becomes (and is, when Miss Pross happens upon him, and claims him as her brother) a spy-gaoler in the prisons of the Republic. Carton seizes the chance. An ex-spy of the British Government living in Paris under a false name is not likely to meet with favour if denounced as a suspect before the Revolutionary Tribunal. Carton threatens to denounce him unless he comes to terms; and adds as an additional threat that he had seen him in conversation with his fellow-spy in the British service, Roger Cly. This Barsad denies; Cly is dead, he says, and buried in St. Pancras churchyard. He produces as proof the certificate of burial.

This brings into play one more of Dickens' ingenuities. Present at the interview between Barsad and Carton is along with Jervis Lorry the latter's body-servant, Jerry Cruncher, normally a messenger at Tellson's Bank. Jerry is, unknown to the bank, a "bodysnatcher" in his spare time. And at this point he interrupts Barsad to tell him—as he has only too good reason to be able to—that what was buried as "Cly" was a coffin-full of paving stones; that the death and burial were a "fake." (All this has been prepared for, in the course of the novel, by the descrption at its time of occurrence, of the fake funeral and Jerry's subsequent disappointment.) Answered thus Barsad surrenders. He agrees to Carton's demand. In his capacity as extra-gaoler he secures Carton access to Darnay in prison, and bears away the unconscious Darnay to the coach which carries him to safety.

It is one of the many charges levelled in disparagement against Dickens' later novels—as compared with his earlier ones—that his plots "grew more mysterious." A generation which has witnessed the rise of the detective novel to the place it occupies to-day, can hardly see in this "mysteriousness" a blemish. The truth is that Dickens, always a workman, paid the greatest possible attention to the construction of his novels. If in his earlier novels he scattered "characters" with a reckless profusion, in his later works he is at infinite pains to bring on the stage only just so many characters as have actual work to do. His devoted "public" combined with his natural genius, made it imperative that he should bring on to his stage a fuller parade of characters than most novelists would care to try to control. And the fact also that his novels all appeared in parts or in instalments made it imperative that his every part or instalment should contain its specially outstanding incident. Few, if any, writers ever attempted so difficult a task as Dickens did every time he tackled the job of making a large crowd work as a team and weaving a whole hierarchy of main and subsidiary plots and counterplots into a perfectly reticulated whole. And Dickens' skill in this direction was seldom shown to finer advantage than in the *Tale of Two Cities.*

Of its class-bias it is superfluous to speak. It ranks as "villains" the whole *ancien régime,* aristocracy, absolute monarchy and all their works. It lumps along with aristocracy for equal condemnation all its sycophantic upholders—such as the blatantly self-seeking, philistine, ignoramus, Stryver of the King's Bench Bar. It exalts as heroic, in opposition to all these, the people in all their activities; the oppressed and suffering peasantry; the well-educated and industrious professional men; the faithful and devoted everywhere, down to and including the "failures" such as Sidney Carton. True, the Defarges and their train are shown in a terrible and implacable light. But since every care is taken to show that this implacable lust for vengeance is the direct product of aristocratic pride, selfishness and insolence, it merely adds an extra count to the indictment against the aristocracy that their rule should convert decent and kindly people into avenging furies like the Defarges. True, Jerry Cruncher is a proletarian and is shown as an ugly customer; but even here there is a defence. Quite justly Jerry defends his nefarious "body-snatching" activities by the retort that the well-to-do surgeons, customers at Tellson's Bank, who bribed him heavily to find them "subjects" for dissection, were at least as much to blame as he.

Most emphatic of all, as an indication of Dickens' standpoint and bias, is his conception of Sidney Carton. That which is usually lost upon readers of the *Tale of Two Cities* and a point which disappears entirely in the dramatized version (for which, of course, Dickens is not responsible), is the fact that the resemblance between Carton and Darnay—which makes possible Carton's substitution-sacrifice—does not end at a mere external physical likeness. Both are attracted by, and fall wholly in love with Lucie Manette, and both possess the same reckless generosity and readiness for sacrifice in a worthy cause which in the end leads Carton to take his heroic "only way" out of Lucie's terrible crisis.

Before Carton makes his sacrifice, Darnay has made his. He has sacrificed his title and his inheritance from a sense of their essential injustice and as the only recompense at his command for the wrong these things—titles and feudal rights and privileges—have entailed. Moreover, he has imperilled his personal safety and indeed, his life, to respond to the appeal for protection from a faithful servant, in peril in consequence of doing his duty. Darnay's large-hearted generosity and self-sacrifice precede and create the occasion (as well as the need) for Carton's ultimate self-sacrifice.

Thus by a whole succession of strokes Dickens makes the resemblance between Carton and Darnay extend from their outward appearance to their fundamental character.

There is, of course, an obvious difference. Darnay is as sober and careful as Carton is drunken and careless. In these regards they are opposites. But—and this is usually overlooked—the same contempt of himself which makes Carton a failure and a drunkard is also the quality which makes him prompt to seize the "only way" out of Lucie's difficulties. Thus his supreme virtue has one and the same root as his chief vice.

Dickens here shows, as he often does, his addiction to the doctrine of Robert Owen: "man's character is made *for* him, and not *by* him." With a little difference in their upbringing and their circumstances, Darnay would have been the failure and the drunkard, and Carton the sober and well-conducted husband. The turn of a hair at a critical stage was enough to separate their respective paths in life, so that their opposition in outward seeming is an expression of the fundamental identity of their characters. Carton is to Darnay and Darnay to Carton only another instance of the great truth: "There, but for the grace of circumstances outside my control, go I!"

That Dickens intends this moral to be drawn is clear from any number of strokes. When Darnay and Carton first meet Carton behaves insolently—behaves, as he admits to himself, as though he hated Darnay because he shows him, concretely, what he himself might have been. Later on, after Lucie and Darnay are married their children show a special fondness for Carton. The soundness of an unspoiled child's instincts is one of Dickens' favourite themes.

Nothing is said about Carton's childhood; but from his complete lack of relatives and connections in his manhood it would seem that his parents must have died while he was still an infant. In Darnay's case we know that he was prepared for the sacrifice of his title and his estates by the teaching of his mother—who felt that so cruel had been the injustices worked in their name that there was a curse upon both. It seems a fair inference, and one quite in keeping with Dickens' usual mode of reasoning to suppose that Carton's habitual lack of self-respect or self-regard came from an early training in which he was treated as of no account.

It will be remembered that the theme of a thoroughly good-natured and generous lad, sinking, through lack of proper self-regard, and of any pur- pose in life, into a drifter, and finally a waster and sot, was one that Dickens had experimented with before. Jingle was nearly in this class, but was rescued from it by a native streak of roguery. Dick Swiveller was clearly a case in point, until he was saved by his discovery of the Marchioness, his illness and the opportune death (and legacy) of his aunt. Steerforth is not of this class; he is too much of a fine gentleman, too lacking in real gener- osity, not fond enough of drink, and altogether too fond of himself to quality. But, as we noted above, Walter, in *Dombey,* was intended to be of this order, until Dickens relented.

With Sidney Carton, therefore, Dickens was able, at last, to work out a theme which he had been wanting for years to work out—the theme of the good man gone wrong through lack of the ballast necessary to compensate for sheer excess of good-nature. It is a theme which, quite clearly, shows the bent of Dickens' mind to have been in the direction of the Helvetius— Owen doctrine of the moral equality of man, and the general perfectability of human-nature. And from this doctrine, as Marx and Engels showed, Communism is a logical deduction.

In sum: the *Tale of Two Cities* takes, as clearly as its predecessors had done, the side of the common people against that of the privileged classes. But it adds, more plainly than any of its predecessors, a warning of an Avenging Fate, from fear of which all the privileged, and all those set in authority, would do well to reconsider their ways.

"Great Expectations"

After the blazing high-lights and the intense shadows of the *Tale of Two Cities* Dickens' next novel, *Great Expectations,* could hardly escape an appearance at any rate of anti-climax. Yet its general movement is forceful enough and its incidental action dramatic enough to make it more than hold its own against anything less titanically enormous than the tension and strife of the revolution scenes of its predecessor.

Its plot is comparatively simple. The tendency of his earlier days to let the sub-plot grow to the over-shadowing of the main plot, Dickens had, by now, brought well under control. As in the *Tale of Two Cities,* the subplots are so closely interwoven with the main plot that together tliey form a perfectly compacted whole. There is, of course, a big use made of dramatic surprise; in fact, the whole plot turns upon such an unexpected revelation. But instead of this making the plot "mysterious" it has the reverse effect.

Interest from the first is concentrated on the central character and his "great expectations." The other characters, leading and secondary, group themselves around this central theme with only a minimum of complication and diversion of interest. Not that the novel lacks diversity; on the contrary it contains as much diversity and variety as most of Dickens' novels. But the diversity is so well subordinated to the unity of the whole that the prevailing tone is grey upon grey, deepening into sombre gloom—and such, too, is the moral of the work as a whole.

If Dickens had not allowed himself to be overpersuaded by Bulwer Lytton, he would have achieved, for once, a novel with a positively "unhappy" ending. Even with its point somewhat self-blunted it remains an exercise on the theme of Frustration—of "great expectations" destroyed and punished by pitiless Reality.

The main plot of the novel is simple. Philip (called "Pip") the child of parents dead before the novel begins, is brought up by his sister (a semi-hysterical, harsh-tempered, house-proud shrew, married to a blacksmith) with at first no prospect beyond an ordinary working-man's life; probably as a blacksmith like his simple, uneducated, but great-hearted brother-in-law, Joe Gargery.

Some unknown benefactor pays for his education and provides means to make him into a "gentleman." He and his relatives imagine that this benefactor must be a three-parts crazy woman of fortune who lives a hermit life near to his place of birth. As this lady (Miss Havisham) has, Pip knows, adopted an orphan girl (with whom Pip, even as a small boy, becomes incurably smitten) it is easy for Pip to suppose that what he most wishes is the truth; that Miss Havisham is turning him into a "gentleman," as she her-self has turned the girl, Estella into a "lady," with the intent that they shall marry, and jointly inheriting her fortune, "live happy ever after."

Under the influence of this imagining, Pip grows from a likeable, good-natured, generous, working lad into something very near to an insuffer-able snob. But his dreams are shattered shortly afier his coming of age. He learns that he owes his "gentility" entirely to the quixotic generosity of a transported convict, whom he, as a child, had befriended.

The convict, released on ticket of leave, had prospered in New South Wales. Having neither kith nor kin (so far as he knew) he conceived the notion of revenging himself upon the "gentlemanly" society which had treated him as a pariah and an outcast all his life, by using his money to turn the simple working-class lad who had befriended him into "as good a gentleman as any of'em." Thus, instead of owing his education and his middle-class income to the caprice of a fine lady, Pip finds that he owes it to the convict whom he had found cowering in the mist on the Dartford Marshes one Christmas Eve, and who had terrified him into bringing him food, drink and a file to remove the ankle-ring of his broken fetters.

That the convict's attempt to escape had, at that time, proved abortive, Pip knew. But he also knew, and had been horrified at the time to see, that the convict's failure to escape was due to his wild beast-like ferocity against another convict who was also attempting to escape. Rather than let this second convict escape, the first convict had assaulted him, battered him, and shouted to attract the pursuing escort, which recaptured the pair of them. And it was to this ferocious brute that, to his dismay, Pip learned he owed the prosperity upon which be had reared his dream vision of Great Expectations. Naturally, along with the theory that his prosperity came from Miss Havisham there was also shattered the theory that Estella was intended for him.

The development from this crisis is made by means of the convict's per-sonal peril. In his eagerness to see, with his own eyes, the "gentleman" he and his money had made he had returned to England, despite the law which imposed death as the penalty for an unlicensed return from trans-portation. It is from the convict's own lips that Pip learns the source from which he had derived his gentility. And in addition to the shocks to his snobbish pride, and to his dream-vision of expectations, Pip has to face the problem of keeping his convict-benefactor safe from the authorities.

The convict (Magwitch) has an enemy—a time-expired fellow convict, Compayson, who was, in fact, that other convict whom Magwitch had assaulted on the marshes. He is in England and will, if he can, work

Magwitch's ruin. Pip enlists the help of a friend, Herbert Pocket, and soon learns that Magwitch is being sought. They attempt to get him out of the country, but at the last minute he is arrested on the Thames in a boat when on the point of boarding the ship that was to carry him to safety. In the struggle Magwitch receives fatal injuries —but he holds Compayson under water long enough to drown him.

All Magwitch's fortune being confiscated by the Crown, Pip has to turn to earning his living by work. In the meantime Miss Havisham has died from an accident, and her fabulous fortune, on which so many expectations had been built, turns out to be next to nothing. What there is goes to Estella.

In the end, Pip, after years spent abroad earning his living, returns to England, and meets Estella again. She has been married (to a surly gentleman-brute) and is now widowed. They meet in what had been the garden of Miss Havisham's house. The house and its attendant buildings had been sold and pulled down and the ground sold too—all except this garden. Here Pip and Estella meet again, and Pip sees "no shadow of another parting from her."

This last touch is the one which was supplied to satisfy Bulwer Lytton. Logically Pip should have lost Estella irrecoverably along with the rest of the "expectations" he had built around Miss Havisham. And this, too, was the end obviously fore-indicated by the story of Miss Havisham herself, out of which grew her relation to Estella.

Miss Havisham loomed so large in Pip's young outlook because she was the heiress of the local big business, a brewery with a large mansion adjoining. The brewery business had been closed down, but Miss Havisham lived on in the mansion as a recluse. On her wedding morning, years before, she had learned that her intended bridegroom was a biga-mous rake and a swindler, who, in collusion with her brother, had swindled her of half her fortune. From that moment she had never looked upon the light of day, but had lived in darkened rooms wearing the same costume in every detail (down to one shoe on and one shoe off) that she had worn when the news struck her down.

The appurtenances of the wedding feast, bride-cake and all, had remained mouldering on the table from that moment—a prey to undisturbed mice and spiders.

In her embittered loneliness Miss Havisham had adopted a foundling, Estella, and had brought her up to be an instrument of revenge. She taught Estella to make the most of her natural beauty. She had her well educated. She did all she could to make Estella irresistibly attractive—and at the same time invincibly cold-hearted—in order that Estella might avenge her by breaking the hearts of all the men whom her beauty fascinated. To that end Miss Havisham trained Estella from girlhood to be as proud and imperious as she was beautiful; to regard men as ineradicably treacherous and base—as vermin fit for destruction—to regard love as a pitiful weakness, and a snare to be shunned like a plague—to regard marriage as a means only to the great end of inflicting supreme tortures upon the worst (and therefore the most torture-deserving) man in sight. Trained in that way, Estella—when the boy Pip is introduced occasionally into Miss Havisham's house, partly as a companion, partly to wheel Miss Havisham about in her invalid chair—naturally excites his admiration, only to insult him and ill-treat him. As a grown woman she, to Pip's mystification, warns him against falling in love with her. And, when Miss Havisham herself, at last, reproaches her for her coldness, she retorts with the unanswerable query: "Who taught me to be cold?" Naturally again, Estella chooses to marry the wealthiest brute in sight, who, equally naturally, ill-treats her. They separate; and (here begins the Lytton after-thought) he is providentially kicked to death by a horse he was ill-treating. Thus, cured by suffering of her cold-blooded man-hatred Estella is set free to marry Pip.

It is clear that the logical consequence of Pip's delusion about his "great expectations" was not only the shock of disillusionment—and the loss of his fortune along with his real benefactor—but also the frustration of all his love expectations. And this, all the more, since, in his infatuated belief that Estella was intended for him, he had been blind to the affection, as well as the good qualities, of the girl Biddy, who instead marries Pip's widowed brother-in-law, Joe Gargery. It is no less clear that the logical consequence of such an upbringing as that in which Estella's disposition was formed, would be to unfit her for any sort of marriage. It is clear, too, in the third place, that Dickens, setting to work to build a novel in which the folly of living in a fool's paradise is demonstrated by making the lure of "great expectations" lead to nothing but disaster, was in a mood, for once, to cut out the conventional wedding bells, and finish on a note of failure and grey disillusionment.

Thus interpreted the net effect of the novel would be to demonstrate even more clearly than the *Tale of Two Cities* that Dickens saw in existing society and its whole crop of "great expectations" (it was the period of the most lurid mid-Victorian optimism, remember) nothing but folly and a headlong rush towards disaster.

The class bias of *Great Expectations* is so evident as almost to be underscored. Miss Havisham is a fine lady, who has been cruelly deceived and robbed. But it was by fine gentlemen that she was deceived and robbed—gentlemen of authentic "gentility," even though both finished their days as "swell mobsmen." And Miss Havisham's plan of revenge is, if possible, even more heartless and cruel than was the injury done to her. To fill the account full a select company of relatives are forever on the prowl round Miss Havisham, hating each other, and scheming and counter-scheming to oust each other from "expectations" under her will. So far the gentlefolks pass scrutiny very badly. There is a partial exception in the case of one of Miss Havisham's relatives, Matthew Pocket, who is the only one who never makes fawning visits to her. He is represented as a good sort, who has to work hard as a tutor, lecturer and writer, to keep a considerable family and an expensive wife— who spends her time lolling about and studying the Peerage. All the other characters in the book are either hard-working professionals, like the lawyer, Jaggers, and Wemmick his clerk; shopkeepers, like the egregious humbug Pumblechook; sea captains, like the drunken and outrageous Bill Barley; commercial men, like Herbert Pocket, son of Matthew; crafismen like the blacksmith Joe Gargery, Pip's brother-in-law; wage-earners, like the blackguard, Orlick; plain "varmints" like the convict Magwitch. Thus such class-antagonism as there is in *Great Expectations* is not that between aristocrats (as such) and common people, but that between, on the one side, the "gentlemen" (who are for one reason or another either crazily vengeful or callously cold-hearted and corrupt) and with them their sycophants and attendant slum-hooligans and on the other, the honest, working section of the population.

By far the most attractive characters in the book are the blacksmith, Joe Gargery, and Biddy, the self-taught school-mistress, who becomes his second wife. Pip himself begins as a proletarian and after his spell of prosperity is proletarianized again—except so far as his superior education equates him with the petit-bourgeoisie.

The two legal characters, Jaggers and his clerk Wemmick, are decisive in this regard. Both are exceedingly well-drawn, and each is quite different from the other. But they have this in common—they are different men, when at work in their Old Bailey practice, from what they are, secretly, in their private lives. They are inverted hypocrites. In business cold, unsentimental, calculating and ruthless; each, in private, is capable of deep affection, sympathy and compassion. It is impossible not to see in these two characters—especially when the care with which they have been drawn is taken into account—Dickens' deepening sense that success in business in the bourgeois world can be won only at the expense of every-thing nobly generous, elevating, sympathetic and humane. And as though to force this upon the reader's notice, Dickens endows Jaggers with the special characteristic that, invariably, after doing some more than usually dirty piece of work, he carefully washes his hands—with *scented soap.*

There is, significantly, no trace whatever in *Great Expectations* of the "Cheeryble" illusion—the notion that the world will be put right by the large-hearted benevolence of the employing class. Instead of Mr. Pickwick, the Cheeryble brothers, the elder Martin Chuzzlewit in his final, benevolent phase, John Jarndyce, or Jervis Lorry (the Cheeryble-illusion died hard!) we have the convict Magwitch; victim of an evil state of society; a neglected and ill-treated outcast from birth; savagely treated by law; tricked, exploited, and victimized by the gentleman swindler and forger, Compayson. After all this he shows, notwithstanding, a finely human and pathetic capacity for unstinted gratitude; and a profoundly human desire for a generously impersonal revenge on the official society which has been his enemy all his life long.

In the character of Magwitch, and in his relation to Pip's "great expectations"—he was Estella's father!—the moral of the novel is clearly indicated.

Self-satisfied, mid-Victorian British society buoyed itself up with as great "expectations" of future wealth and glory as did poor, deluded, Pip. If it had but known, its means of ostentation came from a source (the labour of the depressed and exploited masses) to which it would have been as shocked to acknowledge indebtedness as Pip was to find he owed all his acquired gentility to the patronage of a transported felon. Magwitch differed little from the uncouth monster which respectable society envisaged to itself as the typical "labouring man." And in literal truth, good, respectable society owed as much to these working men, and was as little aware of it, as was Pip of the source of his advantages. And respectable society is as little grateful as Pip, whenever the truth is revealed.

Great Expectations shows Dickens in the trough of the wave, his optimism shattered, and his Radicalism nonplussed in consequence. He had not reached a conception of any revolutionary role open to the proletariat. But, if the bourgeoisie is, after all, made up of nothing but Bentley Drummles, Compaysons, Pumblechooks and their like, even another September 1792, and another Reign of the Guillotine, would be preferable to the continuance of their rule in perpetuity. No inference but this is possible from a novel which preaches so clearly the folly and worse of a refusal to face the ugly actualities of life.

And as though to prove that just this conclusion and none other is the one Dickens is resolved we shall reach, his next novel takes as its theme just these ugly actualities, and has as its chief "villain" the egregious

Podsnap, who "abolishes" with a wave of the hand everything which doesn't fit in with his smug, self-satisfied optimism.

The development of Pip's character bears no other interpretation.

Like *David Copperfield* the story is told in the first person, and the earlier chapters recount Pip's childhood experiences. It was a bold thing in Dickens to thus challenge a comparison with his own masterpiece; but, although many find Pip a much less admirable and likeable character than David, the later work stands the test of comparison well.

Nothing could be finer than the child-psychology of the earlier chapters of *Great Expectations*—nothing in Dickens even, betters the delineation of Pip, his irascible and spiteful sister, Mrs. Gargery, and her splendidly simple and good-hearted husband, Joe. And the highwater mark of a masterly performance—whose lowest level exceeds the best of any other English writer in this vein—is the description of Pip's mental agonies during the Christmas dinner, racked by frightful apprehensions of the inevitable discovery of the depredations he had worked upon the larder for the relief of the hunted convict starving in the fog on the marshes outside.

Another masterly passage is Pip's lapse into romantic lying when called upon to give an account of what had happened on his first summons to visit Miss Havisham. The actual reality was so weirdly uncanny to a sensitive child that Pip simply could not bring himself to disclose the truth. Hence, child-like, he grabs at every suggestion from the stupidly greedy and unimaginative Uncle Pumblechook, and makes it an ingredient in a marvellous romance. Dickens' profundity of grasp of child-psychology was never better shown; nor, for that matter, his grasp of adult-psychology, since his audience, led by Pumblechook, swallows the fiction much more readily than they would have accepted the pathetically morbid truth. Joe Gargery—to whom in private, Pip at once admits he has been lying—is quite upset; and not so much at Pip's lying as at having to part with a genuine gorgeous real-life romance.

No less masterly is Dickens' delineation of Pip's turning—in his days of prosperous expectation—into an appalling little snob: his shameful turning-away from, and growing ashamed of, Joe Gargery and Biddy, the devoted friends of his pre-prosperity years. In fact, these scenes are too well done for the novel to be popular with readers who "take" novels as a "dope." They are so true, and so shrewd, that they strike home to the streak of snobbery in every one of us; and so give, not pleasure, but acute pain.

It is not possible to read the pathetically painful story of Pip's cruel awakening in the midst of his snobbery without realizing that here is the pith and marrow of the author's purpose—that Pip, here, like David Copperfield in another sense, stands for Everyman.

"Our Mutual Friend"

Our Mutual Friend, Dickens' last complete novel, appeared in monthly parts beginning in May 1864 and finishing in November 1865. An interval of over two years separated it from its immediate predecessor in which interval Dickens wrote some of his most popular Christmas sketches. The most popular of these, *Mrs. Lirriper's Lodgings* appeared during the year-end immediately prior to the first number of *Our Mutual Friend*. Its sequel, *Mrs. Lirriper's Legacy,* appeared while the novel was still in progress.

This has a significance of no little weight. The pervading sadness of *Great Expectations,* which deepens into the gloom, shot with exasperation, of *Our Mutual Friend,* has been given a purely subjective interpretation by such critics as admit its existence. Dickens, they say, was reaching the point of mental and emotional exhaustion, and this they assert was exacerbated by his private and domestic circumstances. No doubt both these factors operated to some slight extent. No man could go on for ever, pouring out imaginative work on the scale that Dickens had achieved, without some sense of exhaustion; some difficulty in avoiding self-repetition. But as against this *a priori* conclusion stands the fact of *Mrs. Lirriper,* in which all his earlier qualities, of geniality, fun, pathos, and kindliness, culminating in a happy conclusion, are shown in as spritely a condition as ever. His lavishness —which leads him to squander cheerfully on a short story materials which lesser men would find more than enough for a full-length novel—is there, too, fully as of old.

And if the exhaustion theory is shattered by *Mrs. Lirriper* no less completely is the domestic unhappiness theory shattered. Nobody can say *Mrs. Lirriper* strikes an unhappy note. And, even if it did, the fact remains that Dickens' domestic unhappiness was at least, eased, if not ended, by his separation from his wife, in 1857. It would seem from this fact that the growing sombreness of the novels written after 1857 (the *Tale of Two Cities, Great Expectations,* and *Our Mutual Friend)* was no projection of a casually induced mood, but the expression of a deep-rooted conviction which he was glad to reveal, once the local irritation of domestic exasperation and restraint was removed.

The facts are only accounted for if we conclude that the really fundamental incompatibility between Dickens and his wife lay in the complete
antithesis of their convictions about contemporary society as a whole. It is
as Dickens grows more indignantly a Radical, and as, from the loss of
illusions about reformist-Radicalism, he is impelled further and further in
a revolutionary direction, that the incompatibility of disposition between
himself and his wife becomes unbearable, and has to be eased by separation. It is significant that the break came when *Little Dorrit* reached its culmination. And significant too, that the first novel Dickens wrote after the
separation was constructed on the theme of "Recalled to Life," and
contains passionately moving descriptions of oppressors overthrown by a
violent revolution.

The impelling political passion of Dickens—which, in the circumstances
of the time could find only a literary-imaginative expression—gives the
clue to understanding both his separation from his wife and the significance of his last three novels.

Our Mutual Friend shows in its construction a further development of
the converging or interlocking method Dickens employed as an
alternative to, or in conjunction with, the dispersive or radiating method.
In the latter method, as for instance in *Pickwick,* the main thread of the
story is the progression of a central character from one given point to
another; while variety and contrast are supplied by the other characters
whose orbits intersect that of the main character much as a comet cuts
across the orbit of the solar system. In the interlocking method—of which
Our Mutual Friend, Bleak House, and *Little Dorrit* are examples—a more
complex movement is attempted. A number of different characters or
groups of characters are introduced in succession, each group having its
own distinctive and self-contained inner movement. These groups are
made to interlock at certain points with the result that the main action
emerges as something over and beyond all the subsidiary actions, as the
positive outcome of their *interaction,* and not from the initial impetus of
the central character and his purposes. These contrasted methods, it is
true, are capable of evolution out of and back again into each other.
Beyond a point, the following up of the orbit of a comet, takes the observer
out of the solar system into the wider universe; and, conversely the perfection of the convergence of a number of separate actions gives a main
action which so dominates the result as to re-establish the radiating
method on a higher and more developed plane. It would seem from a
comparison of Dickens' later works with his earlier that this constructional

ideal— one in which Tolstoy *(War and Peace)* and Dostoievsky *(Brothers Karamazoff)* are supreme—was the end he sought to attain.

He did not, perhaps, quite succeed. Readers are apt to get too deeply absorbed in one or other of the subplots to be quite aware of the movement of the whole in its totality. In fact, to many, this method gives the effect of unstudied confusion; and so leads in turn to the judgment that Dickens' novels have "no plots." This judgment is not only ill-based, it is one which ignores most unfairly the immense pains Dickens took to achieve an organic unity—to make each novel a real whole. And, on the view we have adopted (that Dickens sought by means of the incident-plot of his novels, to achieve a moral plot indicative of and symbolizing a politico-ethical criticism of the social life of his time) it is a judgment which is most signally unjust in the case of *Our Mutual Friend*.

In this novel the number of sub-strands which combine to create the whole is not perhaps greater than that in several of his previous works. But the comparative bulk and prominence of these sub-strands is more equal, and their inner development is in each case more elaborate, than it was in any earlier case. Moreover, not from accident but from design, the class-groups into which the characters of the novel fall, are made to make contact incidentally—only at certain points of sharp collision. That is to say: the *separation* between the classes of the poor working folk, the shabby genteel, and the opulent and quasi-aristocratic is much more sharply underscored. Most significantly of all the corrupting influence of Riches, on the one side, and of Poverty, on the other—in their contrast as well as in their conjunction—is made the mainspring of the action. Class contrast and class antagonism, class hatred and class contempt, are woven into the innermost texture of *Our Mutual Friend*.

The main story of *Our Mutual Friend* pivots upon the will of a misanthropic dust-contractor, who had died before the novel opens. Incidentally, here the novel "dates" rather badly, because it presupposes a familiarity with a phenomenon that modern Londoners will find it hard to envisage. All the dust and refuse removal of London was, in Dickens' days, undertaken by private contractors, engaged by the various parish vestries, the City Corporation, or the Metropolitan Board of Works. This dust and refuse was all dumped on what was then open ground between the Coldbath Fields Prison (now the Mountpleasant Post Office) and what is now the Caledonian Market. An area with a radius of roughly three-quarters of a mile, with the point now occupied by King's Cross and St. Pancras stations as its approximate centre, was a wilderness of these dumps, which became with the development of manufacture immensely valuable for various reasons. The dust was sifted and sorted. The bones were sold to makers of fertilizers; the rags, etc., went for paper-making and kindred manufactures; the cinders were saleable to iron smelters; and the fine dust was used extensively in making the concrete which was used in large quantities in railroad construction.

Not long before the time when *Our Mutual Friend* was begun, the newspapers had all carried the story of a surprisingly large fortune left by one such dust-contractor. Hence Dickens takes a dust-contractor's fortune as his jumping-off point and his private "mountain range" of valuable dust-heaps as the scene of its primary action.

This deceased dust-contractor, Harmon, was a misanthrope, and a miser, who quarrelled with everyone about him, except his foreman, Boffin, and the foreman's wife, Mrs. Boffin; and he had "breezes", even with them. When Harmon died his wife had long been dead. So also had his daughter, whom he had turned out of his home, in the best tradition of melodrama, because she had refused the man he had selected for her to marry.

His son, whom he had sent to be educated at a cheap boarding-school in Brussels, returned home to plead for his sister; and got disinherited and driven out in turn for his pains. In his will, however (written shortly after this last incident, but some fourteen years before his decease), the foul-tempered miser seemed to relent. He leaves one of his dust-mountains to his old foreman, Boffin, and the rest of his property (which includes over £100,000 in cash) to his son John Harmon.

There is, however a "string" to this latter benefaction. The son inherits only on condition that he marries a girl (Bella Wilfer) whom old Harmon only knew, casually; and also knew chiefly as an angry child whom he had first seen beating her amiable father with her bonnet, because he wanted to take her somewhere she didn't want to go. Evidently the scoundrelly old miser thought she would grow to be just the woman to give his son a real hell of a life.

The son, John Harmon, meanwhile, being driven from home, went to sea. Later on he established himself at the Cape: making a moderate success as a small-proprietor farmer and fruitgrower. He was found there by advertisements circulated by Nicodemus (otherwise "Nick," otherwise "Noddy") Boffin, who had been left sole executor; and who, in the event of John Harmon's failure to marry Bella Wilfer, was to be sole residuary legatee. The son sold off his Cape possessions and returned to England.

The novel opens with the fact that he is reported "found drowned" in the Thames immediately after his arrival. The subsidiary strands which in their integration compose the main action, begin from this situation.

First there is the group of riverside characters beginning with the old, hardened waterman-*cum*-water-rat, Hexam, who finds the body which is identified, from papers in the pockets of its clothes, as John Harmon. Old Hexam has a daughter Lizzie—who subsequently provides the occasion for the love-rivalry between the self-taught certificated schoolmaster, Bradley Headstone, and the gentleman barrister Eugene Wrayburn. Hexam, himself a truculent illiterate, has a son Charley—as ill-natured as himself—who, mostly at the instigation of his sister, aspires to education, and accordingly becomes a pupil teacher under Bradley Headstone (which establishes the first contact between the latter and Lizzie).

Hexam has a discarded partner, Rogue Riderhood, whom he has repudiated because Riderhood had been jailed on a charge of pocket-picking. Since Old Hexam's chief interest in finding bodies afloat in the river—at which he is an adept—is the loose money found in the pockets of the dead, Rogue Riderhood thinks Hexam's attitude hypocritical. Hexam, however, draws a sharp distinction between taking money from the living, who have a need of it (and therefore a property right in it), and taking money from the dead, to whom it can be of no manner of use. In revenge Riderhood accuses Hexam (falsely) of knocking on the head and throwing into the river the corpses he afterwards "finds." He categorically accuses him of the murder of John Harmon, and leads the police to the arrest of Hexam, only to find Hexam dead—accidentally drowned in his turn. Later on, Riderhood admits that he made the charge partly in revenge, but chiefly attracted by the reward of £1,ooo offered by Boffin for information leading to the conviction of John Harmon's murderer.

In the riverside group are also included the local police; the company in and around the "Six Jolly Fellowship Porters" inn; and Pleasant Riderhood, the daughter of Roger *(alias* "Rogue").

The next strand is that of the Wilfer family. Mr. Wilfer is an amiable, mild-natured, city clerk, with an ever-expanding family and a never-expanding income. He has a wife, who is, or behaves as if she were, a tragedy queen in decayed circumstances (or, as one of her daughters puts it, the Tragic Muse with a Toothache). Her self-and-family-esteem are in inverse ratio to the family income. Above all, she is a monument of ostentatious resignation to a cruel fate. When she meets the Boffins she "sat silently giving them to understand that every breath she drew required to be drawn with a self-denial rarely paralleled in history." Her tragedy-glooms are broken by the sparks that fly from between her and the only two of her children who have not yet left home. The elder, Bella, is vivacious and good-natured, though rather petulant and quick tempered; and the younger, Lavinia, is rather like her mother, only with more dash as well as sense in her.

The common bond which unites the riverside group with the Wilfer group is that of Poverty. Poverty drives Gaffer Hexam to his brutalizing way of making a living on the water, and, drives him near to—and his ex-partner, Riderhood, over—the borderline of crime. It is the brutalization consequent upon Poverty which makes Old Hexam jealously furious at book-learning, and at any sort of education that might take his son Charley into a way of living different from, or higher than, his own. And it is fear and hatred of this brutalization which makes Hexam's daughter Lizzie scheme and contrive until she can find the means of sending Charley away from home to become, in time, a certificated teacher. And it is a snobbish horror of the Poverty from which he has, in part, escaped—combined with a selfish fear lest the circumstances of his origin may militate against his worldly success—that makes Charley seek to force his sister to accept the tuition and patronage of Bradley Headstone—with consequences that he did not foresee, fatal to that gentlenian.

In the Wilfer household Pa Wilfer contrives by simple good-nature to keep mildly cheerful, despite poverty and its exasperations. Mrs. Wilfer revenges herself upon her poverty by adopting the poses of a martyr and behaving as though it had been wilfully inflicted upon her by somebody or other who was jealous of her obvious superiority, and that of her family. Bella frankly hates and detests being poor, and swears (and at first believes) that she will do *anything* to escape from it. Lavvy, who as a junior feels the effects of poverty only indirectly, reacts to these effects by a guerilla warfare of minor shrewishness upon everybody in sight. In the upshot Bella's hatred of being poor has consequences which teach her that Riches can be an even greater curse than Poverty.

A third strand, and one also comprised within the Poverty category, is supplied by the Silas Wegg group. Wegg is the proprietor of a street stall on which sweets, fruits and sheet ballads are displayed for sale. Noddy Boffin hires him to come and read to him for two hours every evening. Wegg has a wooden leg and a warped disposition. Noddy Boffin, in the goodness of his heart and the innocence of his ignorance, mistakes Wegg for a literary man; he is, in fact, only semi-literate, and has all the cunning of a half-wit, along with the envious spitefulness of the traditional gnome. Wegg, too, is a born sycophant, and secretly hates Boffin because he has succeeded to great wealth instead of being born into it, and has become able to buy and inhabit the aristocratic mansion alongside which Wegg used to place his stall.

Wegg is an example of a slave-spirited snob, made meaner and more viciously spiteful by poverty. Part of the main action is supplied by Wegg's scheme to avenge his fancied wrongs upon Boffin ("the minion of fortune and worm of the hour") by means of blackmail.

Associated for a time with Wegg is Mr. Venus, an articulator of skeletons, and a bird and animal stuffer. Mr. Venus supplies mild low comedy relief, of a lugubrious order, by his chagrin at his ill-success in his love pursuit of Pleasant Riderhood, which itself is caused by Pleasant's objection to his occupation.

A fourth strand, also in the Poverty category, is supplied by the Betty Higden group.

Mrs. Boffin, wishing to adopt a boy-child (to preserve the memory of young John Harmon) is introduced to an old lady, Betty Higden, who makes a living by taking in mangling and minding children. Her family, apart from the toddlers she "minds" while their mother is at work, consists of herself, her only living relative, Johnnie, the baby great-grandchild whom Mrs. Boffin wishes to adopt, and Sloppy, her mangle-turner in chief, an overgrown but immensely affectionate "love-child" she has herself adopted. Betty is a noble, hard-working soul whose chief terror is a fear of the workhouse. She is loth to part with little Johnnie and loth to stand in his light; but Mrs. Boffin solves her difficulty by agreeing to leave little Johnnie with her so long as she can "manage" with him—that is, until she grows too feeble to care for him properly. Mr. Boffin offers, for his part, to put Sloppy in the way of learning a trade.

Little Johnnie solves Betty's problem in his own way—by contracting a fever from one of the "minders" and dying in the Children's Hospital. At this, Betty, who knows, in practice, that Sloppy will insist upon trying to work all day at cabinet-making and all night at turning her mangle, decides to "run away" from him. She refuses an offer of free quarters and a post (a nominal one) as "housekeeper" from Mr. Boffin, because it looks too much like "charity," and sets out with a basket to live by hawking trifles at markets. Eventually she dies, worn out, while on her way to visit the grave of her youngest child.

Betty represents that type of over-sensitive poverty which lives in permanent horror and dread of mendicancy, and of being forced upon parish relief.

Yet another poverty strand is supplied by the little cripple Jenny Wren, who makes a living as a doll's dressmaker. She is burdened with a dipsomaniac father, who though a good workman at his trade is afflicted with an inherited craving for rum. Jenny's crippled state is due, in part, to pre-natal causes—the consequence of her father's drunkenness, and of the intensification of poverty which follows therefrom. Jenny (who later on becomes friends with Lizzie Hexam), has a friend in a worthy old Jew, Riah, who for his part is shamelessly exploited by his employer—a "Christian" moneylender and bill broker, who uses Riah, and his nationality, as a camouflage. The friendship between Jenny, Riah and Lizzie gives an example of how the poor help the poor.

Interlocking at different points with all these five poverty strands is the main group. This group, in its class-composition, is a mixed formation in that it shows both poverty and riches in conjunction.

Its central character (who, when Boffin speaks of him to the Wilfers as "Our Mutual Friend," gives the novel its title), is the supposedly-drowned heir, John Harmon. The supposition of his drowning is the result of his accidental resemblance to a "crook"—a steward on the ship upon which he travelled home from the Cape. As a consequence of discovering the resemblance—while unaware of the steward's "crookedness"—John Harmon conceives the notion of putting himself in the way of the girl, "willed" to him as wife by his misanthrope father, in order to "size her up" unknown to her. The "crook" falls in with the notion and takes him to a low riverside haunt to get him a seaman's costume as a disguise. Actually the crook intends to take advantage of their resemblance and so to impersonate John Harmon and collar his fortune. But after he had successfully lured Harmon to a riverside den, drugged him, and effected an exchange of clothes, he himself is set upon, knocked on the head, and robbed by the other crooks who haunted the den.

Both the insensible John Harmon and the murdered crook are flung into the Thames. Harmon, revived by the cold water, manages to get ashore. The body of the crook is found and identified as "John Harmon." Whereupon the real owner of that name, takes advantage of the opportunity thus created to carry out his original scheme.

He takes lodgings with the Wilfers, and also induces Noddy Boffin to employ him as secretary. When the Boffins move into a fashionable mansion and take Bella Wilfer into their house as a kind of ward-companion, the secretary, "Rokesmith," duly falls in love with her. She misunderstands his motives and repels him— when chance circumstances betray him into a declaration.

This repulsion has a double result. It makes him decide not to reveal his true identity until he is more sure whether Bella is the mercenary little snob she believes herself to be—and which, from her destestation of poverty, she is in danger of becoming. But it also leads (when Mrs. Boffin comes unexpectedly upon him, and finds him in a dejection similar to that he had often suffered as a child) to Mrs. Boffin's recognition of him as John Harmon. At this Old Boffin propounds, and induces Mrs. Boffin and John "Rokesmith" to agree to and assist him, in a little plot. He pretends to have been turned misanthropic and miserly by his good fortune. He drags Bella round to all the bookshops in London buying up books about misers — which Wegg has to read to him. He talks about misers with enthusiastic admiration, and (in the presence of Bella) he gets harsher and more exacting with his secretary. In the end Bella is so disgusted with the (seemingly) miserly old wretch, that she turns upon him in a fury of disgust. This is occasioned by Boffin's dismissal of his secretary, "Rokesmith," with every aggravation of contumelious reproach for having had the "impertinence" to make his advances to Bella ("when he knows she is on the look out for money") and for having had the "mercenary cunning" to see in her a profitable catch.

Boffin had learned the fact from one of the fashionables whose acquaintance the Boffins had begun to make, one Mrs. Lammle (she and her husband are financially in Queer Street and hope to re-establish their finances by worming into the good graces of the Boffins at the expense of "Rokesmith," and, perhaps, also of Bella). Mrs. Lammle had learned it in turn from an unguarded admission, under "pumping," by Bella.

For her part, Bella is so shamed by the consequences of her indiscretion, so humiliated by Boffin's "defence" of her, and of her money-marrying intentions — and is also so drawn to John "Rokesmith" — that she flies at Boffin and denounces him as a wealth-ruined monster. She apologizes to "Rokesmith" for being the cause of his humiliation; and then leaves the Boffins' house "for ever."

As was inevitable, her marriage to John "Rokesmith" soon follows, and, after an interval sufficient to permit of the birth of Bella's first child, the disclosure of her husband's true identity follows, and with it a complete reconciliation with the Boffins. The young couple thereupon duly enter into their inheritance.

Meanwhile the Wegg-Venus blackmail conspiracy develops and culminates. Wegg, at first, has no idea beyond nosing round the mounds in the dust yard in the hope of finding (and making away with) hidden valuables. He enlists the help of Venus because of his own handicap — a wooden leg, which makes climbing dustmounds a risky adventure. Wegg does find something. He finds a will, later than the one which had been "proved" by Boffin. By the later will the miser Harmon left everything he possessed (beyond the mound left to Boffin) to the State. Wegg proposes to hold this will over Boffin as an instrument of terror, and to force him to disgorge half the property as the price of silence and suppression. Venus, unknown to Wegg, discloses the fact to Boffin, who in turn makes a counter-disclosure to Venus. Boffin and Venus thereupon agree to let Wegg go ahead in the belief that all is as it was. Wegg eventually "comes down upon" Boffin, who affects to be terrified, and to beg for mercy. Finally a day is appointed for a grand settlement. In the moment of his apparent triumph Wegg is confronted with the crushing truth that he has been "led up the garden"—that Boffin has, all the time, been possessed of a still later will which leaves everything to himself. Out of the simple goodness of his heart he has, after establishing his legal right under this will, used it to endow John Harmon with all that would have been his under the provisions of the first will.

Wegg is suitably humiliated. Venus calls him a "precious old rascal"; John Harmon bumps his head against the wall; while Sloppy hoists him on to his back like a sack, carries him out of the house, and throws him into a slush cart—altogether a satisfactorily comic finish to the great Wegg conspiracy.

A contrasting counter-point to the main Boffin-Harmon-Bella development centres in and about Lizzie Hexam. As we have seen, her father, Old Hexam, had a morbidly brutal hatred of any sort of education. She, therefore, while he lived, remained, perforce, illiterate. But she schemed and contrived ways and means of getting her brother Charley sufficient elementary schooling to enable liim to obtain a place in a better school; from which in turn, he obtained a post as pupil-teacher, which carried with it the prospect of becoming in time a fully certificated teacher.

Lizzie, despite her illiteracy, was a competent and reliable work-woman, and was as fine natured as she was good looking. She has the misfortune to exercise an attraction over two very different men at the same time. Eugene Wrayburn, a briefless barrister, of good family (the friend and rooming-mate of Boffin's solicitor, Mortimer Lightwood), is the first of these. Eugene sees Lizzie first when he goes with Lightwood to get from Old Hexam particulars of the finding of the body supposed to be that of John Harmon. The attraction between them is mutual and obvious. But as Lizzie is an illiterate daughter of a "water-rat" of not too savoury reputation, while Wrayburn is emphatically a "gentleman" of family and education—though only very modestly of "fortune"—anything like marriage between them is socially unthinkable. Equally, both from Eugene's side and from Lizzie's, any sort of affair between them other than a *bona fide* marriage is ruled out—firstly because Eugene, for all his pose of boredom and indifference, is, at bottom, genuinely honourable, and generous; and, secondly, because Lizzie, though unmistakably attracted by Eugene, is anything but frivolous or "frail."

Eugene, unable to resist Lizzie's attractions, finds various excuses for seeing her continually at the home of her friend, the doll's dressmaker, Jenny Wren, with whom she takes refuge after Old Hexam's death. Eugene persuades Lizzie to let him pay the cost of a teacher for herself and Jenny who will give them, in the evenings, the grounding of an education.

Meanwhile, through her brother Charley, Lizzie has been brought to the notice of his schoolmaster-tutor, Bradley Headstone. Headstone, a man of "mean birth" and of violent passions—passions which have been repressed by the need to struggle for so much of education and professional advancement as he has achieved— is attracted by Lizzie as instantly as was Wrayburn. In his case, however, he excites in Lizzie nothing but repulsion and terror. Fearful partly of Headstone's persisting in unwelcome attentions, and partly of her own weakness for Eugene, Lizzie leaves her lodging at Jenny's home, and gets work in a paper-mill on the upper waters of the Thames, in Oxfordshire; keeping the place of her retreat secret from everybody but Jenny and Jenny's friend the Jew, Riah.

Headstone and Charley Hexam are, for different reasons, both furious when Lizzie refuses to accept Headstone's offer to teach her to read and write, and learns instead under a woman-teacher whose fees have been paid by Wrayburn. When Lizzie disappears they are both convinced that Wrayburn has seduced her away, and is keeping her in hiding somewhere. They spend all their spare time in following Wrayburn about in the hope of discovering where Lizzie has been hidden.

Wrayburn, no less perturbed than they at Lizzie's disappearance, knows that he is followed, and by whom. Irritated, he takes a delight in leading them on long aimless tramps around London. By letting them see that he knows he is being followed—and that at the same time he is ostentatiously ignoring the fact—Wrayburn goads Headstone into a state of absolute fury. Headstone, who at his best suffers from an injured sense of his inferior birth and upbringing—a sense exacerbated by the repressions imposed by his life of struggle and his occupation of schoolmaster—is so worked upon by disappointment, jealousy, and rage at Wrayburn's studied affronts that he grows positively homicidal. He longs to come upon Eugene and Lizzie together, because the sight will, he knows, nerve him for the murder he longs to be able to commit. He gets his desire. Wrayburn learns the whereabouts of Lizzie's place of retreat (getting the information from the dipsomaniac father of Jenny Wren—who gets enough money for the news to drink himself rapidly to death). Headstone follows by the towpath as Wrayburn makes his way up the river in a skiff, and witnesses, from a hiding place, Wrayburn's meeting with Lizzie. Headstone is not near enough to hear that Lizzie begs Wrayburn not to persist in his pursuit of her, or that Wrayburn agrees—although he finds it as impossible to leave her as it seems to be to marry her. Headstone sees them part, and as Eugene wanders moodily at the water's edge, Headstone falls upon him from behind with a club, batters him savagely, and flings his senseless body into the river.

Lizzie, who has also wandered by the riverside to compose herself, hears the sound of blows, a moan, and a splash, and runs to the spot. She sees the signs of a struggle and a body floating face upward in the water. Her skilled familiarity with boats enables her to get the battered and insensible Eugene out of the water, and so to a water-side inn, where medical attention is given him. When, eventually, Eugene recovers consciousness, though only intermittently, he tells Lightwood—whom Lizzie has sent for—that he wants to marry Lizzie before he dies (as he feels sure he will). Lightwood makes the necessary arrangements, and the marriage takes place, with Eugene still prostrate in bed, and with Jenny Wren and John and Bella as witnesses, along with Mortimer Lightwood.

Bradley Headstone, meanwhile, has fallen into a pit of his own digging. Knowing that Rogue Riderhood (who had become a lock-keeper on the upper Thames) has a grudge against Eugene, he disguises himself for his final following of Eugene in a costume closely copied from that of Riderhood. He stays to rest at Riderhood's cottage, and there, as he sleeps, Riderhood notes the resemblance between Headstone's garb and his own. By means of a trick (wearing a red neck-scarf, which Headstone, the next time they meet, has copied) he satisfies himself that this is no accident. When Headstone returns from his trip further up the river, Riderhood knows from the state of his garments that he has done what he set out to do. Riderhood follows him, when he continues his journey, and sees Headstone change his clothes at a convenient spot, resuming his schoolmaster's garments and flinging the bargeman's costume, in a bundle, into the river.

With this bundle, reclaimed from the river, Riderhood ferrets out Headstone, and proceeds to blackmail him. In revenge for the attempt to put the blame upon himself, Riderhood resolves to squeeze out of Headstone the last possible drop of profit that can be squeezed. Headstone is already in a state bordering upon frenzy from learning that his murderous assault had not merely miscarried, but had, in fact, had the opposite effect of driving Lizzie and Eugene together. He, therefore, complies with Riderhood's demand and visits him at his lock. There, after an altercation, Headstone seizes Riderhood round the waist and drags him down along with himself into the river. Both are drowned.

The contrast between the two love stories (of Bella and John on the one side, and of Lizzie and Eugene on the other) is complete at every point. In appearance, at any rate, John is a poor man aspiring to marry an heiress. It is Bella who abandons all her prospects with the Boffins to become what her mother describes as a "Mendicant's Bride." In the upshot, Bella finds she has not lost but gained. In the contrasting story it is Eugene who, at the point of death, makes the apparent social "sacrifice" of marrying Lizzie. In fact, the mental satisfaction so gained proves the turning point in his illness. He recovers, resolved to become, in deeds, much more worthy of Lizzie than he had seemed ever likely to be. Bella and Lizzie, who had first met and "made friends" by the body of Betty Higden—when Lizzie tended her in her last moments—establish a permanent and complete bond of friendship between the two households.

Taken in themselves, either the Bella theme or the Lizzie theme might, by the supercilious, be dismissed as mere sentimental comedy in the one case, and sentimental melodrama in the other. But as Dickens was a frank and unashamed sentimental-romantic (for all his realism) to say this is merely to say that Dickens achieved his purpose. His use of the one theme to balance, and provide contrast for, the other, as also his final bringing of the two themes into unison, is a fine example of Dickens' careful management.

But what is most noteworthy of all is that the two love themes are made to serve the purpose of contrasting Bella (who was very nearly ruined morally by poverty, and by her hatred and detestation of being poor) with Eugene (who was even more nearly ruined by his "gentlemanly" upbringing, his idleness and his possession of an unearned income) Bella's reclamation from mercenary wealth-worship, and Eugene's reclamation from gentlemanly boredom and cynical idleness, constitute, between them, the real essence of the novel. They are two facets of its general propaganda—its attack upon a social system which is based upon poverty for the mass of the population with wealth and demoralizing idleness for the privileged few.

This moral is underscored and driven home by a device unique in Dickens' work—the use of a whole group of characters to perform, periodically, the function of a Greek chorus. All the characters in this chorus belong to the (real or supposed) well-to-do class—the class of "good society." Only very incidentally, and in a roundabout fashion, do the members of this class (other than Wrayburn and Lightwood who are of them but not "with" them) make contact with the characters who supply the main action of the novel. Dickens, in fact, takes as much trouble to separate this group from the main body as he does to establish contacts linking the sub-groups of the main body into a synthetically united whole. The result is a clearly indicated class cleavage and class contrast, which deepens into a positive antagonism between the "chorus" of "good society," and the people who supply the main action of the novel. And, lest the significance of this should be lost, every character in this "good society" group (with the beforenoted exception of Eugene and Mortimer) is shown to be either a fraud, a fool, a scoundrel, or all together.

The group consists in the first place of the Veneerings—"new" people, in a new house in a new district, with new furniture, as newly married as is consistent with the possession of a new baby, and with an entirely new stock of "friends" whom they entertain at elaborate dinners, to which each of them comes because the dinner is to be had for the eating and because "everybody" else goes. At a certain stage in the novel Mr. Veneering desires to get elected to Parliament, and achieves his desire—at an expenditure of so many thousands of pounds. In the end (after the action of the novel is concluded) the Veneerings will become bankrupt and disappear from "good society" as quickly as they rose above its horizon. (An instance of how studiously tenuous the connection is between this "good society" group and the main body of the people of the novel is given by the fact that Bella Wilfer's longsuffering and patiently good-natured father is a clerk in the office of the firm in which Veneering becomes a partner—a thread of connection which is snapped before the novel ends.)

Next to the Veneerings in this group is the somewhat shrivelled up gentleman, Mr. Twemlow, who lives on a small allowance from his first cousin, Lord Snigsworth, eked out by continual dining out. As the first cousin of a very noble, very wealthy (and very mean and bad-tempered) peer of the realm, Mr. Twemlow is in very great request at the dinner tables of people like the Veneerings. He makes contact with the main action only indirectly, through falling into the clutches of that money-lender who employs the Jew Riah (the friend of Jenny Wren and of Lizzie) as his camouflage.

This money-lender is, in fact—although this is not known to his associates, to whom he appears as nothing but a normally idle, and more than normally stupid "gentleman" of fortune and leisure—one "Fascination" Fledgby (so called because of his singular lack of fascination—his piggy eyes, and generally unprepossessing behaviour) who is also a member of Veneerings' group. Fledgby makes contact with the main action partly through Riah, and partly through becoming in the course of his covert bill-broking activities the creditor of Wrayburn and Lightwood. This, however, affects the main action only to the very slight extent that, in the upshot, Fledgby is glad to dispose of his claim, at a big discount, to John Harmon.

This last result is one consequence of the conflict between Fledgby and Mr. and Mrs. Alfred Lammle, who are also of the Veneerings' "good society" group. These are a pair of adventurors, with (for "good society") trifling incomes. They met, originally, at one of the Veneerings' dinner-parties, and they married each other, each under the impression that the other possessed a fortune. To make ends meet—for which Alfred Lammle's chief resources are cards and billiards—the Lammles must ingratiate themselves with somebody, and to this end they seek to make a match between Fledgby and the daughter (and only child) of the well-to-do Mr. Podsnap. Georgina Podsnap is a timid little rabbit of a thing, who has an affectionate disposition— when she gets a chance to show she possesses a disposition of any kind. Usually she is much too overawed and overpowered by her pompously pretentious father, and her solemnly overbearing mother, to be anything at all. She is all too grateful for the interest shown in her by Mrs. Lammle, and would have been easily bullied and bamboozled into making a runaway match with the piggy-eyed, rat-faced, Fledgby, but for the intervention of her parents. This intervention is secretly engineered by Mrs. Lammle herself. Despite the urgent need she and her husband have of the money Fledgby (who is incapable of doing his own courting) will pay, in the event of his marriage to Georgina, Mrs. Lammle is so touched by Georgina's affectionately trustful simplicity that she contrives to get a warning conveyed to Mr. and Mrs. Podsnap. This results in a complete break between the Podsnaps and the Lammles, which, of course, puts an end to the scheme. Fledgby, in revenge for the disappointment, takes an early opportunity to put into execution a bill of sale he possesses on the Lammles' furniture. The opportunity to do this synchronizes with an attempt by the Lammles to ingratiate themselves with the Boffins, at the expense first of John, and then (if possible) of Bella. The attempt fails, just when it seemed like succeeding. For reasons already explained Boffin (in secret concert with John) pretends to be grateful for the "information" given by Mrs. Lammle, that John has had the "impudence" to aspire to marriage with Bella. But his "gratitude" goes no further than giving the Lammles a hundred pounds for their trouble, and summarily breaking off the acquaintance. The distraint upon their furniture and effects opens the Lammles, eyes to the identity of their implacable creditor, who had hitherto hidden behind that of the Jew, Riah. Alfred Lammle, before flying to the Continent, calls upon Fledgby and gives him a sound thrashing. Incidentally, Jenny Wren, from whom Fledgby had tried to wheedle the secret of Lizzie's whereabouts, finds him writhing on the floor just as Lammle had left him. This circumstance opens her eyes to the true relation between him and Riah. Previously Fledgby had made Riah to appear (in Jenny's presence) as the unconscionably usurious principal in shady money transactions. Actually Riah, through misfortune, had himself become indebted to Fledgby's father, and in return for a cancellation of the debt, had thereafter served him, and his son, for a wretched pittance. Riah was in the act of terminating his service with Fledgby when Jenny made the discovery which reconciled them.

Further members of the "good society" group are Lady Tippins, a faded piece of frivolity (whose speciality is a senile pretence at juvenility), and Boots, Brewer, and a number of Buffers, a collection of nonentities who help to fill dinner tables. The crowning ornament of the circle is Mr. Podsnap.

Podsnap differs from Pecksniff as insular conceit and self-satisfied humbug differ from unctuous hypocrisy. As Uriah Heep is a meaner, and a more coarsely-malevolent, variant upon Pecksniff, so Podsnap is a more pompous, a more blatant, and a more stupidly self-deceived variant in the opposite direction. Consequently where Uriah Heep and Pecksniff are caricatures of a particular type of man, Podsnap is a blistering satire upon a whole class.

The keynote of "Podsnappery"—it is Dickens' own term—is " satisfaction" with things as they are, and a refusal to believe that anybody in his senses could be other than satisfied:

> He (Podsnap) could never make out why everybody was not quite satisfied, and he felt conscious that he set a brilliant social example in being particularly well satisfied with most things, and above all other things with himself.—*Our Mutual Friend:* Book I, Chap. XI.

That being so, Mr. Podsnap naturally refused to admit the existence of anything that ran at all counter to his self-satisfaction. Anything disagreeable, any sort of social problem, he put behind him (and therefore out of existence) with a wave of his right arm, a flushed face, and:

> "I don't want to know about it; I don't choose to discuss it; I don't admit it!"— *Ibid.*

Podsnap (improving upon Hegel's, "all that is real is rational: all that is rational is real") took his stand upon the conviction that all he approved of was real, while all that was real he approved of. Anything he did not approve of was something that personally affronted him —and was therefore something which could not be:

> Mr. Podsnap's world was not a very large world, morally; no, nor even geographically: seeing that although his business was sustained upon commerce with other countries, he considered other countries, with that important reservation, a mistake, and of their manners and customs would conclusively observe, "Not English!" when, *Presto!* with a flourish of the arm, and a flush of the face they were swept away....
>
> Mr. Podsnap's notion of the Arts in their integrity might have been stated thus. Literature: large print respectfully descriptive of getting-up at eight, shaving close at a quarter past; breakfasting at nine, going to the City at ten, coming home at half-past five, and dining at seven. Painting and sculpture: models and portraits of professors of getting up at eight, shaving close at a quarter past, etc.... Music: a respectable performance (without variations) on stringed and wind instruments, sedately expressive of getting up at eight, etc.... Nothing else to be permitted to these same vagrants the Arts, on pain of excommunication. Nothing else To Be—anywhere!—*Our Mutual Friend:* Book I, Chap. XI.

And that nothing might be lacking in this portrait of the quintessential British bourgeois of the 1860's, Mr. Podsnap's religion is described:

> As a so eminently respectable man, Mr. Podsnap was sensible of its being required of him to take Providence under his protection. Consequently, he always knew exactly what Providence meant. Inferior and less respectable men might fall short of that mark, but Mr. Podsnap was always up to it. And it was very remarkable (and must have been very comfortable) that what Providence meant was invariably what Mr. Podsnap meant.—*Our Mutual Friend:* Book I, Chap. XI.

It is decisive in any estimate of Dickens' political line to note how studiously, and with what effect, he uses Podsnap in *Our Mutual Friend* as the central touchstone to all the human (and humane) actions and reactions of the drama. All the evil, all the villainy, all that is mean, despicable, and hateful in the world in which the Johns and Bellas, the Lizzies and the Eugenes, play out their lives, leads back to and has its roots in, Podsnap and Podsnappery, and in the society which Podsnap and Podsnappery typify and sum up. Rogue Riderhood is a rogue; Silas Wegg is a precious rascal; and Bradley Headstone is a tragic misfit. But they are soon disposed of; and, at worst, they are merely incidentally evil. Podsnap and

Podsnappery, with their attendant train of Veneerings, of Lammles, of Fledgbys, and the rest, *are* evil incarnate—things hateful beyond question, doubt or redemption.

How close Dickens made the likeness of Podsnap to the perennial bourgeois is shown in a comic conversation between Mr. Podsnap and his French guest, on a ceremonial occasion. To this day we can read in the leading articles of the *Daily Mail* and in the correspondence columns of the *Daily Telegraph* sentiments exactly paralleling those which impelled Mr. Podsnap to seek to gain from the French gentleman an admission that even a walk through the streets of London reveals evidence of the superiority of the British Constitution. (Between the obtuseness of the French gentleman on this cardinal point, and the need to correct his pronunciation of English, Mr. Podsnap has a difficult time:)

> "I was inquiring," said Mr. Podsnap, resuming the thread of his discourse, "whether you have observed in our streets as we should say, upon our Pavvy as you would say, any Tokens—"
>
> The foreign gentleman, with patient courtesy, entreated pardon: "But what was tokenz?"
>
> "Marks," said Mr. Podsnap. "Signs, you know, Appearances—Traces."
>
> "Ah! of a'Orse?" inquired the foreign gentleman.—*Our Mutual Friend:* Book I, Chap. XI.

Mr. Podsnap, somewhat nettled, explains patiently that only the Lower Classes in England abandon the aspirate and say 'Orse. He concedes graciously that "Our Language is Difficult and Trying to Strangers." He will, he says, not pursue his question:

> "It merely referred," Mr. Podsnap explained, with a sense of meritorious proprietorship, "to Our Constitution, sir. We Englishmen are Very Proud of Our Constitution, sir. It was Bestowed upon Us by Providence. No other Country is so Favoured as This Country."—*Our Mutual Friend:* Book I, Chap. XI.

With the usual slips in pronunciation, which Mr. Podsnap solemnly and instantly corrects, the foreign gentleman contrives to ask How the other countries manage?

> "They do, sir," said Mr. Podsnap, gravely shaking his head; "they do—I am sorry to be obliged to say it—*as* they do."
>
> "It was a little particular of Providence," said the foreign gentleman, laughing, "for the frontier is not large."
>
> "Undoubtedly," assented Mr. Podsnap. "But so it is. It was the Charter of the Land. This land was Blessed, sir, to the Direct Exclusion of such other countries as —as there may happen to be. And if we were all Englishmen present, I

would say," added Mr. Podsnap, looking round upon his compatriots and sounding solemnly, with his theme, "that there is in the Englishman a combination of qualities, a modesty, an independence, a responsibility, a repose, combined with an absence of everything calculated to call a blush into the cheek of a young person, which one would seek in vain among the Nations of the Earth." — *Our Mutual Friend:* Book I, Chap. XI.

It is more than a little provocative of speculation to remark that this passage was written at exactly the same time when Marx was at work upon the Inaugural Address and the Statutes of the International Workingmen's Association. There is no comment upon Podsnap, conceivable, more apt, or more adequate, than the world-famous first of these Statutes:

The emancipation of the working classes must be conquered by the working classes themselves.

As though he himself had a fear lest his plain intention might be lost upon his more obtuse readers, Dickens concludes *Our Mutual Friend* with a final performance from his "good society" Greek chorus, in which Mr. Podsnap stands out more prominently than ever. Departing from his conventional practice of making the final chapter a clearing house in which all the various characters are tidied up and packed away for life, Dickens concludes *Our Mutual Friend* with another dinner party at the Veneerings (which, *inter alia,* balances a dinner party at the Veneerings at the opening of the novel — one at which the story of the Harmon will is first told, and the supposed death by drowning of John Harmon is first announced.) The company is slightly different at this final dinner, but is, in essence, the same — "only more so." The Lammles (who were scheming to entrap each other at that first dinner) were missing at this last one, having fled their creditors and the country.

Fledgby, beaten like a carpet and flayed by Alfred Lammle, and, thereafter, brought into terror of legal penalties for his usurious trickeries by Mortimer Lightwood (as agent for John Harmon) was absent, too. So also was Eugene Wrayburn, who, by marrying Lizzie Hexam, had given "good society" a concrete defiance. But the places of these absent ones were filled, and more than filled, by a rally of the opulent, the obese and the obtuse.

Mortimer Lightwood is present, having been impelled by a curiosity to learn "good society's" reaction to his friend Eugene's marriage adventure. As he anticipates, Lady Tippins raises the question with him directly. With a contemptuous flippancy intended to appear artless and charming, she asks whether the bride "steered herself, skiffed herself, paddled herself, or whatever the technical term may be, to the ceremony?" "However she got there" Lightwood answers, "she graced it." Which throws Lady Tippins into an ecstasy of derisive indignation: ("He means to tell me a horrid female waterman is graceful!") At her instigation, the whole dinner company is resolved into a quasi-Parliamentary committee, to bring home to Lightwood the fact that "such a ridiculous affair is condemned by the whole voice of society."

One by one she collects the opinions of the company:

"The question before the Committee, she says "is, whether a young man of very fair family, good appearance and some talent, makes a fool or a wise man of himself in marrying a female waterman turned factory girl."

"Hardly so, I think," the stubborn Mortimer strikes in, "I take the question to be whether such a man as you describe, Lady Tippins, does right or wrong in marrying a brave woman (I say nothing of her beauty), who has saved his life with wonderful energy and address; whom he knows to be virtuous; and possessed of remarkable qualities; whom he has long admired, and who is deeply attached to him."

"But, excuse me," says Podsnap with his temper and his shirt collar about equally rumpled; "was this young woman ever a female waterman?"

"Never. But she sometimes rowed in a boat with her father, I believe."

General sensation against the young woman. Boots shakes his head. Brewer shakes his head. Buffer shakes his head.

"And now, Mr. Lightwood, was she ever," pursues Podsnap, with his indignation rising high into those hair brushes of his, "a factory girl?"

"Never. But she had some employment in a paper mill, I believe."

General sensation repeated. Brewer says "Oh dear!" Boots says Oh dear! Buffer says Oh dear! All in a rumbling sort of protest.

"Then all I have to say is," returns Podsnap, putting the thing away with his right arm, "that my gorge rises at such a marriage—that it offends and disgusts me—that it makes me sick—and that I desire to know no more about it."—*Our Mutual Friend:* Book IV, Chap. XVII.

On appeal, most of those present speak to similar effect. The contractor (who is alleged to employ directly and indirectly, five hundred thousand men) thinks the man should have bought the young woman a boat and presented her with an annuity equal to so many pounds of beef steak and so many pints of porter per annum. The railway chairman thinks the young woman should have been found a berth in an electric telegraph office "where young women answer very well."

The speculator, worth three hundred and seventy-five thousand pounds, thinks that, as the young woman had no money it was all "Madness and Moonshine." ("A man may do anything lawful for money. But for no money! Bosh!")

So they all go on, until the lot falls at last upon the timid and faded Twemlow, the first cousin of a very Noble Lord:

> Twemlow has the air of being ill at ease as he takes his hand from his fore-head and replies:
>
> "I am disposed to think," says he, "that this is a question of the feelings of a gentleman."
>
> "A gentleman can have no feelings who contracts such a marriage," flushes Podsnap.
>
> "Pardon me," sir, says Twemlow, rather less mildly than usual, "I don't agree with you. If this gentleman's feelings of gratitude, of respect, of admira-tion, and affection induced him (as I presume they did) to marry this lady—"
>
> "This lady!" echoes Podsnap.
>
> "Sir!" returns Twemlow with his wristbands bristling a little, " *you* repeat the word; I repeat the word. This lady. What else would you call her, if the gentleman were present?"
>
> This being something of a poser for Podsnap, he merely waves it away with a speechless wave.
>
> "I say," resumes Twemlow, "if such feelings on the part of this gentleman, induced the gentleman to marry this lady, I think he is the greater gentleman for the action, and makes her the greater lady. I beg to say that, when I use the word gentleman, I use it in the sense in which the degree may be attained by any man. The feelings of a gentleman I hold sacred, and I confess I am not comfortable when they are made the subject of sport or general discussion."
>
> "I should like to know," sneers Podsnap, "whether your noble relation would be of your opinion."
>
> "Mr. Podsnap," retorts Twemlow, "permit me. He might be, or he might not be. I cannot say. But, I could not allow even him to dictate to me on a point of great delicacy upon which I feel strongly."
>
> Somehow a canopy of wet blanket seems to descend upon the company, and Lady Tippins was never known to turn so very greedy, or so very cross.—*Our Mutual Friend:* Book IV, Chap. XVII.

Though the occasion selected for this self-exposure of "good society's" toadyism, flunkeyism, money-grubbing, success worship, and callous self-seeking, is a relatively trivial one, and although the attack is veiled in a sen-timental romantic guise, it is impossible not to see here a deliberate and studied manifestation of contempt for all the essentials of bourgeois society. The very deliberateness of the anti-climax involved in adding this scene as a species of epilogue or final chorus, after the action proper of the novel has been completely rounded off, gives intensity to its sting.

There were many reasons (his friend Forster among them) why Dickens would not venture to write an avowedly political novel upon contemporary themes. And, indeed, the politics of the period were not such as to give much scope to Dickens' special genius. The American Civil War was still raging, and although Gettysburg had been fought and won when *Our Mutual Friend* was commenced, and Grant had taken Vicksburg, it was not nearly so apparent then, as it became after the event, that the pro-slavery rebellion of the South had shot its bolt. Sherman had not then taken Atlanta, still less had he marched from Atlanta to the sea. Grant had only just been made lieutenant-general; the S.S. *Alabama* was still afloat and destroying. From the angle of London it looked, still, as though what all Podsnappery wished for would come to pass; that the slave-owning South might yet win. Dickens himself, at the opening of the struggle had wavered—as did so many—misled by the propaganda which concealed the real issue of the Civil War under a pretence that the " chivalrous and liberty-loving South" was merely fighting to escape from coercion by the sordid, dollar-greedy North. In France, Bonaparte "the Bastard" was still maintaining his parody of his uncle's Empire, to all seeming as strongly as ever.

Garibaldi had visited London, and had received the most astounding ovation ever accorded to any man by Londoners. But he had been induced, somehow or other, to leave the country shortly after. And even unparalleled ovations could not alter the fact that Garibaldi had been defeated at Aspromonte, and that the troops of France were still protecting the temporal power of the Pope in Rome.

As against all these reasons for gloom a genuine Radical could only put the fact, which, as a Radical, he would hardly be able, rightly, to estimate, that half-way through the birth period of *Our Mutual Friend* the International Workingmen's Association had been founded.

But it is just the depressing quality of the then prevalent world outlook which gives significance and point to the aggressive pessimism of *Our Mutual Friend*.

There can be no doubt about this pessimism. It is true that the Boffins triumph, all along the line. True also that John and Bella triumph; and that this is greatly to the advantage of the long-suffering, but amiable Pa Wilfer. So does Mr. Venus triumph in a mild way, and Pleasant Riderhood with him; so does Sloppy triumph. And so, too, do in the end Jenny Wren, Old Riah, Lizzie, Eugene, and, in his way, Mortimer Lightwood.

Even the shrivelled little gentleman Twemlow has his little triumph. And, though in a tragic sense, Betty Higden triumphs, in that she escapes the workhouse which she dreads. But, when it is all summed up, in every case the triumph is "bought with a price." Only after anxiety, suffering, and loss is the triumph achieved; and, when it comes, it is in nearly every case, the negative triumph of an escape from long suffering and peril, rather than the positive triumph of an achieved advance.

Thus the Boffins triumph, in that they are able to do in the end what the novel opens with them wishing to be able to do—-namely, devolve the bulk of their inheritance upon John Harmon and Bella Wilfer his wife. That this end is achieved only after all sorts of difficulties, involving a considerable amount of suffering all round, evidences the negative kind of achievement which constitutes objective triumph in *Old Mutual Friend.*

There is, of course, a positive achievement, subjectively. If John Harmon had not been waylaid and robbed and reported drowned, he would, presumably, have married Bella Wilfer, and have entered upon his inheritance straight away. In the material sense the characters end in the situation in which, but for the intervening mischance, they would have been before the novel began. But in that case there would have been none of that subjective development whereby John, Bella, and the Boffins learn so thoroughly to understand and to appreciate each other. But for the greed, suspicion, and ingratitude of the half-witted Wegg, and his blackmail conspiracy, John Harmon would never have known of the will, which, in fact, left everything to the Boffins. The development of the novel achieves, therefore (for the main characters) just this: John Harmon acquires wealth, not as of right from his misanthropic father, who inflicts injury upon him, even from the grave, but by the grace and favour of a promoted proletarian, Noddy Boffin. Bella Wilfer acquires the escape from poverty she yearns for (and happiness and affection along with it) but only at the price of learning that there are worse things than poverty, courageously endured; that easily-gotten, and unearned, wealth can be even more debasing and corrupting than poverty. Lizzie Hexam escapes from the horrible associations of the riverside, and achieves love and happiness. But she does so at the price of losing her father, and seeing her brother turn out to be a hollow-hearted little monster of selfishness—as well as having to endure the double agony of pursuit by the darkly-furious Bradley Headstone and the, as yet, unregenerate Eugene. Eugene gains, relatively, most of all; he gains Lizzie, and a purpose in life—at the expense of a beating, which brings him close to death's door. Jenny Wren gains in the end, but has paid the price "full measure, pressed down, and running over" in her be-cripplement and in having to endure a rum-sodden horror of a father. Sloppy gains—but only what he has well and truly earned. In fact, so far as the characters representing the common people are concerned, the moral of *Our Mutual Friend* is that, in the lower walks of society, one gets, at best, only what one has earned—if so much.

So far it might seem that there is in *Our Mutual Friend*—at the poverty-pole—a slight balance to the credit of optimism; a balance which is enhanced by the fate of the bad characters, i.e., the elimination of Bradley Headstone, of Rogue Riderhood, and of old Hexam; and the humiliation of Wegg. But quite a different account is rendered at the opposite pole of society. Nemesis, it is true, overtakes the fortune-hunting Lammles; but even here it is not the same sort of Nemesis as is allotted to their opposite numbers in the lower strata of society Rogue Riderhood, for instance, and to Bradley Headstone. And, as though to accentuate this disparity, Mrs. Lammle, shown as one in whom are latent the possibilities of far better things, is left tied for life to the foul-tempered rogue, Alfred Lammle. Fledgby gets his deserts to the extent of a thrashing, and is forced to gorge some—but only some, and no considerable proportion—of his ill-gotten gains. He fares, that is to say, considerably better on the whole than does his opposite number Silas Wegg.

The Veneerings will, we are told, pay the penalty of living beyond their means, and come to smash. But there is no reason to doubt that they will survive it, and find ways and means of acquiring a fresh veneer. That is to say their fate is pretty much the converse of that of John and Bella, in that they are, after the close of the novel, pretty much where they were before it opened. But whereas John and Bella have undergone a chastening suffering in the interval, the Veneerings have undergone an interval of unearned and undeserved opulence and gratifying ostentation. Mr. Twemlow, who has the rudiments of humanity in his shrivelled little carcass, gets a negative reward in that he escapes from Fledgby. But when all is said and done the bulk of the Good Society class—the opulent contractors, the wealthy railway directors, the well-fed and prosperous nonentities, Boots, Brewer, and all the Buffers—remain exactly as they were—stolidly established as the ruling class and power in society. And in the forefront of their phalanx rears his undiminished head the egregious and preposterous Podsnap.

Contrast Podsnap with his opposite number Noddy Boffin, and note that, at the end of the novel, Noddy is actually (though by his own act) poorer than at its opening—while Podsnap has in various ways been protected by fate from any sort of loss—and the class moral of the novel, along with its general balance between optimism and pessimism, is made daylight clear.

In the chapter already quoted, in which Mr. Podsnap instructs the French gentleman on the glories of the British Constitution, occurs a passage directly pertinent to the point we have reached. A sedate, Podsnappian, dance is in progress:

> In the meantime, a stray personage of a meek demeanour, who had wandered to the hearth-rug and got among the heads of tribes assembled there, in conference with Mr. Podsnap, elicited Mr. Podsnap's flush and flourish by a highly unpolite remark; no less than a reference to the circumstance that some half-dozen people had died in the streets of starvation. It was clearly ill-timed after dinner. It was not adapted to the cheek of the young person. It was not in good taste.
>
> "I don't believe it," said Mr. Podsnap, putting it behind him.
>
> The meek man was afraid we might take it as proved because there were the inquests and the Registrar's returns.
>
> "Then it was their own fault," said Mr. Podsnap.
>
> Veneering and other elders of the tribe commended this way out of it. At once a short cut and a broad road.
>
> The man of meek demeanour intimated that truly it would seem, from the facts, as if starvation had been forced upon the culprits in question—as if, in their wretched manner, they had made their weak protests against it—as if they would have taken the liberty of staving it off if they could—as if they would rather not have been starved upon the whole, if perfectly agreeable to all parties.
>
> "There is not," said Mr. Podsnap, flushing angrily, "there is not a country in the world, sir, where so noble a provision is made for the poor as in this country."
>
> The meek man was quite willing to concede that; but perhaps it rendered the matter even worse, as showing that there must be something appallingly wrong somewhere.
>
> "Where?" said Mr. Podsnap.
>
> The meek man hinted, Wouldn't it be well to try, very seriously, to find out where?
>
> "Ah!" said Mr. Podsnap. "Easy to say somewhere; not so easy to say where! But I see what you are driving at. I knew it from the first. Centralization; no. Never with my consent. Not English."
>
> An approving murmur arose from the heads of tribes; as saying, "There you have him! Hold him!"
>
> He was not aware (the meek man submitted of himself) that he was driving at any ization. He had no favourite ization that he knew of. But he certainly was more staggered by these terrible occurrences than he was by names, of howsoever so many syllables. Might he ask, was dying of destitution and neglect necessarily English?
>
> "You know what the population of London is, I suppose?" said Mr. Podsnap. The meek man supposed he did, but supposed that had absolutely nothing to do with it, if its laws were well administered.

"And you know, at least, I hope you know," said Mr. Podsnap with severity, "that Providence has declared that you shall have the poor always with you?" The meek man hoped he knew that.

"I am glad to hear it," said Mr. Podsnap with a portentous air. "I am glad to hear it. It will render you cautious how you fly in the face of Providence."

In reference to that absurd and conventional phrase, the meek man said, for which Mr. Podsnap was not responsible, he the meek man, had no fear of doing anything so impossible; but—

But Mr. Podsnap felt that the time had come for flushing and flourishing this meek man down for good.... —*Our Mutual Friend:* Book I, Chap. XI.

And accordingly he flushed and flourished him down —affirming that it was not for *him* to impugn the workings of Providence, and that, besides, the subject was an odious one, not one to be introduced among "our wives and young persons," etc.

It is obvious that under the figure of the meek man Dickens indicates himself, and under the figure of Podsnap, he indicates that which he hates—the whole self-satisfied, callous, money-greedy, success-worshipping bourgeoisie. That the novel should end—and with it (except for the after-thought of Edwin *Drood* Dickens' whole novel-producing career—with Mr. Podsnap, paunched and prosperous, still dominant—Mr. Twemlow notwithstanding—over all the Boffins, Johns, Bellas, Eugenes, and Lizzies in creation, sums up, in one blast of furious scorn, the net outcome of the works of Dickens' final period.

A comparison of this last-completed novel with his first brings out sharply the nature of the development he had achieved. In point of plot-construction the end-novel is as carefully reticulated and planned as the beginning-novel is planless and tumbled together. *Per contra*—the end-novel is as deliberately grim, scornful and bitter as the beginning-novel is irresponsibly festive, frivolous, and light-hearted.

There is much more in this than a simple quantitative progression from exuberant youth to sober maturity. There is no note, for instance, of disillusionment as to human nature. On the contrary, it is the earlier work which in places affects an adolescent cynicism which in the mature work would have jarred inexpressibly. Fundamentally Samuel Pickwick, Esq., and Noddy Boffin each finish in an identical position—as each a minor-providence to his little world. But contrast the gorgeous absurdity of the Pickwick Club, in full session, with the repulsive and vulpine pseudo-rationality of the dinner company at the Veneerings and there is revealed in a flash a complete revolution in Dickens' attitude towards bourgeois society.

That Samuel Pickwick belonged as essentially to the bourgeoisie as Noddy Boffin belonged to the proletariat, underscores the moral beyond all cavil.

Certainly we miss profoundly the whole multitude of delightful freaks and oddities who play their pranks and tumble over each other in every chapter in *Pickwick*. Certainly Alfred Lammle the fortune-hunter is a sour mouthful after his opposite number Alfred Jingle. But no less certainly the whole riotous company of coach-men, country-men, medical students, editors, politicians, lawyers, preachers and old women who frisk their way through *Pickwick* would have been as out of place in the world of *Our Mutual Friend* as a Hitler, or a Goering in fairy-land.

It was not that the sense of fun had died down in Dickens or that his power of creation had been exhausted. It was the world that had changed for Dickens, and with it his sense of responsibility to, and for, that world.

With *Our Mutual Friend* finished, Dickens turned his energies to public readings, in the strain, excitement and exhaustion of which he wore himself out. And so in 1870, he found peace at last. Whole troops of working-men got leave from work that they might file past his open grave and pay their last tribute to the writer whom they had literally loved as a close personal friend—though in the flesh their eyes had never lighted upon him.

PART III.

DICKENS' OUTLOOK
AS A WHOLE

DICKENS' friend and biographer, Forster, was clearly worried by the change that came over Dickens' politico-social outlook. He puts the best possible face upon it, and defends his friend stoutly; but he is clearly ill at ease about it all the same. He half tries to dismiss it as a mere mannerism—the result of "periodical writing." The effect of this type of writing was, he says:

> ...observable in the increased impatience of allusions to national institutions and conventional distinctions to be found in his later books. Party divisions he cared for less and less, as life moved on; but the decisive peremptory, dog-matic style into which a habit of rapid remark on topics of the day will betray the most candid and considerate commentator, displayed its influence, per-haps not always consciously to himself, in the underlying tone of bitterness that runs through the books that followed *Copperfield.*—Forster: *Dickens,* Book Eleventh, III.

In August 1854, Forster tells us, Dickens wrote to him to say that he had "with regret," abandoned a project:

> "and with it my hope to have made every man in England feel something of the contempt for the House of Commons that I have. We shall never do any-thing until the sentiment is universal."

To this belief Dickens, in his letters to Forster, returns again and again. It finds expression, for instance, in a paper included in his *Uncommercial Traveller,* one written in 1867, in praise of a co-operative effort, a "Self supporting, Cooking Depot for the Working Classes" in Commercial Street, Whitechapel:

> If working men have seemed rather slow to appreciate advantages of combi-nation which have saved the pockets of gentlemen, and enhanced their comforts, it is because working men could scarcely, for want of capital, origi-nate such combinations without help, and because help has not been sepa-rable from that great impertinence Patronage. The instinctive revolt of his spirit against patronage is a quality much to be respected in the English working man. It is the base of the base of his best qualities. ...It is to me a

proof of his self-control that he never strikes out pugilistically right and left when addressed as one of "My friends" or "My assembled friends," that he does not become unappeasable and run-amuck like a Malay when he sees a biped in broadcloth getting on to a platform to talk to him; that any pretence of improving his mind does not instantly drive him out of his mind, and cause him to toss his obliging patron like a mad bull.—*Uncommercial Traveller:* loc cit.

Dickens goes on to describe vividly how often he has heard the working man lectured as if he were a little charity child. If the tools the worker works with— spades, axes, forges, engines, etc.—were all toys in a paper box, and he the baby who played with them, the workers, Dickens says, "could not have been discoursed to more impertinently and absurdly than I have heard him discoursed to times innumerable."

> Consequently, not being a fool or a fawner, he has come to acknowledge his patronage by virtually saying: "Let me alone. If you understand me no better than *that,* sir or madam, let me alone. You mean very well, I dare say, but I don't like it, and I won't come here again to have any more of it."
> Whatever is done for the comfort and advancement of the working man must be so far done by himself as that it is maintained by himself. And there must be in it no touch of condescension or shadow of patronage.—*Ibid.*

And in the last public speech Dickens ever made, less than twelve months before he died, he affirmed that his faith in the people who do the governing of the country was "infinitesimal" while his faith in the People they govern was "illimitable."

Forster agrees that in his "political discontents" Dickens was "perfectly sincere," (in passing, it is notable that one of the chief counts in the indictment Dickens draws against Podsnap is the fact that he was "quite satisfied") and Forster admits, too, that the things Dickens said ("with too much bitterness") "he not only believed, but had (Alas!) too much ground for believing." Forster cites a letter from Dickens of April 27th. 1855:

> A country which is discovered to be in this tremendous condition as to its war affairs; with an enormous black cloud of poverty in every town which is spreading and deepening every hour; and not one man in two thousand knowing anything about, or even believing in, its existence; with a non-working aristocracy and a silent parliament; and everybody for himself and nobody for the rest; this is the prospect, and I think it a very deplorable one.

This was written while Dickens was at work upon *Little Dorrit,* and it expresses, concretely, the whole pervading atmosphere and implied background of that novel. It was not the Marshalsea as such (which in fact had been abolished several years before the novel was written, along with the cruder forms of imprisonment for debt) against which Dickens levelled his attack in *Little Dorrit;* he attacked fiercely all the things indicated in that letter of April 27th, 1855, down to and including the sense that at its best (though *Little Dorrit* does marry her Arthur, and they do live in moderate happiness "ever after") the prospect is most definitely "a deplorable one."

Forster agrees that the facts are pretty much as Dickens states them. Yet he still maintains that Dickens was "too bitter," and "too angry." For that reason he seeks an explanation for this excess of feeling partly in the bad habits induced by journalism, and partly in Dickens' "unhappy experiences as a child."

This latter explanation is worse than worthless, and shows, incidentally, how very much greater Dickens was than his biographer. Dickens' childhood-experience was not at all as unique as Forster suggests. And Dickens knew that it was not at all exceptional. Other men had suffered in childhood, and that too less acutely than Dickens suffered—and men, too, who rose less rapidly and to a lower degree of fame and affluence—but they remembered their early sufferings only in the Bounderby fashion, as an enhancement of the personal merit of their eventual success. That instead of treating his own case thus as cruelly exceptional, and taking the Bounderby line (saying, I had to put up with worse than they, and still I rose above it!) Dickens should have flamed with increasing indignation against the Bounderbys to the end showed him to be the fine, large-hearted Radical he was. When Dickens himself tasted suffering as a child, it gave him a reason why no child ought ever to have such sufferings to endure.

Forster's philistine imperviousness to the obvious is accentuated by the fact that he himself reveals the real explanation for Dickens' growing bitterness—without being aware of it. "It will be remembered of Dickens always," he said,

> that he desired to set right what was wrong, that he held no abuse to be unimprovable, that he left none of the evils named exactly as he found them, and that to influences drawn from his writings were due not a few of the salutary changes which marked the age in which he lived.— Forster: *Life of Dickens,* Book Eleventh, III.

Forster says here both too much and too little; but he also reveals incidentally the secret he himself has missed. He says too much in attributing to Dickens the sole, or at any rate the primary, credit for the reform of such abuses as were reformed in Dickens' lifetime. Dickens himself would have maintained stoutly—what was indeed the truth—that he only joined in, and lent a hand to, a fight that others had started before him. That Dickens' contribution to the fight put the issue in some cases beyond doubt, is, of course, true beyond question. But there were other evils against which Dickens fought which, far from being abated in consequence of his onslaught, grew worse; evils which still, more or less, endure. And of these Forster says nothing, though in them lies the explanation of the thing he is seeking.

He sees, as is most just, that with Dickens the desire to set right what was wrong, was the paramount cause of his attack. But since, unlike Dickens, he sees only incidental social abuses awaiting remedy, and does not see, as Dickens came to see, that it was not incidentals only, but bourgeois society itself, that constituted the wrong, Forster cannot see the cause of Dickens' growing bitterness—his growing sense that the only possible remedy for so vast an evil, that of complete social revolution, was one that then seemed completely unattainable.

Dickens as an Observer

Forster speaks of Dickens' recollections of his childhood sufferings, and notes, as he could hardly fail to note, Dickens' amazingly detailed memory. He does not note, as he should, how this super acuteness of physical vision contributed a basic element to Dickens' artistic method. For with that acuteness of physical vision, and that unerring recollection of every detail in the thing seen, went an abnormally complete grasp of the thing in the totality of its natural connections. It is often said that Dickens could only draw characters "in the flat"—never "in the round"—and it is usual to cite in proof the cases of Mrs. Micawber who would "never leave" Mr. Micawber, and of Uriah Heep who was always *"umble."* This criticism is simply suicidal. The point about Mrs. Micawber is that she has every reason for leaving Mr. Micawber—especially as she belongs to a family which strongly disapproves of him—but that never for an instant would she dream of letting him leave *her.* Whole chapters of pseudo-analytical psychologizing would not tell us more about Mrs. Micawber than is told in her absurdly romantic utterance at every moment of crisis that she "will never leave Mr. Micawber." So too, with Uriah Heep; it is not that he is, in fact, humble; but, on the contrary, the fact that he most emphatically is *not* in the least capable of humility, or even of being humbled, which is the essence of the malignantly self-seeking Uriah Heep. That he should, in his malevolent cunning, think (and, in fact, find, up to a point) that the pose of cringing humility "pays"—that he most affects to be *'umble* where he has most intent to do mischief—this is the essence of Uriah Heep. And here again by means of a sensory image, and all that it implies, the whole nature of the villain is revealed—in the cold clamminess of his hands—as surely as a whole skeleton is revealed to a skilled anatomist by a single bone.

Dickens in fact grasped intuitively and presented artistically, a truth which only Marx and Engels have comprehended and explained theoretically. In bourgeois society—the highest form of society based upon the division of labour in production, as distinct from the synthetic organization of labour in a Socialist system of production—there goes on necessarily that "fractionalizing" of the whole man which to the Greeks (Aristotle particularly) constituted the essence of slavery. Engels states the case thus:

In every society in which production has developed spontaneously—and our present society is of this type—it is not the producers who control the means of production, but the means of production which control the producers. In such a society each new lever of production is necessarily transformed into a new means of subjecting the producers to the means of production. This is most of all true of that lever of production which, prior to the introduction of large-scale industry, was by far the most powerful—the division of labour. The first great division of labour, the separation of town and country, condemned the rural population to thousands of years of degradation, and the people of the towns to subjection to each one's individual trade. It destroyed the basis of the intellectual development of the former, and the physical development of the latter. When the peasant appropriates his land and the citizen his trade, to just the same extent the land appropriates the peasant and his trade the citizen. *In the division of labour man is also divided.* All other physical and mental faculties are sacrificed to the development of one single activity. This stunting of man's faculties grows in the same measure as the division of labour, which attains its highest development in manufacture.... And not only the labourers but also the classes directly or indirectly exploiting the labourers are made subject, through the division of labour, to the tool of their function; the empty-minded bourgeois to his own capital and his own thirst for profits; the lawyer to his fossilized legal conceptions, which dominate him as a power independent of him; the "educated classes" in general to their manifold local limitations and one-sidedness, to their own physical and mental short-sightedness, to their stunted specialized education and the fact that they are chained for life to this specialized activity itself—even when this specialized activity is merely that of doing nothing—ENGELS: *Anti-Duhring,* Chap. III, iii.

Dickens was neither philosopher enough, nor sociologist enough, to grasp this truth theoretically. But he was, being probably the greatest master of reportage that ever lived, acutely conscious of the fact intuitively in its empirical-phenomenal forms. He drew men "in the flat" because he saw them primarily "in the flat." And he saw them so because so they were—because the constitution of society had flattened them, past repair.

That which is charged against Dickens as a defect— that he drew not personalities but caricatures—should, in fact, be credited to him as a virtue. He saw men so, as caricatures of themselves, because so they were in actual life and reality, and so, in the circumstances, they could not help but be.

Dickens, it is well known, only became a novelist by accident. He had not—which again is charged against him as a demerit—any of that adoring regard for the novel *per se* as a distinct and distinctive Art form, with its own peculiar and uniquely distinguishing laws of motion, which was erected into a cult by Gustave Flaubert and his school. Dickens, for himself, remained all his life, just a plain "writer." He remained, in fact, to the end, that which he was when he began to live by his own exertions—a reporter. His first impetus towards creative writing came from one of his first editors, John Black, who edited the *Morning Chronicle*—the organ of the Nonconformist Liberals—from 1818 to 1843. John Stuart Mill said of him:

> I have always considered Black as the first journalist who carried criticism and the spirit of reform into the details of English institutions. Those who are not old enough to remember those times can hardly believe what the state of public discussion then was.—MILL: *Autobiography.*

From John Black,Dickens received just the encouragement he needed to induce him to make the most of his marvellous natural gift of observation—of seeing things in all their detail, just as, in actuality, they were. From John Black too, he received the needful encouragement to release, instead of suppressing, his talent for satirical and denunciatory reforming attack. Dickens lacked that pseudo "artistic" detachment—that leisured class aloofness from actuality—which makes it possible for a man to see his characters with the personal unconcern of a naturalist studying cheese-mites under a microscope. For Dickens there was always present the consciousness of a personal responsibility for "doing something about it." And this all the more because, while he wrote, he *was*, subjectively, each of his characters in turn.

It did not satisfy Dickens to make it plain that such scoundrels as Squeers, Pecksniff and Fledgby existed; he simply had to give them before he had done with them, if only on paper, the physical thrashing he would, undoubtedly, have wished to give them in real life. Did his art suffer from this excess of propagandist passion? For the "all art is useless" school it did most assuredly. But by the same token, for the "all art is propaganda" school, this quality must be counted unto him as a superlative merit.

Let the aesthetic problem be solved as it may, it remains a fact that for good or ill, Dickens never lost the initial, reforming impetus which John Black helped to confirm in him as well as to release.

Dickens and the Conventionally Pious

As we have seen it was the growing sense of the nonadequacy of all the conventional "reforms"—of the lack of any available remedy—which caused the intensifying bitterness expressed in Dickens' later novels. Early on he learned to be more than dissatisfied with the moralizing Nonconformists; the hole-and-corner temperance reformers and tract distributing "philanthropists." He attacked them in the persons of Stiggins (and the Brick Lane Branch) in *Pickwick;* he attacked them again, in passing, in the *Old Curiosity Shop* and in *Dombey.* In the *Old Curiosity Shop,* the boy Kit's mother goes to a Little Bethel, where, much to Kit's indignation, the cheerful, hardworking soul is made miserable; and little Jacob, Kit's brother, is informed that he is a "child of the devil." In *Dombey* the termagant Mrs. MacStinger attends, appropriately, the ministrations of the Rev. Melchizedek Howler, who is, theologically, a match for her at her worst. In *Bleak House* Dickens delivers his heaviest assault upon this brood of free-lance evangelists in the person of the ineffable Chadband, who is to Stiggins as Pecksniff is to Job Trotter, before his reformation.

It was, probably (though the fact seems to have been too thoroughly suppressed by Forster to be recoverable) Dickens' hatred of self-glorifying, evangelical-teetotal, tract-distributing ("Come to Jesus or Go to Hell") Nonconformity that was at the back of the failure of his attempt to edit the *Daily News*—the journal which replaced the *Morning Chronicle* as the organ of the Liberal Dissenters in 1846. Certainly it was his hatred of the "Exeter Hall gang" which led him into the worst political mistake of his life; his support in 1865-7 of the agitation got up by Thomas Carlyle in defence of Governor Eyre of Jamaica.

Carlyle was the means of dragging both Dickens and Ruskin into that piratical "galley," and both became heartily ashamed of themselves when they fully realized what they had done. All three were actuated by the one motive—hatred of ranting-canting-evangelical-humbug; but Carlyle in addition had reached, *via* his pet dogma of Great Man worship, the stage of being ready to take any Colonel Blimp who hanged an evangelist as a World Deliverer. The Exeter Hall Nonconformists were greatly chagrined when they learned that the pious Negro Baptists over whom they were agitating had been actually concerned for real material grievances; had been, indeed, engaged upon a distinctly revolutionary agitation. Carlyle and the Strong Man worshippers were equally chagrined when they learned that their hero had been, in actuality, a fussy old gentleman with the wind up; who was so little of a strong man, that he meekly allowed himself to be made responsible for every piece of cowardly savagery indulged in by the military juniors he was supposed to control.

The episode is interesting to us in so far as it shows, firstly, how strong was Dickens' bias against proselytizing evangelical piety; and secondly, how greatly his anti-parliamentarian prejudice served, by keeping him out of concrete political struggle, to deprive him of a guiding chart and compass just when he most had need of them.

If Dickens had an unconcealed grudge against the Nonconformists he shows no great love for the established Church, either. And while, like a good Liberal, he is vigorously opposed to the legal subjection of Catholics, he has clearly, and avowedly, no love at all or liking, for the Roman Church. In truth, although Dickens, at times, is rather prone to intrude his sentimental Jesusism —and to talk with what, nowadays, we should call downright unctuousness about "Our Saviour" (if, that is to say, Forster was not responsible for inserting these passages in Dickens' MS.) none the less for that Dickens is a singularly non-religious writer.

Gladstone, at the time of its appearance, made a diary note of *Nicholas Nickleby*. He was much impressed—but he noted that there was "no Church in the book, and the motives are not those of religion." That is true more or less of all Dickens' novels. There is no churchgoing in *Pickwick;* none in *Oliver Twist,* beyond the very casual fact that Henry Maylie becomes, in the end, a clergyman; none in *Nickleby;* and even in the *Old Curiosity Shop* Little Nell visits the old church, usually, only in the periods when there is no religious service. Although *Barnaby Rudge* turns on the theme of the No Popery riots, there is no church-going in it. Neither is there in *Martin Chuzzlewit,* although Tom Pinch is the church organist and, of course, Pecksniff has a pew in the church. Some casual church-going is described in *Bleak House,* but so little, and that so much a mere matter of form, as to throw into sharp contrast the gloomy piety of Esther's godmother-aunt, the assiduous early morning church-going of Mrs. Pardiggle and her unfortunate offspring, and the oozing piety of Mr. Chadband. From *Hard Times* we have already quoted the scornful passage in which Dickens describes the many denominations competing for recruits from the workers of Coketown, and the uniform antipathy with which these workers regarded them all. *Little Dorrit* in a sense has, as its chief "villain," the gaoler-like theology that made Mrs. Clennam a monster of vengeful tyranny. In the *Tale of Two Cities* religion is mentioned, only in so far as Mrs. Cruncher "flops (i.e., on to her knees to pray) against" Mr. Cruncher's spare time occupation of body-snatching; while the aristocratic Princes of the Church in France play their part in precipitating the revolution. In *Great Expectations* religion is mentioned mainly because the grotesque Mr. Wopsle is a parish clerk, before he ventures upon the stage. In *Our Mutual Friend* a Church of England clergyman plays a minor part, with credit. But this is in his capacity of distributor of material benefits, and even here Dickens takes the chance of having a fling at the hypocritical pretences of the tea-and-sugar-greedy old women who become filled with anxiety for theological information, whenever they feel a new dole distribution ought to be due. Also, although the parson's wife is shown in quite a favourable light generally, even she develops bigoted suspicions (as to possible proselytizing) when she finds that Lizzie's employers are not only the biggest employers in the village, but are also Jews. (She finds to her relief that their only interference with the village school is to stock its garden with shrubs and flowers!)

All things considered, the absence of any theological bias in Dickens is remarkable. He is not, it must be conceded, openly anti-religious; and there are to be found in his novels passages, as we have noted, which imply a belief in Jesus, in the "excellence" of the Sermon on the Mount, and in immortal life in "Heaven." But, on the other hand, as to this last item, Ruskin expressly affirms (in *Fors Clavigera)* that Dickens did "not a whit" believe in any such thing. And although Ruskin is not too safe a witness in such a matter as this (since having lost all religious faith himself he had a way of supposing that everybody he had any respect for must have done the same), these passages have so much the tang of labels stuck on for effect as to rouse a suspicion that Ruskin was, possibly, speaking from knowledge.

Quite definitely it can be said that, if every passage in Dickens which implies a belief in "Our Saviour," or in a future life, were eliminated, the novels would suffer no recognizable change—beyond their gain from the removal of a discordant note. In his admiration for the Sermon on the Mount, as also for the character of Jesus as indicated in the Gospels, Dickens does no more than strike an attitude previously struck by Voltaire, by Thomas Paine and by most of the Deists of their school. Even the future life passages (interpreted with some latitude) might be matched with parallel passages from the works of these great "Infidels." Forster is, of course, of little help here. He says that Dickens for many years rented a pew in the nearest parish church. But how far this was done as a compliance with convention—how far for himself, and how far for Mrs. Dickens and the children—Forster does not say. He admits that, for a period, Dickens transferred his spiritual "custom" to a Unitarian Chapel. And that, of itself, is, when the temper of the time is considered, significant of much.

There is, of course, the evidence of Dickens' will. In this document (dated May 12th, 1869) Dickens "commits his soul to the mercy of God, through Our Lord and Saviour Jesus Christ"—a phrase pious enough to satisfy even Little Bethel. But the estimation to be placed upon its literal truthfulness is rendered doubtful by two weighty considerations.

It is followed by these words: "and I exhort my dear children humbly to try to guide themselves by the teaching of the New Testament *in its broad spirit* [our italics] and to put no faith in any man's narrow construction of its letter here or there." This is as near to a repudiation of a literal interpretation of the New Testament as words could go without actually affirming it. The omission of the Old Testament is very significant; the warning against "any man's narrow construction" is in all but actual terms a repudiation of all the creeds and formularies of all the churches. Very many avowed "freethinkers" of Dickens' day could have used, and did use, similar language. It is less "religious" in form and in content, than many a passage from Strauss, from Renan, or from Auguste Comte. Even taken at its face value this clause is clearly at fisticuffs with the sentence preceding, with its "soul" and its "Lord and Saviour Jesus Christ."

Two alternatives seem to offer: either Dickens was (in the "Lord and Saviour" sentence) indulging in a deliberate humbug, or, Dickens was, to the end, still halting between two opinions. It is even possible that, to an extent, both causes were operating.

The Blasphemy Laws in Dickens' Day

The most natural explanation is, however, that the phrase is a legal, conventional one, inserted by the legal draughtsman of the will as a matter of course and rote, and retained by Dickens as a safeguard against a possible attempt to upset the will.

Until Lord Chief Justice Coleridge's judgment in the case of *Regina v. Foote and Ramsay* in 1883, the common law of England held that "Christianity was parcel of the laws of England," that any denial of the truth of Christianity was, however temperately worded, a misdemeanour punishable by fine and/or imprisonment. Bequests for purposes deemed by the High Court to be in contravention of this law (as, for instance, bequests to secular societies for the purposes of their association, or to notorious freethinkers such as Charles Bradlaugh) were set aside as void in law.

As late as 1887—Lord Chief Justice Coleridge's judgment notwithstanding—it was held by the Vice Chancellor in the County Palatine of Lancaster Chancery Court, that a bequest of £500 as a trust to Chas. Bradlaugh and George Payne for purposes privately communicated to them by the testator, was void and inoperative. The Vice Chancellor accepted the view that if, for example, the trust were for such a purpose as the establishment of "a college to teach that the Scriptures were to be disregarded by all sensible men, and were a mere collection of fables and myths" it would be illegal. As the legatees could not prove, in law, that the trust was not for any such purpose, the court held that these provisions of the will must be set aside. And this view was upheld by the Court of Appeal.

A similar view was taken later still in the case of the will of John Beswick who left £400 to the Oldham Secular Society to be paid on the death of his wife, should she survive him. Mrs. Beswick died in 1902 and the will was contested successfully. The Vice Chancellor held that, Lord Chief Justice Coleridge's judgment notwithstanding, the Oldham Secular Society, while not being in itself an unlawful association, was not one that could lawfully take a bequest. That is to say, according to Vice Chancellor Sir Charles Hall, while this secular society was not one prohibited by law, it was not one that could claim the protection of the law either. It was legally a nonrecognizable body, and that because, particularly, it held that, "Theology is condemned by reason as superstitious and mischievous, an enemy of progress."

These decisions, coming after the date of Dickens' death, cannot, of course, have influenced the wording of his will. But they were based upon earlier decisions in cases which determined the state of the law as it stood in 1869. The leading case was Briggs *v.* Hartley in 1850. Here a legacy was left for "the best essay on natural theology, treating it as a science, and demonstrating the truth, harmony, and infallibility of the evidence on which it is founded, and the perfect accordance of such evidence with reason... tending, as other sciences do, but in a higher degree, to improve and elevate man's nature, and to render him a wise, happy, and exalted being." This legacy was set aside on the ground that the bequest was "inconsistent with Christianity." Readers will not fail to note that the terms in which "natural theology" is described, are just those which Dickens himself would have chosen to describe his own standpoint.

This judgment was given, it will be seen, while Dickens was at work upon the concluding chapters of *David Copperfield.* Hence it is safe to conclude that even if Dickens himself had not been as well acquainted with the law as he was, such a judgment was bound to be known to his friend, the lawyer John Forster. So that, even if Dickens himself had wished otherwise, John Forster (who drafted his will) would never have regarded it as "safe" without the pious "tag" about "committing" his "soul" to the care of "Our Lord and Saviour Jesus Christ." In itself this sentence proves, therefore, just nothing at all about Dickens' private theological beliefs; while the sentence which follows it implies a great deal in the anti-religious sense. Taken in conjunction they give a very characteristic picture of the time of which it was said that the foremost and most progressive group then living—the group which derived directly from Jeremy Bentham and the elder Mill, and which had as its outstanding members John Stuart Mill, George Henry Lewes, "George Eliot" and Herbert Spencer—held as the first article of their faith the dictum: "There is no God; but that is a family secret!"

Dickens was not one of this group; in fact, on points, he was definitely hostile to it. At the same time, his orbit intersected that of this group, and he was on friendly terms with most of its members. He was one of the very first to see the merit of, and to acclaim, the first work to appear under the name "George Eliot." And he knew, and shared theatre-going enthusiasms with, George Henry Lewes. That his theological views did not differ very widely from those of the translator of Strauss and Feuerbach (who later adopted the penname of "George Eliot") or of her free-marriage husband, the English apostle of Auguste Comte, seems a very probable conclusion.

Must we conclude that the "Our Saviour" and "gone to Heaven" passages in Dickens' novels were nothing but conscious and deliberate pieces of humbug? Hardly so, although there was at that time plenty of excuse if a popular writer who depended wholly upon the month by month sale of his writings for the support of himself and a large family of dependants, played for safety even at the cost of a little pious humbug. (Self-consciousness of guilt may have added extra venom to Dickens' picture of Pecksniff, just as guilty self-consciousness seems certainly to have added an extra stroke or two to Bella Wilfer's temporary lapse into the vice of mercenariness, from which she, to her creator's joy, so splendidly recovers). In the circumstances, some measure of humbug in regard to the conventional creed was almost unavoidable.

Dickens, it must be remembered, began his public career during a brief lull between two fierce periods of legal repression of "blasphemy" and "sedition." The furious wave of prosecutions which followed the publication first of Paine's *Rights of Man* (1792) and then of his *Age of Reason* (1797) had slackened slightly after the suppression of all working-class political and corresponding societies by the Act of 1799. It broke out again with the prosecution in 1811 of Daniel Isaac Eaton, for the publication of the (so-called) third part of the *Age of Reason,* and swelled into a raging storm after the close of the Napoleonic Wars in 1815.

In 1817 Shelley was deprived of the custody of his children (on the grounds of his irreligion) by a judgment of Lord Chancellor Eldon. In the same year a bookseller in Portsea was charged with publishing blasphemous publications and making no defence was given twelve months' imprisonment and mulcted in a fine of £100. William Hone, the bookseller, in the same year, successfully defended himself against three distinct indictments for blasphemy—one of the very few occasions on which anyone charged with this offence has ever escaped. Richard Carlile, who was under arrest for selling the "blasphemies" Hone was charged with publishing, was discharged without a trial after Hone's third acquittal. Carlile was, however, charged again in 1819, for selling Paine's *Age of Reason,* and was sentenced to three years' imprisonment and a fine of £1,5oo (he to be kept imprisoned until the fine was paid, which in the end cost him three more years in prison). With this began the great battle of Richard Carlile and his shopmen. Carlile's wife took his place, and got two years' imprisonment. His sister took her place, and got two years, plus £500 fine (which actually meant another year in gaol). Thereafter the breach was filled by volunteers after volunteers, who quietly took their places, first behind the counter, then in the dock, and ultimately in gaol. In the end over 150 persons, all obscure working men and working women, served between them 250 years' imprisonment, and kept it up, until the Government sickened and the prosecution of the *Age of Reason* (and similar works such as Shelley's *Queen Mab* and Palmer's *Principles of Nature)* came to an end.

By the beginning of 1827 Carlile and his shopmen were all at liberty, and the sale of the *Age of Reason* and kindred publications, went on without interference.

Prosecutions for blasphemy and sedition did not, however, end. In 1827, and again in 1831, the Rev. Robert Taylor, Carlile's chief associate, was indicted for blasphemy and sentenced first to one, and on the next occasion, to two years' imprisonment. Carlile himself was attacked for "sedition"—which mainly consisted in references to the mummery of monarchism and to the discontents of the Dorsetshire labourers (at the time reported to be in revolt) in speeches delivered at the Rotunda, Blackfriars, and reprinted in Carlile's (unstamped and therefore illegal) paper, the *Republican*. He was sentenced to two years' imprisonment and a fine of £200. Cobbett was also prosecuted for his reference to the Dorsetshire labourers, but the jury failed to agree, and the prosecution was abandoned.

From then onward public attention was too much occupied with the Reform Bill, and following that with the battle of the "unstamped press" (which Carlile helped to open) for blasphemy prosecutions to be fashionable. But with the rise of Owenite Socialism and Chartism, these prosecutions began again.

John Cleave, a Chartist, was convicted of publishing "blasphemy" in London in 1840. In the same year, Henry Heywood, a Radical publisher, was similarly convicted in Manchester; while Henry Hetherington, the editor and publisher of the *Poor Man's Guardian* (the leading champion of the "great unstamped") was indicted, and convicted, in London.

Hetherington, always a fighter, hit upon a clever mode of reprisal. In the interval, then customary, between conviction and sentence, he caused "information and complaint" to be laid as from the "common informer" against the leading booksellers and publishers of London, headed by Edward Moxon (publisher of the works of Tupper, Tennyson, Browning and other poets) for publishing and circulating a "blasphemous" work, namely Shelley's *Queen Mab!* As the convictions against this work lay thick and heavy in the law reports of the days of the great Carlile battle, no defence was possible. However reluctantly, the Judge had to direct the jury to convict, which accordingly they did. Hetherington, however, did not attend to "pray a sentence." He had scored his point. The Attorney General, who had appeared in his private capacity as counsel for Moxon, had been forced to bring forward every plea possible as to the undesirability of prosecutions for "blasphemy," and the Judge on the bench had had to do the same, out of deference to the character of the accused, and to the pleadings of the leader of the Bar. Besides, instead of the usual savage sentence, Hetherington himself had escaped with no more than four months' imprisonment—in the Marshalsea! It was the beginning of an end to blasphemy prosecutions, for a generation. True, a batch of "Socialists" were convicted; Charles Southwell, editor of the *Oracle of Reason,* an Owenite journal, was sentenced, in January 1842, to twelve months' imprisonment, and £100 fine. In May of the same year, his successor as editor, George Jacob Holyoake, an Owenite "social missionary," was sentenced to six months, imprisonment at Cheltenham. Holyoake's successor, Thomas Patterson, was sentenced in London in January 1843, to a fine of forty shillings (which he refused to pay) or one month in default (which he "did"). In the same year the same Thomas Patterson was sentenced to fifteen months in Edinburgh, while Thomas Finlay, in June 1843, was sentenced to sixty days in default of a fine of £40, also in Edinburgh. In January 1844, Matilda Roalfe was sentenced, also in Edinburgh, to two months' imprisonment. All these charges were based upon the publications issued from an Owenite bookshop Patterson and his associates had attempted to establish first in London, then in Edinburgh.

Except for the solitary case of Thomas Pooley, which, in 1857, roused the fury of both John Stuart Mill and Henry Thomas Buckle, this was the end of blasphemy prosecutions until 1883, when they were revived as part of the struggle to exclude Bradlaugh from Parliament.

In all these blasphemy cases, which continued, it will have been noted, down to and beyond the end of *Martin Chuzzlewit* and of Dickens' first period, it was held that "Christianity is parcel of the laws of England," that any denial of the "inspiration" and "authority" of the Bible, or of the existence of God, or of the divinity of Jesus Christ, was a crime in law. And that was the state of the law during the whole of Dickens' lifetime. That he should rather choose to seem a humbug than run the risk of having his will set aside would be quite forgivable in Dickens, even if we were not sure that his lawyer would be bound anyway to want to insert the customary references to "God," "soul," and "Saviour" as a matter of legal obligation.

Religion: The Law: The Family

But, all speculation and guesswork apart, Dickens' theology, even taken at its face value as shown in the novels, was too closely similar to that prevalent in educated middle-class circles in his day to cause surprise.

He seems to have believed in some sort of God—or, as it has been defined, "in a sort of a kind of a *something,* that does something or other, somehow"—but he obviously has as little patience as Jerry Cruncher had with people who "flop" as a substitute for working. And he hates without disguise the Fire-and-Brimstone theology of the Hell-fire school. His Mrs. Clennam, and still more his drawing of the Murdstones, is enough to show that. Towards the end of *David Copperfield* he makes Mr. Chillip discourse on Murdstone's religion:

> "Mrs. Chillip... quite electrified me, by pointing out that Mr. Murdstone sets up an image of himself and calls it the Divine Nature.... The ladies are great observers, sir!"
>
> "Intuitively," said I, to his great delight.
>
> "I am very happy to receive such support in my opinion, sir," he rejoined... "Mr. Murdstone delivers public addresses sometimes, and it is said—in short, sir, it is said by Mrs. Chillip—that the darker the tyrant he has lately been, the more ferocious is his doctrine."
>
> "I believe Mrs. Chillip to be perfectly right," said I.
>
> "Mrs. Chillip does go so far as to say," pursued that meekest of little men, much encouraged, "that what such people miscall their religion, is a vent for their bad humours and arrogance. And do you know, I must say sir," he continued, mildly laying his head on one side, "that I *don't* find authority for Mr. and Miss Murdstone in the New Testament?"
>
> "I never found it either!" said I.—*David Copperfield:* Chap. LIX.

This is a recurring note in Dickens; the disbelief in, and active dislike of the punitive theology of the Hellfire school. He was, no doubt, among the many who rejoiced when, in 1865—just as *Our Mutual Friend* was concluding—Lord Chancellor Westbury, after a famous appeal case, "dismissed Hell with costs, and took away from orthodox members of the Church of England their last hope of everlasting damnation." In plain English, the Lord Chancellor held, in the case of the authors of *Essays and Reviews,* that a belief in an eternity of punishment in Hell could not be proved from Scripture, and was not therefore obligatory upon members of the Church of England. That the action should have been brought at all, and in the case of a work so mildly rationalistic as the *Essays and Reviews,* as late as 1865, speaks volumes for the state of mind of even the educated well-to-do in Early and Middle Victorian England. Dickens, in the main, judged on the evidence of his novels, clung as long as he could—possibly, with misgivings, to the end of his life—to the view typical of the English (petit-bourgeois) "genius for compromise." He did not apparently believe in Hell, nor in the sort of God who would use a Hell, as a Tory Government would use Newgate or the Marshalsea to keep the poor, and the rebellious, in order. But he seems, positively, to have yearned for excuses to believe in Heaven— especially for little chidren who die young!

Much of what seems to us extravagant and mawkish sentimentalizing (such as that over the death-beds of Little Nell and Paul Dombey) seems to have at the back of it this pathetic dilemma, that he, like so many of his contemporaries, could not quite believe in Heaven, really—not for grown-ups—but at the same time he could not bear to part with the belief that something other than extinction awaited a bright and dearly-loved child.

Marx's contention that it is not possible wholly to break away from supernaturalism and superstition without breaking finally away from the standpoint of bourgeois society, was never better exemplified than in the inconsistency and vacillation in regard to religion of so great a man, and so genuine a realist as Charles Dickens.

For, however weak and inconsistent Dickens may have been and was, in clinging to a sentimental half-belief in a Heaven for little children, and in his uncritical acceptance of the conventional clap-trap about the "unique" excellence of the Sermon on the Mount—which is most admired by those who understand it least—Dickens never allowed these things to impose upon him, or to obscure his judgment upon the actual issues confronting the poor and the oppressed in real life. One can search his novels with a microscope and find no shred of support for the reactionary imposture of a reward in Heaven for the ills endured by the poor and the oppressed in this life—or for the equally reactionary immorality of "turning the other cheek to the smiter."

As we have seen, long before the end of his literary life-time Dickens had shed completely all trace of the "Cheeryble illusion." He had, for all practical purposes reached the very brink of the conviction that "the emancipation of the working classes must be *conquered* by the working classes themselves." He had completely lost faith in bourgeois society; but, unfortunately for himself—although he went as near to its attainment as a man can go without actually achieving it—he never quite acquired a faith in the proletariat and its historical future.

It is this fact—that he had lost the old optimist faith in bourgeois society on which his youthful Radicalism was based, but had not yet acquired the only possible alternative—faith in the proletariat and its revolutionary mission—which constitutes the real tragedy of Charles Dickens. And it is to this that we must attribute, along with the deepening gloom of his later novels, his weakness and hesitation in the matter of religion.

But even if we admit, as we must, that Dickens showed—if only in a measure—weakness and uncertainty in his critical attitude towards religion, he showed none in his attitude towards those other pillars of bourgeois society, Law and the Family.

Towards the Law, Dickens' attitude was contemptuous and aggressive from the first. Hardly one of his novels can be named which does not contain some fling at the elaborate imposture which is The Law, or that revolting and irrational cruelty that passes under the name of Justice. And this hostility is expressed through the medium of a multitude of characters which exhibit between them every phase of the legal profession from the wretched and pitiable law-writer (a craft which the typewriter has rendered obsolete) up to and including the Lord Chancellor.

It is not that Dickens represents all solicitors as touting pettyfoggers like Dodson and Fogg in *Pickwick,* or scoundrels and swindlers like Sampson Brass in the *Old Curiosity Shop.* On the contrary: from Mr. Perker and his clerk Lowton *(in Pickwick)* to Mr. Jaggers and his clerk Wemmick (in *Great Expectations)* Dickens gives a whole gallery of legal portraits of which no lawyer could conplain—since all in this category are men who, apart from foibles harmless in themselves, are admirable and respectworthy characters. And yet the effect of the whole—even because of the Perkers, the Wemmicks, and the Sidney Cartons—is to widen and deepen our sense of disgust at and distrust of the Law as a system basically compounded of irrationality, meaningless ritual, chicanery, self-seeking, and downright fraud. Mr. Perker is an admirable little man who is willing to agree that Dodson and Fogg have been guilty of "sharp practice." But Mr. Perker is positively pained at the suggestion that there is anything radically wrong with the system which not only makes it possible for Dodson and Fogg to flourish, but protects them in the possession of their ill-gotten gains. Conversation Kenge is not only a highly polished gentleman, but a highly respected and trustworthy family solicitor. Yet Conversation Kenge—though he knows Mr. Vholes to be taking advantage of Richard Carstone's infatuation to the extent of every last penny Richard possesses, and most of Ada's pennies into the bargain—will not hear a word said in favour of so altering the legal system as to eliminate Mr. Vholes. Everybody concerned knows the evil the great suit of Jarndyce *v.* Jarndyce has wrought, in common with other such cases; everybody knows of Tom

Jarndyce's suicide, of Gridley's premature death, and of poor crazed Miss Flite. Yet no lawyer can speak of Jarndyce *v.* Jarndyce other than with reverence as "a monument of Chancery procedure." Mr. Jaggers and his clerk Wemmick both know that their thriving practice is based upon the well justified belief, widespread in criminal circles, that if there exists the tiniest possibility, however remote, of getting a man off, Mr. Jaggers is the man who will do the trick. Mr. Jaggers can wash his hands with scented soap—like a male Lady Macbeth with a tougher conscience—but no soap exists to wash from the reader's mind the impression created by the cumulative force of the whole of Dickens' novels in sequence—the impression that the whole legal system from top to bottom is positively as well as relatively evil; something inimical to, and destructive of, the very roots of Truth and Justice.

It is a commonplace of criticism to credit Dickens with having attacked, exposed, and secured the amendment of incidental abuses—such as the ignorance and brutality of the magistrate's bench exposed in the cases of Nupkins in *Pickwick,* and Fang in *Oliver Twist;* the swaggering witness-bullying counsel exposed in the person of Sergeant Buzfuz in *Pickwick,* the scandal of Doctors' Commons exposed in *Copperfield* (and exposed, too, with so much subtlety that only well-qualified students knew how thorough the exposure was); the scandal of imprisonment for debt exposed in *Pickwick,* in *David Copperfield* and in *Little Dorrit;* the scandal of the Court of Chancery exposed in *Bleak House;* the scandal of the whole state of the criminal law exposed in *Great Expectations;* the scandal of the marriage law, exposed with deadly force in *Hard Times;* the whole notion of a savagely repressive punitive system attacked and exposed in *Oliver Twist,* in *Barnaby Rudge,* and in *Great Expectations;*—all these things are quite generally scored to Dickens' credit, as incidental evils he exposed and with remedial effect. But these things were at best only the externalities of the evil, and, also, the extent to which they have been remedied has been grossly exaggerated too.

What has not been remedied, and will not be so long as the bourgeois order lasts, is the fundamental wrong upon which the whole pretentious edifice of the Law has been reared—the wrong implicit in, and inseparable from, a class-divided state of society: the two-fold wrong of pretending that "all are equal in the eyes of the law" (when everybody knows that they are not), and the even greater wrong of imposing one common standard of conduct upon people in circumstances as widely different as the opposite poles of a magnet, those from the two main classes in society, the bourgeoisie and the proletariat.

In the face of this class cleavage, and of the antagonism it involves, any system of justice which pretends to absoluteness and to superiority to circumstances of time, place, birth and upbringing and so forth is branded as a fraud and pretence from the start. And everybody concerned with maintaining the gigantic pretence must, at some point or another, and in some degree, become himself tainted with the fraud, the humbug, and the wilful blindness to wrong committed in the name of Right and Justice which such a huge system of fraud entails. One despises as one must, the John Barsacs, the Roger Clys, and all the brood of informers from Noah Claypole down to and including Rogue Riderhood. But that brood is as inseparable from the legal system of bourgeois society. as is the Lord Chancellor on his Bench, the Law Serjeants and King's Counsel in their wigs and gowns, the juniors with their red and blue bags, the solicitors— Perkers and Kenges, or Vholeses, Dodsons, Foggs, and Sampson Brasses as they may be— and behind them the whole apparatus of clerks—Guppys and Smallweeds prominent among them—and auxiliaries such as law-stationers like Snagsby and law-writers like Nemo.

Social evolution has modified certain details. The lawwriters have gone before the onset of the typewriter. Doctors' Commnons has gone and with it the Spenlows and Jorkinses. Law Serjeants exist only as a relic from the Irish Bar, whence they too are disappearing. Buzfuz would need to be a little more circumspect nowadays, and Nupkins and Fang have been rendered not quite so blatantly harmful. The more obvious anomalies of Doctors' Commons, and the more grossly indefensible aspects of Chancery procedure have been removed, and the law of evidence amended. But when all is said and done the evil of the Law remains in substance just what it was in Dickens' day, and must remain until the social system it expresses has been completely revolutionized.

As to the Family: Dickens' criticism is, though equally unflinching, more oblique. We have noted in the first part of this essay how Dickens makes his stand for the rights of the child, and how that entails a protest against the tyranny of parents. No less critical of the essential basis of the bourgeois family is Dickens' attitude to illegitimacy. It is of first-rate significance that Dickens allots in no fewer than three cases, or possibly, four, the part of hero or heroine in major novels to the illegitimate child of a "free-marriage" union. Oliver Twist, Esther Summerson, Arthur Clennam, and (probably, though not certainly) Estella "Havisham" are all of this category; and it is more than clear from Dickens' handling of their cases, that not only did he sympathize heartily with them, but still more, did he sympathize with the parents who gave them birth. These things alone would be decisive, but it is clear from a whole number of other strokes, scattered through his novels generally, that Dickens attitude to the bourgeois family was a radically critical one.

Two instances, both in *Hard Times* (which is, in so many respects, one long outspoken manifesto of defiance to bourgeois society) illustrate this point.

The first is the advice on the question of divorce given by Bounderby to the workman Stephen Blackpool.

Stephen is married to a woman who is a complete waster in every sense. Not only is she a hopeless drunkard, who, when she lives under the same roof with him, wrecks, pawns or sells every stitch she can lay hands on to raise the money for drink, but she has a habit of leaving him for long spells and returning only when in a maudlin frenzy in order to plague him. Supplementing all these reasons for wishing to be free is the fact that Stephen knows of a mill lass of his own age who is a dear friend, and as good as his wife is bad. He has paid his wife for years to stay away from him, which for years she does. Then once again she turns up, half-dead, and frenzied with drink. Stephen, in despair, goes to his employer, Bounderby, for advice how to get rid of his torment. The aristocratic Mrs. Sparsit penetrates his secret:

> "He wishes to be free to marry the female of whom he speaks, I fear, sir," observed Mrs. Sparsit in an undertone and much dejected by the immorality of the people.
>
> "I do. The lady says what's right. I were a-coming to it. I ha' read i' th' papers that great fo'k (fair faw'em a'! I wishes'em no hurt!) are not bonded together for better or for worse so fast, but that they can be set free fro' *their* misfortnet marriages, an' marry ower agen. When they dun not agree, for that their tempers is ill-sorted, they has rooms o' one kind an' another in their houses, above a bit, and they can live asunder. We fok ha' only one room, and we can't. When that won't do they ha' gowd an' other cash, an' the'y can say, 'This for yo and that for me,' an' they can go their separate ways. We can't. Spite o' all that they can be set free for smaller wrongs than mine. So, I mun be ridden o' this woman, an' I want t'know how?"—*Hard Times:* Book I, Chap. X.

Stephen goes over all the things that can be done to him if he does any hurt to the woman he is tied to or if he deserts her, and all the punishment (social if not legal) that will fall on him if he lives with the woman he loves without marriage. Bounderby agrees with his every point, but on being pressed to show Stephen a law to help him, answers lamely:

"Hem! There's a sanctity in this relation of life," said Mr. Bounderby, "and—and—it must be kept up."

Blackpool's answer is devastating:

"No, no, dunnot say that, sir. 'Tain't kept up that way. Not that way. 'Tis kep' down that way. I'm a weaver, I were in a fact'ry when a chilt, but I ha' gotten een to see wi' and eern to year wi'. I read in th' papers every Sizes, every Sessions—and you read too—I know it!—with dismay—how th'supposed impossibility of our getting unchained from one another, at any price, on any terms, brings blood upon this land, and brings many common married folk to battle, murder, an' sudden death. Let us ha' this right understood. Mine's a grievous case, an, I want—if you will be so good—t'know the law that helps me."—*Ibid.*

This rouses Bounderby in his turn, and accordingly he tells Stephens that there *is* such a law:

"But it's not for you at all. It costs money. It costs a mint of money."
"How much might that be?" Stephen calmly asked.
"Why, you'd have to go to Doctor's Commons with a suit, and you'd have to go to a court of common law with a suit, and you'd have to go to the House of Lords with a suit, and you'd have to get an Act of Parliament to enable you to marry again and it would cost you (if it was a case of very plain sailing), I suppose from a thousand to fifteen hundred pounds," said Mr. Bounderby. "Perhaps twice the money."
"There's no other law?"
"Certainly not."— *Ibid.*

What makes this passage—striking enough in itself—all the more remarkable, is the closeness of the parallel between it and a famous judgment given in a bigamy case, some two years after *Hard Times* was written.

Mr. Justice Maule had before him, in 1857, a case almost exactly paralleling the case of Stephen Blackpool with one exception—in this case the man had several children who needed looking after and so he (illegally as it proved) married the woman who was willing to take charge of them. In words that repeat those of Dickens at point after point the Judge expressed himself in bitter irony and told the prisoner what he "ought to have done" according to the law — just as Bounderby recites the procedure, only Mr. Justice Maule made it even more grotesquely absurd, by dwelling upon the amount of time it would take and the difficulty of proving the case at each of its stages. Finally, to show how "indignant" he was at the prisoner for taking the law into his own hands, Mr. Justice Maule imposed a sentence of *one day's imprisonment*—" and inasmuch as the present Assize is three days' old, the result is that you will be immediately discharged."

Mr. Justice Maule's judgment (which it is impossible to read without a conviction that a reading of *Hard Times* must have inspired it) created a sensation and an agitation which led to the first Divorce Law in England. But despite amendments, things remain for the ordinary worker pretty much what they were in Stephen Blackpool's time; and that all the more so as reactionaries continually endeavour to undo every slight amendment which makes divorce either easier or more accessible to the poor.

Dickens, though in a skilfully covert way, misses no chance of striking a blow at the "for better for worse" theory of marriage so beloved of the pious Victorian bourgeoisie; particularly along the line of the atrocious cruelty involved in the marrying-off by greedy fortune and position-hunting parents of attractive young daughters to wealthy men of twice their age and more. A melodramatic example is the attempt by Madeline Bray's father (in *Nicholas Nickleby*) to force her into a marriage with the repulsive old miser, Gride. Something of the same kind is indicated as the background of Quilp's marriage to Mrs. Quilp, for which, however, her mother pays dearly, as she deserves. A more gruesome example is that of Pecksniff's forcing his daughter to marry Jonas Chuzzlewit, followed by his own attempt to force himself upon Mary Graham; while the most obviously tragic example is that of Mrs. Skewton, who forces her daughter Edith into two loveless marriages in succession; the second of which—to Mr. Dombey—ends, as it was bound to end, in disaster all round.

But only less tragic in its outcome, and, in its way, even more horrible, is Louisa Gradgrind's marriage— morally forced upon her by her father and the manner in which he had educated her—to that monster of coarse egotism, Josiah Bounderby. He is as old as her father, and has known her from birth; and Dickens takes a great deal of care to show that even as a child the mere touch of his hand was unendurably repulsive to her. She marries him only because she sees no prospect of a successful resistance in the teeth of Bounderby's coarse persistence, her father's desire to gratify his friend Bounderby, and her mother's all but imbecile incapacity for anything beyond bemoaning her own unfortunate state of health—her mother's fear that she "will never hear the last of it" if she offers any sort of opinion of her own. Suffering unendurable torments from her forced association with Bounderby, Louisa is driven to the limit of endurance and beyond by the advent of her would-be seducer James Harthouse, who, though less repulsive externally than Bounderby, has as little regard for any feelings other than his own. As we have noted earlier Louisa solves the difficulty by flying for refuge to her father, and lapsing into a brain fever. And to his credit, her father has the grace to be horrified at what he has done. The whole episode is an unanswerable demonstration of Dickens' abhorrence of, and contempt for, the Victorian bourgeois conception of marriage and the married state.

It is almost superfluous to add the minor circumstances which round off Dickens' assault upon the bourgeois order. His attack upon the private-property basis of society is spread all over his novels. His attack upon conventional religion and religiosity is, despite weakness and vacillation, none the less an attack. His crushing indictment of the Law is, as we have seen, complete and unanswerable. And his attack upon the Family, though more subtly veiled, is none the less mordant. His contempt for Parliament aid Parliamentarians we have shown at length. His contempt for bureaucracy, whether in the minor form of Bumble and Bumbledom, or in the major form of the Circumlocution Office—with the swarms of Tite-Barnacles and Stiltstalkings who batten upon it—is no less open and devastating. It is almost an anti-climax to add that his contempt for the Army—though much more incidentally shown—is as complete as is his contempt for the Law. Only once, in *Bleak House,* in the persons of the ex-soldiers George Rouncewell and his friend Matthew Bagnet does he show any sort of respect for the military, and they, as private soldiers, are the exception which proves the rule. And even in their case they serve mainly as a means of bringing upon the scene and exhibiting in all their admirable qualities, Mrs. Bagnet, her children, and her management of her household.

It is an illustration of Dickens' unerring instinct that he never once falls into the bourgeois trick of treating the hen-pecked husband as a comic figure. On the contrary, as in the case of the Bagnet household, he makes a mild jest of the opposite kind. He shows Matthew Bagnet as invariably, and quite properly, subordinate in every crisis to the quicker understanding and the better judgment of his amazingly capable wife—and this without the least trace of any sort of "hen-pecking." But he also shows Mat Bagnet as quite innocently believing that "he never admits" his wife's superiority openly to her, since "discipline must be maintained." That he invariably admits it in his deeds doesn't occur to old "Lignum Vitae" Bagnet. The Bagnet household, taken over all, constitutes not only a charming study in itself, but a complete indictment by comparison of all the bourgeois households described by Dickens with which it can be compared. Hence the merely incidental fact that the presiding genius of the household happens to be a soldier's wife serves only to reinforce the implied condemnation which becomes apparent at sight on comparing the Bagnet household with that of such a character as Major Joey Bagstock in *Dombey.*

Dickens and Christmas

British journalists seem obsessed with the notion that the works of Dickens are full of descriptions of what, nowadays, it is usual to call an "old-fashioned Christmas." So much is this the case that it has been asserted that "Dickens *invented* Christmas." The notion has, of course, its germ of truth; but relative to Dickens' total output this germ is so disproportionately small as to be ludicrously insufficient for the use which has been made of it.

The fact is that in one, and one only, of his major novels does Dickens describe a Christmas celebration, or, indeed, make any allusion to Christmas, and that one was his earliest, the *Pickwick Papers.* True, in his (quantitatively considered) minor writings there are other allusions. A Christmas dinner is described in his own serio-comic, pathetic-satiric fashion, in one of the *Sketches by Boz.* And between 1850 and 1867 inclusive he contributed twenty sketches, stories, or parts of stories, to the Christmas numbers of *Household Words* and *All the Year Round.* But charming though many of these stories are—two of them, *Mrs. Lirriper's Lodgings* and *Mrs. Lirriper's Legacy* being worthy to rank with his finest work—only *three* of them contain any reference to Christmas at all, and one *only* includes a reference to Christmas feasting.

This, if it were all, would be a slender basis indeed for the mountain of myth which has been built upon it, but (with what significance we shall see) it is not all.

In the years 1843, 1844, 1845, 1846 and 1848—years, it will be observed which fall within the middle or transitional period into which we have divided his literary lifetime—Dickens produced five "Christmas Books." He did not invent the practice—it was a custom with which he complied. He was not the only popular writer of the time to do so, since Thackeray also produced five Christmas books. But most of all is it significant that in only two of his Christmas books does Dickens lay his scene at Christmas time, and in only *one* does he give any sort of description of Christmas festivity—of the turkey, roast beef, plum pudding, and hot punch kind. In short, Dickens' repute as an "inventor of Christmas rests almost wholly upon this one Christmas book—A *Christmas Carol*—supported somewhat, though not greatly, by the Christmas at Dingley Dell chapters in *Pickwick*.

In the formal sense the journalistic myth above cited is therwfore all but baseless. It is rescued fron absolute falsity by two facts—first, the astonishing and abiding popularity of the *Christmas Carol*, a popularity sufficient to have made a lasting reputation for its author even if he had written nothing else, and second, by the fact that the implicit thesis of Dickens' Christmas books (and especially the first three of them, the *Carol*, *The Chimes*, and *The Cricket on the Hearth)* forms an ingredient in all Dickens wrote, and does so increasingly in all his work after his visit to America in 1842. In his Christmas books especially, Dickens, as though in spite of himself, revealed to himself in explosive outbursts, his gathering hatred of that which lies at the heart of the bourgeois system of society—the subordination of all men, and of every human capacity to the tyrannical dominance of a vast, impersonal, process of *money-gaining*.

The technique of these Christmas books is noteworthy in that avowedly Dickens sought to achieve in a prose narrative something parallel to the results achieved by a masque, or an old "morality" play. In the *Christmas Carol* the miserly Scrooge is presented, first of all as a repulsive grotesque who has crushed out of himself every sympathetic human emotion and made of himself a machine for meanly adding pound to pound, shilling to shilling, and pence to pence. He is in short a grotesquely exaggerated version of the miserly side of old Anthony Chuzzlewit and of his son Jonas, in the novel Dickens was then producing, *Martin Chuzzlewit*. Later on, after seeing a vision of himself as he had been, and as he most probably would be—in the one case a normal, likeable lad, capable of generosity, sympathy and enthusiasm, and in the other a wizened, solitary miser, robbed ruthlessly in death by ghouls as pitilessly mercenary as he had, at the opening of the story, advocated that everybody should be—Scrooge repents and is converted. He wakes to find Christmas Day, is dawning and celebrates the occasion with a generosity and a gaiety as fantastic as his miserliness and moroseness had been grotesque.

In the second Christmas book, *The Chimes*, Dickens locates the story at the New Year. Again the machinery of the story is deliberately fantastic and supernatural. The central character, a "ticket-porter" (i.e., a licensed messenger) undergoes a vision in which he sees realized the worst prophecies of the group of Manchester School "Utilitarians" into contact with whom he comes, and who reprove him for his (alleged) thriftlessness and that of his class. In these pompous, prosperous, and sententious bourgeois—men who have not a single redeeming virtue but the bourgeois virtue of financial solvency—we have a fantastically exaggerated version of the characters Dickens afterwards worked out in sober earnest in *Hard Times* (Gradgrind, Bounderby, M'Choakumchild and the boy Bitzer).

In both the third and the fourth Christmas books—*The Cricket on the Hearth* and the *Battle of Life*—the action is not located at any special season, and hence has no formal connection with Christmas at all and the machinery is naturalistic throughout. They continue the same thesis as their predecessors, however, in that they each preach the doctrine that self-forgetfulness even to the point of pain, patiently endured, and with it an actively sympathetic consideration for others, brings, in the end, a fuller measure of reward, and a more abiding happiness than any alternative line of conduct does or can bring.

The fifth and last Christmas book, *The Haunted Man,* returns to the semi-supernaturalistic method of the first of the series. A man, haunted by a painful sense of personal wrong inflicted by a false friend, prays in his agony for the power to forget. He gains his wish only to find that along with the wrong he forgets all the good that he has ever done and that has ever been done to him. He becomes callously self-centred and positively antisocial since his fellows are now to him merely means to the end of, or obstacles to, his own momentary satisfaction—which ceases to be satisfaction since it is, and can be, only momentary. His curse is intensified by the fact that everyone he meets catches from him the evil which afflicts him. This goes on until he meets with two people whom he fails to affect—a neglected waif who had never known any emotions but selfish ones, and a woman so devoid of selfishness that she had no harboured wrong, and no sense of injury or infliction to forget. Thus defeated in his power to radiate harm the Haunted Man is restored to his normal state, plus, of course, the enlightenment gained while under the curse. A Christmas scene is introduced, casually, as part of the culmination of the story.

Taking these five Christmas books together it is impossible to miss the significance, firstly of their common theme, and secondly of this theme considered in connection with the date at which they were written. Their theme broadly stated is the folly and worse than folly of all narrow, calculating egoism—in short, the viciousness of that self-regarding principle which to the *epigoni* of degenerate Benthamism constituted the real essence of human nature. This being so, it comes with treble force to realize that the first of the series was written when *Martin Chuzzlewit*—the novel which is wholly a dissertation on the theme of Greed—was drawing to its close; while the last of the series similarly appeared at a corresponding period in the production of Dickens' next novel *Dombey and Son,* whose theme is the cognate one of Pride.

We saw earlier how Dickens' visit to America had the effect of opening his eyes to the extent to which the *cash nexus* between man and man was the basic (and only seriously respected) relation binding man to man in bourgeois society. And we saw, too, how on his return to England, this experience caused him to see English society in a new and grimmer light. For the time being the shock to his Radical optimism was so great as to drive Dickens into a state of excited confusion and semi-bewilderment from which he vainly sought relief in foreign travel, and such abortive experiments as the editorship of the *Daily News* at the beginning of 1846. The whole series of Christmas books can, therefore, be regarded quite fairly as "escape fantasies"—projections of Dickens' desire for a way out of the conflicts and crises of class struggle and revolution which had culminated in concrete political explosions—in the "mad year" of 1848—just before the last of the series was written.

The whole transitional period in Dickens' development culminated and completed itself *after* the fate of the revolution had been objectively decided, in 1849, by the production of the semi-autobiographical, *David Copperfield,* in which, once again, Dickens got his feet firmly on the ground. Not for nothing does Dickens in that novel use emigration to Australia as the means of escape into a new life of prosperity and happiness for his best-loved characters, for Wilkins Micawber and his family, for Little Em'ly and her kinsfolk, and for Mr. Mell, the ill-used usher in Creakle's school.

Dickens' repute as a Champion of Christmas rests primarily—in fact, almost exclusively—on the basis of his Christmas books in general, and his *Christmas Carol* in particular. Take away the Christmas books and what is left amounts to less than many a writer might claim—virtually to nothing at all by comparison with the extent and intensity of his repute. Take from his Christmas books the *Christmas Carol* and the rest are merely somewhat sentimental exercises on the theme of the need for generosity and imaginative sympathy in men's dealings with each other. With the *Christmas Carol* added all the rest of the Christmas books, and each and every allusion he makes to these themes of benevolence, largehearted charity, and understanding sympathy—and there is not one of his writings which fails to strike that note —becomes a contribution in support of the thesis of the *Christmas Carol.*

What is there special in the thesis of the *Christmas Carol?* Its special quality can best be brought out by a comparison with the Christmas at Dingley Dell described in *Pickwick.*

In *Pickwick* the Christmas feast is still in essence a feudal institution, a feast given by the squire to his servants, his tenants, and his poor relations. Just as the aboriginal Yule feast, with its mystico-magical Yule log as a culminating ritual presupposes the spacious garth of a substantial Scandinavian Jarl, so its feudal and quasi-feudal descendant presupposed either a baronial hall or a spacious farmhouse to provide room for the huge fires, and the numerous company required to do justice to the boars' heads, the barons of beef, the vast turkeys and geese, and all the rest of the Christmas appurtenances down to and including the huge bowls of rum punch. With all its modernistic modifications, the Christmas Dickens described in 1836 was still feudal in its essence.

In the *Christmas Carol* the situation has been revolutionized. The scene, now, is set not in any baronial hall, or spacious farmhouse, but in a poor man's home—a tenement lodging so ill-equipped for such festivities that the turkey (or whatever it is that is to serve as the main item of the feast) must be sent out to be cooked *at the baker's.* It must be fifty years, or close upon it, since it was the general custom of Londoners of the lower middle class and the proletariat to send their Sunday joint or their Christmas turkey to the baker's to be cooked. The bakers have changed their habits, and the invention of the "kitchener" range, the gas stove and the electric cooker have made home cooking more practicable. But in the 1840's the situation was just as Dickens describes it. Every one of his works contains flash after flash of amazingly acute observation, but worthy to rank with his best efforts are the passages in the *Christmas Carol* which describe the happy procession with the joint or bird from the baker's, and the baker's shop itself with the pavement over the oven not only melted clear of snow, but *steaming* — as though it itself were cooking too. It does not always — or even often — snow at Christmas in England (tradition to the contrary notwithstanding) but sometimes it does. And just such a sight as Dickens describes down to and including the smoking pavement many still living must have seen.

From one angle the *Christmas Carol* appears as propaganda in favour of pathetic resignation. Bob Cratchit, the ill-used, fifteen-bob-a-week clerk, has little enough to be thankful for, and yet is presented as still finding excuses for his wretched old screw of an employer, Scrooge. But submission, especially to injustice, is fundamentally at variance with Dickens' whole nature, so that this cannot be the interpretation Dickens intended us to adopt. When we remember that Dickens knew next to nothing of trade unions, and in any case would never have conceived such a thing as operating in the case of an office worker, we see his meaning clearly. For Bob Cratchit a miserly boss was, in a time of economic depression such as prevailed in 1843, just one more of those ills which, since it could not be cured, must be endured. It was only from the outside, and from the hands of writers with some hold upon the interest of the public—such as Dickens was—that any sort of alleviation could come to Bob Cratchit and his like. Hence in his scathing attack upon the unregenerate Scrooge, and his glorification by contrast of the kindliness, altruism, and general good-nature of the Cratchit family, Dickens was in his own special way joining in the fight for the cruelly exploited and under-esteemed workers in commerce and in industry. It is a significant coincidence that Tom Hood's *Song of the Shirt* appeared (in the Christmas number of *Punch*) during the same Christmas season that saw the appearance of Dickens' *Christmas Carol.* Kingsley's *Alton Locke,* with its preface on "Cheap Clothes and Nasty"—a stinging protest on behalf of the sweated clothing workers—did not appear until 1850. Elizabeth Barrett Browning's *Cry of the Children* —a noble protest on behalf of the child-slaves in factory, mill, and mine, appeared in a magazine alniost exactly at the same time as Dickens began to write the *Christmas Carol.* That three works of such first-class merit as those of Dickens, Tom Hood and Mrs. Browning should have been written virtually simultaneously and under circumstances which entirely preclude any theory of collusion, throws a great light both upon the conditions then prevailing, and the reactions of these three great artists to them.

With this clue the whole of Dickens' Christmas books —treated as a single category—can be placed accurately. The foregleams of the attack upon the Manchester School to be found in the *Chimes,* and the almost excessive glorification of the atmosphere of the working-man's hearth and home in The *Cricket on the Hearth,* all fit in with this general theme. Dickens had shed—or, at any rate, was rapidly shedding—the Cheeryble illusion. The supernaturally induced repentance of Scrooge gives only a very superficial appearance of support to the notion that the employers in bulk could ever be relied upon for spontaneous benevolence. Rather does the whole parable seem to hint that only a thorough shaming, reinforced by the fear of terrors to come, could induce them to behave with decency. And even so much of hope has faded away from the *Chimes.* From thence to the end of the Christmas books the implied moral is, firstly, that the finest qualities of humanity flourish more fully in the homes of the working poor; and secondly, that "it is the poor, and the poor only, who help the poor."

Thus the Christmas books form a complete demonstration of the mode of transition from the earlier to the later Dickens; and, in their own special way, lead us, yet again, to the very brink of the slogan: "the emancipation of the working class must be *conquered* by the working class *itself!*"

Dickens' Imaginative Realism

It is no doubt true that Dickens never fully realized the cumulative force of his own indictment of bourgeois society. Hence he did not draw the theoretical conclusions that, to us, seem to have been staring him in the face. Much of his failure to do so must, no doubt, be attributed to the fact that the very strength of his prejudice against Parliament and Parliamentarism held him back from participation in actual, practical, political struggles from which he would have learned both the need for and how to achieve the theoretical comprehension of his own work which was the chief thing that he lacked.

But another source of his failure seems to have been the curiously revealing fact that Dickens was afraid of the very power of his own astounding imagination— a quality in which not even Shakespeare was his superior. It is here that the effects of his own childhood experiences— those of the economic vicissitudes he suffered in consequence of the Micawber-like character of his father—are most clearly apparent. When he draws Mr. Micawber away on an imaginative flight, or Harold Skimpole indulging in butterfly-like flittings from flower to flower in the sunlight of fancy, Dickens seems constantly to be reminding himself that he simply must keep his fancy under restraint—that imagination divorced from contact with reality produces nothing but suffering and disaster—that however much one's head may be among the stars, one's feet must always be kept firmly planted upon good solid ground.

The moral is so patently true as to be, to a philistine, positively trite. It says much for Dickens' imaginative power, and for that amazing power of visualization which must repeatedly have made it difficult for him to separate things he had actually experienced from things that he had only fancied, that he should have felt the need to remind himself so often of something which is a prosaic commonplace to less gifted men. That he did so need to remind himself is apparent; the character of Harold Skimpole (a failure in the sense that it was too successful a portrait) is of itself sufficient to show Dickens' consciousness of the need.

The character of Harold Skimpole is usually regarded as a blemish upon the work *(Bleak House)* in which it appears. Certainly as it stands, it lacks clarity of outline and spontaneous freshness. But that is more than sufficiently accounted for by the fact that Dickens, who thought he was only borrowing a few hints from his friend Leigh Hunt, achieved in fact and to his own horror, a masterpiece of portraiture which he tried to alter, but only succeeded in blurring. The truth seems to have been that while Leigh Hunt was not, actually, quite the swine that Skimpole turns out to be, at the same time Harold Skimpole was, to an extent, *potential* in Leigh Hunt, just as Boythorne in the same novel was potential in Walter Savage Landor, upon whom he was modelled. In any case, what stands proved is that Dickens, while pleading as eloquently as any man the claims of the imagination, felt the need of a character who would demonstrate that slavery to the imagination can be as grievous an affliction as enslavement to lack of imagination. The romantic imagination of how things might be needs yoking in double-harness with the realistic power of seeing things as they actually are. Only so can be generated the scientific imagination which sees in things as they are things as they could be, and *should be made to become.*

And if ever a man had the gift of the eye—and not merely of the eye but of the ear, and of the nose—and the faculty of remembering with microscopic accuracy of detail everything ever seen, or heard, or tasted, smelled, or felt, that man was Charles Dickens.

Every single thing he ever wrote is full to overflowing with examples of his marvellous gift. The whole picture arises before us in sight, sound, touch, taste, and pervading odour, just exactly as in real life, and with a vividness that becomes positively uncanny.

To readers less sensitive than Dickens, this very vividness with which he visualizes plain things in plain everyday life appears to be "exaggeration." It is no such thing. The truth is that Dickens always sees instantly, and in every last, least, tiny detail, *all* that there is to be seen; while lesser mortals see only a part, and sometimes a trifling part at that. And since Dickens' unerring instinct always led him to see, in dealing with the plain life of plain working folk, that which was essentially real in those lives, there runs through all his work an obstinate—even if theoretically blind—conviction that somehow or other a way out will be found, and justice be done to all who suffer and are oppressed.

It is this understanding faculty in Dickens—his romantic realism which endeared him to his working-class contemporaries and made Dickens supreme—made him that one writer of all writers who really knew and understood their lives, and life conditions, their hopes, their fears, their aspirations and their prejudices, and knew them, sympathetically, from the *inside*.

When Dickens described in microscopic detail all the things they were familiar with—and in so doing showed he knew them even more intimately than the workers themselves did—observing all sorts of details and oddities they had never before noticed, but which once pointed out could never be missed—when Dickens did this the common people knew him at once for *one of themselves*.

Almost any page of any of his novels opened by chance will give examples of his wonderful gift. Peggotty's buttons, always flying off as she bends; Peggotty's workbox with the picture of the dome of St. Paul's on its lid! This workbox in one or other of its forms (it crops up again in the hands of Berry in *Dombey*—where, since the scene is at Brighton it has, of course, a picture of the Royal Pavilion on the lid) must have been a sight reminiscent of the childhood of every single one of his readers, not only in his own lifetime, but of the generation next succeeding. A similar case—again to take a seemingly trivial example—is that of the mode of salute used invariably by the coach-drivers in *Pickwick*—the solemn lifting of the little finger of the right hand. Everyone now living in London who can remember the days of the old horse buses (especially those who ever enjoyed the thrill of riding on the box-seat, alongside the driver) can remember that salute as still in use years after Dickens' death, and half a century after the first appearance of *Pickwick*. (With the left hand fully occupied with the reins, and the right hand almost wholly occupied with the whip the right hand little finger was all that a driver had left with which to salute a passing comrade.) Every character in Dickens (apart from the fine "gentlemen" and "ladies" about whom they knew nothing at firsthand) appeared to the common people who devoured his pages as somebody whom they had seen in the flesh, and known, met, talked with, and worked with in real life. And all are described, not as things seen by an outsider—by an alien from afar—but as things intimate and familiar, things so much part of the life of the observer that he has a natural right to laugh at them or be furious about them since they are the people who make up his own world.

Since every novel contains scores of illustrations of this ability in Dickens to identify himself and his own private world with the private world of his workingclass readers, an example can only be chosen at haphazard. Thus at haphazard take as an example, the scene in the street where Pecksniff calls upon Sairey Gamp:

> This lady lodged 'in Kingsgate Street, Holborn', at a bird-fancier's, next door but one to the celebrated mutton-pie shop, and directly opposite to the original cat's-meat warehouse; the renown of which establishments was duly heralded on their respective fronts. It was a little house, and this was the more convenient; for Miss Gamp being, in her highest walk of art, a monthly-nurse, or, as her sign-board boldly had it, "Midwife," and lodging in the first-floor front, was easily assailable at night by pebbles, walking-sticks, and fragments of tobacco-pipe; all much more efficacious than the street-door knocker, which was so constructed as to wake the street with ease, and even spread alarms offire in Holborn without making the smallest impression on the premises to which it was addressed....—*Martin Chuzzlewit:* Chap. XIX.

Mrs. Gamp, having been out nursing all night is asleep; the bird-fancier downstairs is out; so, when Mr. Pecksniff arrives he has to apply himself to this knocker:

> Mr. Pecksniff, in the innocence of his heart, applied himself to the knocker; but at the first double knock every window in the street became alive with female heads; and before he could repeat the performance, whole troops of married ladies (some about to trouble Mrs. Gamp themselves, very shortly) came flocking round the steps, all crying with one accord, and with uncommon interest "Knock at the winder, sir, knock at the winder. Lord bless you, don't lose no more time than you can help—knock at the winder!"
>
> Acting on this suggestion, and borrowing the driver's whip for the purpose, Mr. Pecksniff soon made a commotion among the first-floor flower pots and roused Mrs. Gamp, whose voice—to the great satisfaction of the matrons—was heard to say, "I'm coming."
>
> "He's as pale as a muffin," said one lady, in allusion to Mr. Pecksniff.
>
> "So he ought to be, if he's the feelings of a man," observed another.
>
> A third lady (with her arms folded) said she wished he had chosen any other time for fetching Mrs. Gamp, but it always happened so with *her.*
>
> It gave Mr. Pecksniff much uneasiness to find, from these remarks, that he was supposed to have come to Mrs Gamp upon an errand touching—not the close of life, but the other end. Mrs. Gamp herself was under the same impression, for, throwing open the window she cried behind the curtains, as she hastily attired herself:
>
> "Is it Mrs. Perkins?"
>
> "No!" returned Mr. Pecksniff sharply, "nothing of the sort."
>
> "What, Mr. Whilks!" cried Mrs. Gamp. "Don't say it's you, Mr. Whilks, and that poor creetur Mrs. Whilks with not even a pin-cushion ready. Don't say it's you, Mr. Whilks!"

"It isn't Mr. Whilks," said Pecksniff. "I don't know the man. Nothing of the kind. A gentleman is dead; and some person being wanted in the house you are recommended by Mr. Mould the undertaker."

As she was by this time in a condition to appear, Mrs. Gamp, who had a face for all occasions, looked out of her window with her mourning countenance, and said she would be down directly. But the matrons took it very ill, that Mr. Pecksniff's mission was of so unimportant a kind; and the lady with her arms folded, rated him in good round terms, signifying that she would be glad to know what he meant by terrifying delicate females "with his corpses," and giving it as her opinion that he was quite ugly enough to know better. The other ladies were not at all behind-hand in expressing similar sentiments; and the children, of whom some scores had now collected, hooted and defied Mr. Pecksniff quite savagely. So when Mrs. Gamp appeared, the unoffending gentleman was glad to hustle her with very little ceremony into the cabriolet, and drive off, overwhelmed with popular execration.—*Martin Chuzzlewit:* Chap. XIX.

There is nothing here in the least of a demagogic tendency; on the contrary, in the hands of anybody less than a master this would have become a scornful satire on the squalor and stupidity of the "lower orders." Yet no proletarian would ever mistake this description for other than what it is— microscopically acute observation presented with just that tiny bit of exaggeration which gives it warmth and feeling, and makes it into splendid good fun. There are half a dozen strokes in it, too, that could only have come from one who had actually lived in one such street and seen, and enjoyed, just exactly such a sight. That door knocker is a masterstroke. How well some of us remember just that sort of knocker. And those "fragments of tobacco-pipe"—reminders of the days of the all-but-universal clay-pipe....

It was just that sort of thing that revealed Dickens to the common people as immovably and unchangeably one of themselves.

All his life long, according to his lights, Dickens fought for the poor and for the oppressed as stoutly as any man who ever struck a blow on their side. There have been probably quite a number of greater artists in the field of prose fiction. But very few indeed of them had so much as a tithe of his genius; and not one of them had a truer or a kinder heart.

The common people loved him living, and mourned him dead, and in these matters the common people are always right.